W9-BAR-335

Ready® Common Core

7 Reading INSTRUCTION

Acknowledgments

President Barack Obama, "Remarks by the President in Back-to-School Speech," Sept 28, 2011.

"Extraordinary People: Tim Berners-Lee" adapted from *HowStuffWorks.com*. Copyright © by Discovery Communications. Reprinted with permission.

O. Henry, excerpt from "The Ransom of Red Chief" (1918).

Saki, excerpt from "Dusk" from *Beasts and Superbeasts* (1914).

Mark Twain, excerpt from *The Prince and the Pauper* (1909).

Louisa May Alcott, excerpt from *Little Women* (1880).

"The Discovery of DNA's Structure" adapted from *Evolution* website at http://www.pbs.org/wgbh/evolution/library-06/3/1_063_01.html. Copyright © 2001 by WGBH Educational Foundation and Clear Blue Sky Productions, Inc. Reprinted with permission.

Emily Sohn, "A Dire Shortage of Water" adapted from *Science News for Kids*, August 16, 2004, and "A Prime Time for Cicadas," adapted from *Science News for Kids*, May 18, 2004. Copyright © 2004 by Emily Sohn. Reprinted with permission of Science News.

William Wordsworth, "Composed Upon Westminster Bridge" from *Poems in Two Volumes* (1807).

Paul Laurence Dunbar, "At Loafing-Holt" from *The Complete Poems of Paul Laurence Dunbar* (1922).

Martha Baird, "Man and Nature in New York and Kansas" from *Nice Deity*. Copyright © 1955 by Martha Baird. Published by Definition Press, New York, NY. Reprinted with permission of the publisher.

Eloise Greenfield, "Harriet Tubman" from *Honey I Love and Other Poems*. Text copyright © 1978 by Louise Greenfield. Reprinted with permission.

William Butler Yeats, "Song of the Old Mother" from *Modern British Poetry*, Louis Untermeyer, ed. (1920).

Richard Wilbur, "A Barred Owl" from *Mayflies: New Poems and Translations*. Copyright © 2000 by Richard Wilbur. Reprinted with permission of Houghton Mifflin Harcourt Publishing Company. All rights reserved.

Elizabeth Barrett Browning, "How Do I Love Thee?" from *Sonnets from the Portuguese* (1910).

Gary Soto, "Ode to Family Photographs" from *Neighborhood Odes: Poems*. Copyright © 1992 by Gary Soto. Reprinted with permission of Harcourt Children's Books, an imprint of Houghton Mifflin Publishing Company. All rights reserved.

Edgar Guest, "A Boy and His Dad" from *Rhymes of Childhood* (1922).

Francis Goodrich Hacket and Otto Frank, Act One, Scenes 1 and 2 and Act Two, Scene Four adapted from *The Diary of Anne Frank* (PLAY). Print copyright © 1956 by Albert Hackett, Frances Goodrich Hackett and Otto Frank. Reproduced with permission of Random House, Inc. Any third party use of this publication is prohibited. Interested parties must apply directly to Random House, Inc. for permission. Electronic copyright © 1956 by Albert Hackett. Copyright © renewed 1986 by David Huntoon and France Neuwirth. Reproduced with permission of Flora Roberts, Inc.

Pearl S. Buck, adapted excerpts from *The Good Earth*. Copyright © 1931 by Pearl S. Buck. Copyright renewed 1958 by Pearl S. Buck. Reprinted with permission of Washington Square Press, a Division of Simon & Schuster, Inc. Electronic rights granted by Open Road Media. All rights reserved.

Emily Dickinson, "The Sky Is Low" from *Poems by Emily Dickinson, Series One* (1886).

Al Gore, "A Generational Challenge to Repower America" from *The Huffington Post*, July 17, 2008. Copyright © 2008 by Al Gore. Reprinted with permission of The Wylie Agency LLC.

"Clean Cars for California" February 7, 2012, adapted from www.einow.org. Copyright © 2012 by Energy Independence Now. Reprinted with permission.

Stephen Ornes, "Big Fish in Troubled Waters" from *Science News for Kids*, April 20, 2011. Copyright © 2011 by Stephen Ornes. Reprinted with permission of Science News.

Lucy Stone, "The Progress of Fifty Years," speech to the Congress of Women at the World's Fair in Chicago (1893).

Common Core State Standards copyright © 2010 National Governors Association Center for Best Practices and Council of Chief State School Officers. All rights reserved.

All third-party content has been permissioned or is in the process of being permissioned.

Project Manager: Susan James
Cover Designer and Illustrator: Julia Bourque
Book Design: Mark Nodland

ISBN 978-0-7609-8558-8
©2014—Curriculum Associates, LLC
North Billerica, MA 01862

Table of Contents

Table of Contents

Table of Contents

Unit 1
Key Ideas and Details in Informational Text

Imagine you are in a scientist's laboratory. You see flasks of bubbling liquids, test tubes, and rubber tubing. The scientist is analyzing a substance by boiling it down to identify its parts. This will help her understand important ideas about the substance and how it can be used. How is a reader like a scientist? A reader also analyzes a text, breaking it down to identify important **details**. Then, like scientists, readers examine those details carefully to see how they are used to develop the **key ideas** in the text. Sometimes those details provide all the information you need. At other times, though, readers must use those details to make inferences, or figure out what the author really means.

In this unit, you will learn how to read closely and to use evidence, or details, to support your understanding of an informational text. You will also learn how to use the details to summarize the text. You will read about important people, events, and ideas and learn how they affect each other in a text. Put on your lab coats as you fill your test tubes with fascinating information. Don't forget your goggles!

✔ **Self Check** **Fill out the Self Check on the next page.** ▶

Before starting this unit, check off the skills you know below. As you complete each lesson, see how many more you can check off!

✔ Self Check

I know how to:	Before this unit	After this unit
find two or more central ideas in a text and the details that help support them.	☐	☐
explain how the facts, details, and other evidence develop central ideas in a text.	☐	☐
summarize a text without giving personal opinions.	☐	☐
cite several pieces of evidence to support inferences about a text.	☐	☐
explain how individuals, events, or ideas influence each other in a text.	☐	☐

Analyzing the Development of Central Ideas

CCSS

RI.7.2: Determine two or more central ideas in a text and analyze their development over the course of the text. . . .

Theme: *Careers*

As you read, do you wonder what the author is trying to tell you in the text? Try to figure out the **central idea**, or the most important point (or points) an author is trying to make about the topic. Sometimes a central idea may be stated directly, but more often it is implied. Then you must figure it out by analyzing the **supporting details**. These facts, examples, reasons, and other pieces of information are meant to explain and expand on the central idea.

Examine the cartoon below. Think about the central idea and its supporting details.

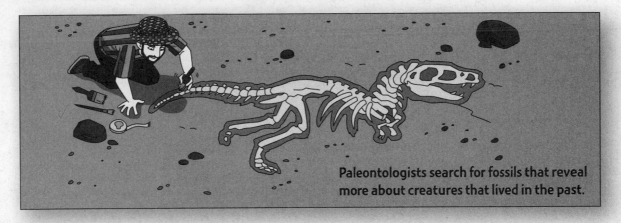

Paleontologists search for fossils that reveal more about creatures that lived in the past.

What central idea is shown? Circle parts of the picture and caption that support the central idea.

Study the web below that shows the central idea of the picture and details that support it.

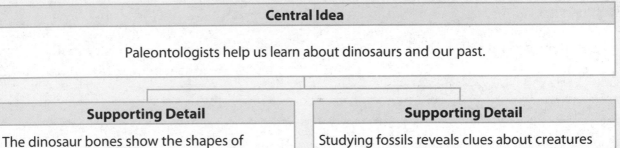

Central Idea
Paleontologists help us learn about dinosaurs and our past.

Supporting Detail	Supporting Detail
The dinosaur bones show the shapes of creatures from the past.	Studying fossils reveals clues about creatures that lived in the past.

As a good reader, make sure you figure out how the supporting details work together to develop the central idea in the text. This will help you understand each important point the author wants to make.

Read the first two paragraphs of an account about deep-sea divers.

Genre: **Social Studies Account**

Deep-Sea Treasure Hunters   *by Ramona Rivera*

Deep-sea diving is a dangerous but fascinating activity. Some people dive for fun or sport, and some make a career out of hunting for sunken treasure. These types of career divers fall into one of two categories: those who want to study their discoveries and those who want to sell the treasures they find.

The divers who study sunken treasures are concerned with preservation of the sites. These divers often locate, map, and study shipwrecks. When they find a site, the divers are interested in using the information that the treasure provides to form a story about the ship that wrecked. By studying artifacts such coins or jewelry found at a site, these divers learn many things about the lives of the ship's passengers. They also learn more about the cargo and the daily lives of the sailors aboard the ship. Sometimes they even learn why the ship sank.

(continued)

Explore how to answer these questions: *"What is the central idea of paragraph 2? What details are given to support it?"*

The author describes two career paths: deep-sea treasure diving for money, and deep-sea treasure diving for gathering information. Which career path is described in paragraph 2? How do the details help you learn more about it?

Study the account to figure out the central idea and supporting details in paragraph 2. Then complete the idea web below. Add more supporting details if necessary.

Central Idea
The goal of some deep-sea divers is to . . .

Supporting Detail	Supporting Detail
The divers study artifacts, like jewelry and coins.	

Work in a group and compare your web with your classmates'. Are your supporting details similar? Discuss how you chose each detail. Revise your web as needed, but remember that your answers can vary from your classmates' and still be correct.

Continue reading about deep-sea treasure hunters. Use the Close Reading and the Hint to help you answer the question.

Close Reading

The author mentions two central ideas in these paragraphs. **Circle** the first central idea and **underline** the second central idea.

(continued from page 4)

The deep-sea divers pursuing profit must carefully research their sites to make sure it is legal to take artifacts from the location. They must also take measures to preserve the artifacts so that they don't corrode and lose value once they are recovered. For these deep-sea divers, the measure of their success is the dollar value of the treasure they find.

Whether deep-sea divers wish to study treasure or collect it, divers must obey the laws, dive in teams, and be careful at all times. We must respect the power and mystery of our oceans if we hope to uncover their many hidden treasures.

Hint

Which choice explains more about the central idea you circled?

Circle the correct answer.

Which sentence provides a supporting detail for the idea that we must respect the oceans and their treasures?

A Some divers spend a lot of time searching for sunken treasures.

B Deep-sea diving involves a great deal of physical training.

C Divers must identify sites that are legal before they collect artifacts.

D Profit is the main motivation for some deep-sea divers.

Show Your Thinking

Explain how the supporting details given by the author develop the central idea about divers searching for profit.

_____

_____

_____

_____

With a partner, discuss details about each of the two careers described in the account. Then analyze the author's statement in the concluding sentence of the account.

Read the biography. Use the Study Buddy and Close Reading to guide your reading.

As I read, I'll think about the central ideas the author is telling me about Suni Williams. Why is she famous? What details about her life does the author want to share?

Close Reading

What does Suni say about why she hadn't yet become an astronaut? **Underline** the quote in paragraph 3.

Reread paragraph 1. Find and **star** (*) a sentence that gives a central idea about Suni Williams. Then **underline** sentences with details that support this idea.

Genre: **Biography**

Commander Suni Williams

by Margo Carlin

1   As 5-year-old Sunita "Suni" Williams watched Neil Armstrong's fascinating moon walk on television, she thought, "That's what I would like to do." While she never thought of moon walking as a realistic career goal, Williams' story proves that we can't always know where our path is going to lead us. If we believe in ourselves, though, we'll end up in the right place.

2   Williams' career path was far from predictable. She says she was just an "okay" high school student. Because her brother had gone to the U.S. Naval Academy, she was drawn there, too.

3   Williams graduated from the Naval Academy and trained to become a Navy helicopter test pilot. Listening to a former astronaut talk about flying a helicopter as preparation for flying a moon lander, a light bulb went on in Williams's head. It dawned on her that her helicopter training could be her ticket to space. She realized: "The only one who's telling me I'm not going to be an astronaut is me."

4   Williams eventually trained to become a member of the *International Space Station* crew, where she served as flight engineer and set a new record for women in space. Another first: She "ran" the Boston Marathon—on a space station treadmill.

5   Williams believes there is a message for young people in learning about the twists and turns that led to her space station adventure. "Maybe you want something, but you get something else. But if you make the best of it, things sorta work out."

Hints

Use the Hints on this page to help you answer the questions.

Which choice matches one of the central ideas from the previous page?

1 Which sentence best captures a central idea of the biography?

    A Career paths are not always easy to identify and follow.

    B Suni Williams did not face any difficult challenges in her career.

    C The career path chosen by Suni Williams was very predictable.

    D People should never change their career path.

Which sentence tells something about Williams not believing in herself?

2 Which sentence from the biography best captures a second central idea of the text?

    A "She says she was just an "okay" high school student."

    B "It dawned on her that her helicopter training could be her ticket to space."

    C ""The only one who's telling me I'm not going to be an astronaut is me.""

    D "Williams eventually trained to become a member of the *International Space Station* crew, where she served as flight engineer and set a new record for women in space."

Which central idea did you choose in the second Close Reading activity?

3 Describe one central idea about Suni Williams' life. List at least three details from the text that support this idea.

_____

_____

_____

_____

_____

_____

_____

_____

_____

_____

Read the biography about a famous dancer. Then answer the questions that follow.

Martha Graham: Modern Dance Innovator

by Eva Milner

1   In the world of dance, Martha Graham is a giant. A true innovator, it was she who led the way into the brave new world of modern dance, leaving behind the constraints of classical ballet. Through her work as a dancer, choreographer, and teacher, Martha has inspired both audiences and generations of dance students. Her institute, the Martha Graham Dance Company, has produced some of the finest dancers in the world today.

2   Martha Graham was born in 1894 in a small town near Pittsburgh, Pennsylvania. Her father was a doctor who specialized in nervous disorders. He was interested in how illnesses and disorders could be revealed through the way a patient's body moved. Martha also believed in the body's ability to express what is inside. She would channel this belief through dance, not medicine, however.

3   Martha was an athletic child, but it wasn't until after seeing the ballet dancer Ruth St. Denis in her teens that she became interested in dance. Martha was so inspired by the performance that she enrolled at an arts college where she studied theater and dance. After graduating in 1916, she joined the Denishawn School, a dance company founded by Ruth St. Denis and Ted Shawn to teach both American dance and world dance.

4   Though Martha began her eight years at Denishawn as a student, it wasn't long before she became a teacher and one of the school's best-known performers. It was during this time that Martha costarred with Ted Shawn in "Xochital," a duet that Ted created specifically for Martha. In this ballet, Martha played the role of an Aztec maiden attacked by an Aztec emperor. Her wildly emotional performance brought her critical acclaim.

5   By 1923, however, Martha felt ready to try new things. She took a job dancing in a vaudeville show in New York City. Here Martha had the opportunity to create her own dances. While there was some room for creativity, she still had to please the audience. Soon she longed for someplace she could take her experimental dance techniques even further. Her search led her to a job teaching at the Eastman School of Music, where she had complete control over her classes and the dance program. This was her chance to truly experiment.

6   Martha felt that classical ballet focused too much on fluidity and grace and ignored deeper, darker emotions and themes. At Eastman, Martha began to use jerky, trembling movements and falls to express ideas and feelings. She developed a fresh, new method of muscle control she called "contraction and release." Through this method, a dancer creates movement by first contracting a muscle and then allowing the movement to flow as the muscle relaxes. This method of muscle control gives the dancer's motions a hard, angular look. This was a big change from the dance style found in classical ballet.

7   Audiences did not always appreciate Martha's style. They were used to the more graceful, flowing motions of ballet dancers, and Martha's choppy, angular style was shocking to them. Many reviewers criticized her for dancing in an "ugly" way. During her first performance in Paris, she and her dancers were booed by the audience.

8   In 1926, Martha formed her own dance company, the now-famous Martha Graham School for Contemporary Dance. She brought in several of her students from the Eastman school and also began

working with Louis Horst, the musical director from her days at Denishawn. Under Horst's influence, Martha began to use music by modern composers, rather than music from the eighteenth and nineteenth centuries. This was yet another way in which Martha's work departed from classical ballet.

9   Many of Martha's dances explored emotional and psychological themes. One example is her solo piece "Lamentation." In this dance, a grieving figure sits alone on a bench and moves to a mournful piano score. The dancer wears a tube of stretchy, purple fabric. Only the dancer's head, hands, and feet show. The movements of the dancer's body within the fabric create a sort of moving sculpture. The dancer represents the raw emotions of grief.

10   Martha was also interested in exploring social issues and political themes. Her dance "Deep Song" was a statement about the Civil War in Spain, and "Chronicle" looked at the menace of fascism and war in Europe. This second dance was created the same year Martha had turned down an invitation to the 1936 Olympic Games being held in Germany. Both the dance itself and her refusal to attend the games expressed Martha's integrity and desire to highlight important political issues.

11   Martha Graham's career spanned her entire life. Health issues forced her to quit dancing at the age of 76, but she continued teaching and creating works until her death in 1991. In her lifetime, she created 181 masterpieces of dance, which continue to inspire dancers and audiences alike.

Answer the questions. Mark your answers to questions 1–3 on the Answer Form to the right.

Answer Form

1 Ⓐ Ⓑ Ⓒ Ⓓ
2 Ⓐ Ⓑ Ⓒ Ⓓ   **Number**
3 Ⓐ Ⓑ Ⓒ Ⓓ   **Correct** /3

1   Study the idea web below.

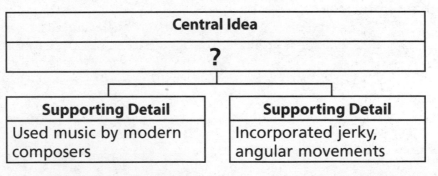

Which sentence completes the idea web?

A   Classical ballet focused on flowing, graceful movements.

B   Martha's dance style was very different from classical ballet.

C   Martha was one of the best dancers in America.

D   Louis Horst was the musical director at Denishawn.

2　Which sentence **best** supports the central idea that Martha Graham was an innovator?

　　A　"While there was some room for creativity, she still had to please the audience."

　　B　"Her search led her to a job teaching at the Eastman School of Music, where she had complete control over her classes and the dance program."

　　C　"She developed a fresh, new method of muscle control she called 'contraction and release.'"

　　D　"In 1926, Martha formed her own dance company, the now-famous Martha Graham School for Contemporary Dance."

3　Which sentence could be added to **best** support the idea that Graham was an innovator?

　　A　By 1927, Graham was working full-time as a dancer and choreographer.

　　B　Graham was the first choreographer to fully collaborate with other modern artists.

　　C　During the Depression in the 1930s, Graham sewed her dance costumes herself.

　　D　Graham was given the title "Dancer of the Century" by *Time* magazine in 1998.

4　Describe the central idea of paragraphs 9 and 10. Identify at least **two** details the author used to develop that central idea.

_____

_____

_____

_____

_____

_____

_____

✓ **Self Check**　*Go back and see what you can check off on the Self Check on page 2.*

Summarizing Informational Texts

CCSS

RI.7.2: . . . provide an objective summary of the text.

Theme: *Invasive Species*

What do you do when a friend sees you reading and asks, "What is that article about?" You don't recite the article word for word or read it aloud. The best response is to give a **summary**, or a brief restatement of the article's important details and central ideas in your own words. A summary should be **objective**, or free of any opinions or personal beliefs.

Read the news report below. Think about what its most important points might be.

A local woman was injured while water-skiing when a large silver carp jumped across her path and broke her jaw. State park officials indicate that this non-native species is known to "fly" over the water when it is disturbed. Many consider the fish to be a public nuisance.

Now read the report again. Underline the most important details in the report.

Read the chart below to see how to summarize information.

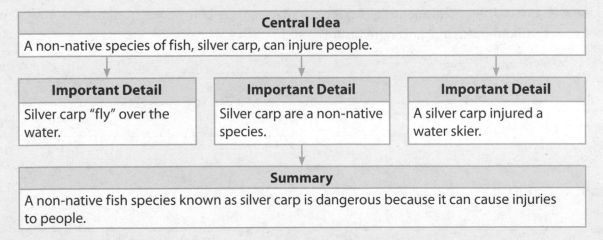

Central Idea
A non-native species of fish, silver carp, can injure people.

Important Detail	Important Detail	Important Detail
Silver carp "fly" over the water.	Silver carp are a non-native species.	A silver carp injured a water skier.

Summary
A non-native fish species known as silver carp is dangerous because it can cause injuries to people.

Good readers recognize central ideas, whether stated or implied, and identify important details in a text. They use those ideas and details when they summarize the text, and they do not include any nonessential information or opinions.

Read the first two paragraphs of a government bulletin about invasive species.

Genre: **Public Document**

The Invaders   *by Mark Sanchez*

During the early 1900s, two kinds of invasive organisms turned up in waterways in the United States. One was the Asiatic clam, a fast-growing shellfish that crowds out other aquatic animals. The other was milfoil, a fast-growing aquatic plant that overcomes and displaces native water plants.

Wildlife officials are seeing once-smooth freshwater beaches littered with sharp, tiny shells. Though Asiatic clams are rarely larger than 1.5 inches across, the sheer number of the shells is cause for concern. The highest populations occur near power and wastewater plants. The clams cause problems by biofouling, or clogging intake valves. Biofouling also occurs in irrigation canals and pipes and drinking water facilities. Repairing damage caused by Asiatic clams is expensive. Experts estimate that the price tag has reached one billion dollars per year in the United States.

(continued)

Explore how to answer this question: *"How can I best summarize this bulletin?"*

The author presents a central idea in each paragraph but does not state it directly. The important text details support the central idea, so identifying them will help you determine the central idea. This in turn will help you summarize the text.

Reread the bulletin. Underline the important details. Then fill in the missing information below.

Central idea of paragraph 2: Biofouling by Asiatic clams, one type of invasive species in U.S. waterways, causes costly repairs to industrial and agricultural water facilities.

Important detail from the text: _____

_____.

Important detail from the text: _____

_____.

Summary: _____

_____

_____

_____.

With a partner, take turns summarizing this part of the bulletin objectively. Remember, summarizing means restating the central idea and important details *in your own words*.

Continue reading the government bulletin about invasive species. Use the Close Reading and the Hint to help you answer the question.

Close Reading

On page 12, the author does not directly state the central idea. Jot your ideas in the margin about the implied central idea of this part of the bulletin.

Hint

Which answer choice restates important details and does not include opinions?

(continued from page 12)

The fern-like and harmless-looking milfoil has also become a threat. It too can clog valves at water facilities. In addition, milfoil poses problems for recreational water users. Dense growths of the Eurasian native create unfavorable conditions for swimmers, boaters, and fishers. Milfoil grows aggressively and crowds out other vegetation. The resulting ecosystem lacks food sources and habitats for native fish, amphibians, and waterfowl. Milfoil spreads naturally when fragments travel by water currents. It spreads with human help when fragments are carried from one waterway to another on boats and boat trailers.

Circle the correct answer.

Which of the following statements best summarizes the text above?

A The annoying milfoil plant does extensive harm to human facilities as well as to fragile ecosystems. It spreads ruthlessly by water current and should be a major concern to outdoor enthusiasts.

B Fern-like and harmless-looking, milfoil is a secret threat. Dense growths of the Eurasian native crowd the waterways, creating unfavorable conditions for swimmers, boaters, and fishers.

C Milfoil, a non-native species of water plant, ruins recreational water activities and heartlessly wipes out food sources and habitats for animals.

D Eurasian milfoil is an invasive species that spreads both naturally and with human help. Milfoil is an "invader" because it can harm water facilities, destroy animal habitats, and crowd out native plants.

✎ Show Your Thinking

Choose an answer choice that includes an opinion. Explain what clues helped you recognize that it was not objective.

_____

_____

With a partner, take turns summarizing the central ideas and important details in the government bulletin. Be sure to avoid using judgments and opinions in your summary.

Read the scientific account. Use the Study Buddy and the Close Reading to guide your reading.

The passage's title is "Kudzu: From Pretty Vine to Invasive Pest." I'm going to look for text that supports the ideas of the vine being "pretty" or a "pest." I'll underline those ideas when I find them.

Close Reading

Paragraph 2 mentions two important details about problems with kudzu. **Circle** phrases that name those two details.

The author describes the rapid growth of kudzu in the last paragraph. **Star** (*) the sentences that explain the problem caused by this plant's size.

Genre: **Scientific Account**

Kudzu: From Pretty Vine to Invasive Pest

by Aaron Hartman

1   Like many plants that are in the news, kudzu originated in Asia. Unlike other invasive species, this plant was purposely brought here and, at first, everyone loved it. At the 1876 Centennial Exposition in Philadelphia, Pennsylvania, the Japanese government filled its display with plants native to Japan. <u>The attractive kudzu vine, with its large leaves and sweet-smelling blooms, was greatly admired by the Americans.</u> People began planting the vine for decorative purposes. Some years later, kudzu was promoted as forage, or food, for cattle and goats. And during the 1930s and 1940s, the government fostered the spread of kudzu by planting it to control erosion.

2   Modern-day experts agree that kudzu is good for forage. However, it is easily overgrazed, so farmers need to have an alternate food source so that the animals can be removed from the kudzu field to allow the vines time to regrow. And no one denies that kudzu is effective at controlling erosion. However, kudzu vines have a tendency to take over. Farmers and homeowners all over the southeastern United States know that only too well.

3   Kudzu can grow about a foot a day, or approximately 60 feet in a growing season. Huge tap roots help the plant survive dry periods and make kudzu impossible to pull up. The vigorous vines completely cover abandoned fields and trees. The large leaves block out the sun and smother existing plants. As is the case with all invasives, the absence of natural checks and balances is what has turned kudzu from a pretty plant into a noxious weed.

Hints

Which choice *restates* paragraph 2's central idea and does *not* include opinions or judgments?

Use the Hints on this page to help you answer the questions.

1. Which of the following statements best summarizes the central idea and important details of paragraph 2?

   A   Modern-day experts agree that kudzu is good for forage. Kudzu also is very effective at controlling erosion.

   B   Kudzu is only of limited value as animal forage. It is also an effective erosion controller, but it can take over in an undesirable way.

   C   As forage for animals, kudzu is useless because it is easily overgrazed. It is also useless at controlling erosion because it grows too much.

   D   Farmers and homeowners in the southeastern United States agree that kudzu grows too much to be useful, either as forage or as an erosion control.

To help with question 2, I'll look back at the ideas I underlined.

2. Which of the following statements best restates one central idea that should be included in a summary of the passage?

   A   Though once considered a desirable plant, kudzu has invasive tendencies that make it a harmful weed.

   B   Kudzu has become the most troublesome invasive plant species, partly because it was once thought to be attractive.

   C   As is the case with other invasives, natural checks and balances are effective at controlling kudzu.

   D   Kudzu is native to Asia but was brought to the United States on purpose.

What is the implied central idea of the whole passage? What important details does each paragraph provide?

3. Write a brief summary of the passage. Use at least three specific details from the passage in your summary.

   _____

   _____

   _____

   _____

   _____

   _____

Read the scientific account. Then answer the questions that follow.

Python Invasion!

by Leigh Driver

1   For years, the number-one, most feared animal in Florida has been the
alligator. But recently the Burmese python has been challenging the alligators'
long-held position. Burmese pythons are native to Asia, but they have found a new
home in Florida. Their numbers are increasing dramatically. Today they can be
found in the wild and in suburbs across the state. Burmese pythons have lightly-
colored skin with brown patches, and they are admired for their skin patterns and
size. But they are also massive hunters—among the largest top six snakes in the
world—and they pose a danger to people, other animals, and the environment.

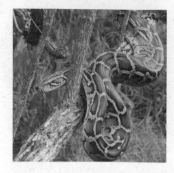

How Did They Get There?

2   The Burmese python has become more and more popular as a house pet. This caused a surge of
imports of the snake to Florida. This is not the first time Florida has become home to a species of reptile
intended to be kept as a pet. The state is the adopted home of several types of reptiles. The green iguana and
the speckled caiman, a type of alligator, were brought to Florida as family pets. Now, many of these creatures
live in the wild. These animals may seem like exotic and fascinating alternatives to the family cat, but they
are also very difficult to maintain. People often found them hard to keep at home so they released them to
the wild.

3   The same thing is happening with the Burmese python, an animal that begins at a manageable 3 feet
long on average but can grow up to 20 feet long and weigh up to 250 pounds. There have been several reports
of deaths in homes where pythons are kept. When a python is fully grown, many owners find they can no
longer handle their exotic reptile, and they simply release it outdoors.

4   Another factor has been the destructive hurricanes that Florida has suffered over the years.
Sometimes storms damage pet stores and animal shelters, and the reptiles get loose. When people bring their
other pets to shelters, it is sometimes easier to free the snakes because of overcrowding.

Environmental Impact

5   A python can survive very well in the Florida climate. In fact, the Florida Everglades are the perfect
home for these snakes. Some experts estimate that there are up to 100,000 Burmese pythons living in the
Everglades alone. But this surge of wild pythons is not without problems.

6   Releasing animals into an environment where they do not belong affects that environment and the
species within it. Such animal populations are referred to as non-native species. While few creatures prey on
it, the python competes with other animals in the territory. For example, alligators compete for prey with
pythons. As these snakes breed and thrive, they threaten the survival of the alligators. Other animal
populations may also be harmed by the presence of pythons, and Floridians who are concerned about
conservation have publicized the dangers of this situation.

Danger to People

7   Another growing concern is that the Burmese python can seriously harm people. A python can eat an animal as large as a full-grown deer, and it is extremely difficult to control the powerful creature. Some Floridians believe that keeping these snakes as pets is simply not safe.

What Can Be Done?

8   Scientists and citizens have become more and more worried about the "invasion" of the Burmese python into the Florida wild. There have been proposals to ban the importation of snakes or to make it illegal to keep these animals as pets, but so far no laws have been passed. Some have even proposed destroying the pythons living in the Everglades to get rid of the problem.

Answer Form

1 Ⓐ Ⓑ Ⓒ Ⓓ
2 Ⓐ Ⓑ Ⓒ Ⓓ   **Number** ╱ **3**
3 Ⓐ Ⓑ Ⓒ Ⓓ   **Correct**

1   Which of these sentences would most likely **not** be included in a summary of this passage?

    A   Burmese pythons have light-colored skin with interesting patterns.

    B   Due to their weight and strength, Burmese pythons may endanger their human owners.

    C   Some Floridians have made house pets of this exotic species of reptiles.

    D   Non-native species threaten native animal populations in the Everglades.

2   Read these sentences from the passage.

    Burmese pythons are native to Asia, but they have found a new home in Florida. Their numbers are increasing dramatically. Today they can be found in the wild and in suburbs across the state.

What is the **best** summary of this section of the passage?

    A   Burmese pythons are now at home in many suburbs in the state of Florida.

    B   Though Burmese pythons are native to Asia, they now live in Florida's suburbs.

    C   Native to Asia, Burmese pythons now occupy wild and suburban areas of Florida in growing numbers.

    D   Visitors to the state of Florida can study populations of the Burmese python in many wild and suburban areas.

3　Which of the following statements **best** restates a central idea that should be included in a summary of the passage?

　　A　Exotic creatures such as the Burmese python or the speckled caiman are becoming very popular as house pets in Florida.

　　B　With few natural enemies in the wild, the Burmese python has become a threat to the survival of native animal species in Florida.

　　C　When homes or stores are damaged during a hurricane, Burmese pythons and other exotic pets may escape into the Florida wilderness.

　　D　With hard work, Florida conservationists hope they can succeed in changing the law to make it illegal to keep Burmese pythons as pets.

4　Based on the information in the text "Python Invasion," write an essay that summarizes and explains not just the problems caused by Burmese pythons but also the proposed solutions. Use at least **three** details from the text to support your ideas.

_____

_____

_____

_____

_____

_____

_____

_____

_____

_____

_____

_____

✓ **Self Check**　*Go back and see what you can check off on the Self Check on page 2.*

Citing Evidence to Make Inferences

CCSS

RI.7.1: Cite several pieces of textual evidence to support analysis of what the text says explicitly as well as inferences drawn from the text.

Theme: *The Competitive Spirit*

When you **analyze** something, you examine its parts to see how they work together. For example, you might analyze how the parts of a bicycle work to help a person move forward.

Reading involves analyzing, too. When you analyze a text, you sometimes look at what the text says **explicitly**, or directly. "The crowd clapped and cheered wildly when the home team won" is an example of explicit information because you know what happened and why. Other times, though, you must make an inference to figure out what the text is really saying. An **inference** is a reasonable guess based on textual evidence and what you already know.

Find the slowest runner in the picture below. Is he sad about losing? How can you tell?

I love this sport!

Circle details in the picture that support an inference that the runner isn't sad about losing. Then complete the chart below to describe what details support this inference.

Text Evidence	+	Background Knowledge	=	Inference
• The expression on the runner's face is _____ _____. • This runner says _____ _____.		A person who loves a sport also enjoys participating in it.		The runner is just happy to compete. Competing is more important to him than winning.

To get the most out of your reading, you must analyze texts to understand what they say directly and make inferences about what they say indirectly. When you find evidence to make and support inferences, you'll find you won't get stuck as often trying to figure out what a text is saying—like when a bike is stuck in gear and can't move forward.

Read the first three paragraphs of an article that showcases Michael Jordan.

Genre: **Article**

The Flu Game   *by Maureen McBride*

Game 5 of the 1997 basketball playoffs should have been the game that the Chicago Bulls lost. It should, in fact, have marked the Utah Jazz's first NBA championship win. Michael Jordan, the Bulls' star player, had spent the previous 24 hours bedridden and dehydrated with what doctors had diagnosed as the stomach flu. He had lost weight and had missed two key days of practice leading up to the game. It was a recipe for disaster.

But three hours before the start of Game 5, the best player in the history of basketball suited up and appeared on the court.

Though Jordan was visibly weak in the first quarter, he had scored 17 points by the second, putting the Bulls ahead at half time. However, while Jordan spent the third quarter overcome by nausea and fatigue, Utah managed to reclaim the lead.

(continued)

Explore how to answer these questions: *"What is Michael Jordan's attitude toward competition? What text evidence supports your idea?"*

Michael Jordan's attitude is not stated, so you must use evidence in the text to infer what he thinks.

Look for evidence of Jordan's feelings about competition. One detail is shown in the chart below. Write another detail in column 1. Use this information to complete the inference in the last column.

Text Evidence	+	Background Knowledge	=	Inference
• Jordan was diagnosed with the flu before Game 5. •		• Jordan's team depended on him greatly. • Playing sports while sick requires determination.		Michael believes that competition _____.

What text evidence supports the inference that Michael Jordan is a fierce competitor? With a partner, find evidence in the article that supports your answer, and write it on the lines below.

_____

_____

Continue reading about Michael Jordan in "The Flu Game." Use the Close Reading and the Hint to help you answer the question.

Close Reading

Which sentence best shows that Jordan is a talented player? Find and **underline** a sentence on this page showing this.

(continued from page 20)

"In the third quarter, I felt like I couldn't catch my wind," Jordan said. "I was just trying to get myself through it."

In the fourth quarter, Jordan scored 18 more points. Then, with only 25 seconds left in the game, he scored a 3-point shot, and the Bulls beat the Jazz by only two points. At the end of the game, Jordan collapsed into the arms of his teammate Scottie Pippen.

"I almost played myself into passing out just to win a basketball game," Jordan admitted later. "If we had lost, I would have been devastated."

Hint

Look for the choice that shows Jordan's talent, not his dedication or his luck.

Circle the correct answer.

Which sentence from the passage best supports the idea that Michael Jordan is a talented basketball player?

A "'In the third quarter, I felt like I couldn't catch my wind,' Jordan said. 'I was just trying to get myself through it.'"

B "In the fourth quarter, Jordan scored 18 more points."

C "Then, with only 25 seconds left in the game, he scored a 3-point shot, and the Bulls beat the Jazz by only two points."

D "'I almost played myself into passing out just to win a basketball game,' Jordan admitted later."

Show Your Thinking

Michael Jordan is a dedicated basketball player. Find and write down a sentence from the passage that supports this statement. Then explain your answer.

_____

_____

_____

With a partner, make an inference about why Michael Jordan collapsed into Scottie Pippen's arms. Support your inference with evidence from the text and background knowledge.

Read the following historical account. Use the Study Buddy and the Close Reading to guide your reading.

As I read, I'll look for evidence that tells more about each explorer. Then I can make inferences about what each one was like.

Close Reading

What factors led to Scott's failure? **Underline** details from the text that show the kind of trouble he and his men ran into.

What did Amundsen have going for him that Scott did not? **Circle** details that show Amundsen's advantages.

Genre: **Historical Account**

Race to Reach the South Pole: Scott vs. Amundsen   *by Alarik Fjelstad*

1   In 1911, Englishman Robert Falcon Scott and Norwegian Roald Amundsen raced to reach the South Pole first. Scott, captain of the *Terra Nova,* had nearly made it to the South Pole seven years earlier. He was confident he would succeed this time. Scott publicly announced that he would be using the latest in technology: motor sleds. He recruited scientists, sailors, and even a paying guest who insisted on bringing ponies to the coldest place on Earth.

2   Amundsen worried that competitors might try to prevent his attempt to reach the South Pole. He refused to share his dream with anyone, including his shipmates. Amundsen finally told his men where they were going midway through the Atlantic. Though he told them they could quit, they decided to continue the journey with him. They were all veteran Arctic explorers trained to use skis and sled dogs. At this time, Amundsen sent Scott an unsettling telegram telling him he was on his way to Antarctica.

3   Both vessels landed in Antarctica in January of 1911, but Amundsen set up his base camp deep inland on ice, while Scott made camp at the shoreline. With expert planning, Amundsen and his crew arrived at the South Pole with sled dogs on December 15, 1911. Meanwhile, Scott's motor sleds failed to work in the minus 40 degree Celsius cold, and the ponies died and were eaten by Scott's crew. Scott arrived at the Pole 33 days after Amundsen and was shocked to find the Norwegian flag. Disillusioned and weak, Scott and his men died of starvation on the return trip, just 11 miles from their nearest supply station.

Hints

Which choice provides evidence that Amundsen was not very trusting?

Use the Hints on this page to help you answer the questions.

1 A student makes the following inference about Captain Amundsen:

   Amundsen was a very secretive person.

   Which sentence from the text best supports this inference?

   A ". . . Admundsen set up his base camp deep inland on ice, while Scott made camp at the shoreline."

   B "Admundsen finally told his men where they were going midway through the Atlantic."

   C "At this time, Amundsen sent Scott an unsettling telegram telling him he was on his way to Antarctica. "

   D "Scott arrived at the Pole 33 days after Amundsen and was shocked to find the Norwegian flag."

Think about what finally happened to Scott and his men. Which choice explains their fate?

2 Based on the text, which of the following statements explains why Scott and his men were unsuccessful?

   A Scott and his men were not truly prepared for the trip's hardships.

   B Scott planned to use outdated technology on the trip.

   C The English expedition camped at the shoreline instead of inland.

   D They were unfamiliar with the challenge of Arctic exploration.

What did Amundsen have in his favor that Scott did not? Think about his shipmates and forms of transportation.

3 Explain why Amundsen succeeded. Include at least two details from the text that support your inference about what led to his success.

   _____

   _____

   _____

   _____

   _____

   _____

   _____

   _____

Read this excerpt from a back-to-school speech. Then answer the questions that follow.

from "The President's Speech to Students"

by President Barack Obama

1   You're this country's future. You're young leaders. And whether we fall behind or race ahead as a nation is going to depend in large part on you. So I want to talk to you a little bit about meeting that responsibility.

2   It starts, obviously, with being the best student that you can be. Now, that doesn't always mean that you have to have a perfect score on every assignment. It doesn't mean that you've got to get straight As all the time—although that's not a bad goal to have. It means that you have to stay at it. You have to be determined and you have to persevere. It means you've got to work as hard as you know how to work. And it means that you've got to take some risks once in a while. You can't avoid the class that you think might be hard because you're worried about getting the best grade if that's a subject that you think you need to prepare you for your future. You've got to wonder. You've got to question. You've got to explore. And every once in a while, you need to color outside of the lines.

3   That's what school is for: discovering new passions, acquiring new skills, making use of this incredible time that you have to prepare yourself and give yourself the skills that you're going to need to pursue the kind of careers that you want. And that's why when you're still a student you can explore a wide range of possibilities. One hour you can be an artist; the next, an author; the next, a scientist, or a historian, or a carpenter. This is the time where you can try out new interests and test new ideas. And the more you do, the sooner you'll figure out what makes you come alive, what stirs you, what makes you excited—the career that you want to pursue....

4   So that's a big part of your responsibility, to test things out. Take risks. Try new things. Work hard. Don't be embarrassed if you're not good at something right away. You're not supposed to be good at everything right away. That's why you're in school. The idea, though, is that you keep on expanding your horizons and your sense of possibility. Now is the time for you to do that. And those are also, by the way, the things that will make school more fun.

5   Down the road, those will be the traits that will help you succeed, as well—the traits that will lead you to invent a device that makes an iPad look like a stone tablet. Or what will help you figure out a way to use the sun and the wind to power a city and give us new energy sources that are less polluting. Or maybe you'll write the next great American novel....

6   But I also want to emphasize this: With all the challenges that our country is facing right now, we don't just need you for the future; we actually need you now. America needs young people's passion and their ideas. We need your energy right now. I know you're up to it because I've seen it. Nothing inspires me more than knowing that young people all across the country are already making their marks. They're not waiting. They're making a difference now....

7   There are students like Will Kim from Fremont, California, who launched a nonprofit that gives loans to students from low-income schools who want to start their own business. Think about that. So he's giving loans to other students. He set up a not-for-profit. He's raising the money doing what he loves—through dodgeball tournaments and capture-the-flag games. But he's creative. He took initiative. And now he's helping other young people be able to afford the schooling that they need....

8   The point is you don't have to wait to make a difference. Your first obligation is to do well in school. Your first obligation is to make sure that you're preparing yourself for college and career. But you can also start making your mark right now. A lot of times young people may have better ideas than us old people do anyway. We just need those ideas out in the open, in and out of the classroom....

9   When I meet young people like yourselves, when I sit and talk to [a student at this school], I have no doubt that America's best days are still ahead of us, because I know the potential that lies in each of you. Soon enough, you will be the ones leading our businesses and leading our government. You will be the one who are making sure that the next generation gets what they need to succeed. You will be the ones that are charting the course of our unwritten history. And all that starts right now—starts this year....

Answer Form

1 Ⓐ Ⓑ Ⓒ Ⓓ
2 Ⓐ Ⓑ Ⓒ Ⓓ   **Number**   / 3
3 Ⓐ Ⓑ Ⓒ Ⓓ   **Correct**

1   Which of these statements is **not** supported by the remarks made in President Obama's speech?

   A   Work hard in school and try out new possibilities.

   B   While in school, acquire a variety of skills and interests.

   C   Figure out different ways to become energetic leaders.

   D   Explore a wide range of ideas and career options.

2   What evidence from the speech **best** shows how students can prepare themselves for the future?

   A   Students need to act responsibly during their time in school.

   B   Students should focus on courses that will help them earn good grades.

   C   Students should realize that they will not excel at everything that they try.

   D   Students need to try new possibilities to discover what excites them.

3   Which sentence from the passage **best** supports the idea that President Obama thinks students must take responsibility for their own futures?

   A   "Now, that doesn't always mean that you have to have a perfect score on every assignment."

   B   "Down the road, those will be the traits that will help you succeed, as well—the traits that will lead you to invent a device that makes an iPad look like a stone tablet."

   C   "Your first obligation is to make sure that you're preparing yourself for college and career."

   D   "Soon enough, you will be the ones leading our businesses and leading our government."

4   Read the statement below, and then answer the question that follows it.

    President Obama believes that creativity is a valuable trait for people to have.

Explain how you can tell that the above statement is true. Write a paragraph responding to this question. Use at least **two** details from the passage to support your response.

_____

_____

_____

_____

_____

_____

_____

_____

_____

_____

_____

✓ **Self Check**   *Go back and see what you can check off on the Self Check on page 2.*

Lesson 4   Part 1: Introduction 👥

Analyzing Interactions in a Text

CCSS
RI.7.3: Analyze the interactions between individuals, events, and ideas in a text (e.g., how ideas influence individuals or events, or how individuals influence ideas or events).

Theme: *Inventors and Inventions*

Why does an individual invent something new? Is it a response to a question, a dream, or a need? Most often, different factors work in combination to **influence**, or affect, the inventor.

Consider the events in the cartoon below. What effect does Ogg's complaint have on his wife, Urg? What is her response? How do these factors result in a new invention?

Complete the chart below to show how the different factors in the cartoon are related.

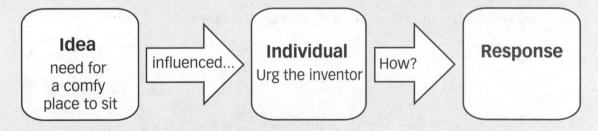

The cartoon shows that a single idea influenced Urg, which led to her response. In contrast, consider an invention as complicated as the airplane. *Many* individuals, events, and ideas influenced the Wright brothers' thinking and responses over the years. Ultimately, their invention was the result of a series of **interactions**, or the direct effects the factors had on one another. With your classmates, brainstorm the different factors that might have interacted to result in the invention of the airplane.

Throughout history, important outcomes result from the interactions among individuals, events, and ideas, and informational texts often explore these relationships. As a good reader, analyze the interactions carefully. Note how they shape the course and development of later events and ideas as well as the choices individuals make.

Read the first paragraphs of the historical account about the photographer Eadweard Muybridge.

Genre: **Historical Account**

Flying Horses   *by Cynthia Hernandez*

Do horses fly? Intelligent, well-educated people were still asking this question at the end of the nineteenth century. Although the age of believing in winged horses had long since passed, people still wondered if a horse ever lifted all four hooves off the ground at the same time. If someone could prove that a horse's hooves left the ground, then the answer would indicate that, yes, in a sense, horses do fly! Eadweard Muybridge, photographer and adventurer, put an end to years of speculation. Through the use of a new technology, photography, he laid the question to rest at last.

In 1872, Muybridge was working as a photographer in San Francisco when Leland Stanford, former California governor, hired Muybridge to photograph his racehorse. Stanford wanted to know if all four hooves of a trotting horse actually leave the ground, even for an instant. Muybridge rapidly hatched a plan. Unfortunately, his early efforts were unsuccessful.

(continued)

Explore how to answer this question: *"What people, events, and ideas led to Muybridge's plan to photograph a horse?"*

Think of the way the question about horses influenced Muybridge's actions.

Fill in the chart below with the idea that led to Muybridge's response.

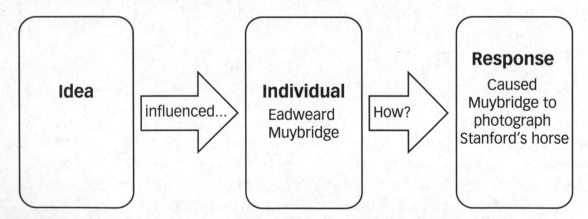

How did people, events, and ideas influence Muybridge's plan? On the lines below, explain the interaction among the factors. Support your ideas with evidence from the text.

_____

_____

_____

Continue reading about Eadweard Muybridge. Use the Close Reading and the Hint to help you answer the question.

Close Reading

How did Muybridge's ideas about photography and cameras help him figure out how horses moved? **Underline** the sentence that explains what his high-speed photographs revealed.

(continued from page 28)

After several attempts, Muybridge finally succeeded in getting the proof Stanford needed. Muybridge set up a series of cameras in a line down the side of a horse track. As the horse passed by, its hooves snapped wires stretched across the track, which activated the camera shutters. A series of high-speed photographs resulted.

The results amazed the public. The photographs showed clearly that a trotting horse had all four hooves off the ground at the same time. The pictures were a sensation, and Muybridge became an international figure. His successful camera techniques led him to photograph other animal movements too fast for people to see.

Hint

Which answer choice best describes the images caught by the cameras?

Circle the correct answer.

Which sentence from the text best explains why the evidence provided by Muybridge changed the public's thinking about horses?

A "Stanford wanted to know if all four hooves of a trotting horse actually leave the ground, even for an instant."

B "Muybridge set up a series of cameras in a line down the side of a horse track."

C "The photographs showed clearly that a trotting horse had all four hooves off the ground at the same time."

D "His successful camera techniques led him to photograph other animal movements too fast for people to see."

✎ Show Your Thinking

Explain why the answer you chose illustrates the effect that Muybridge's photographs had on people's ideas about horses.

_____

_____

With a partner, discuss how Muybridge's knowledge about the new technology of photography influenced events in his life as well as the thoughts and actions of others.

Read the historical account. Use the Study Buddy and the Close Reading to guide your reading.

I wonder how changes in England affected Eli Whitney in America. I'll have to read carefully to figure out how the interactions between events and ideas resulted in his response.

Close Reading

Why couldn't Southern states make money by growing cotton in 1792? **Underline** the sentence explaining the problem Whitney hoped to solve.

Underline clues in the text that show how Whitney's invention changed life in the South.

Genre: **Historical Account**

Eli Whitney and the Cotton Gin

by Timothy Morris

1   In the late 1700s, England was hungry for cotton. Until this time, women and girls of the family generally did the spinning and weaving. Then improvements were made to the spinning wheel and loom, making them faster and more efficient. As a result, the process became mechanized, and new textile mills opened to meet the growing demand for cotton cloth.

2   In America in 1792, Eli Whitney recognized that the mechanization of the cloth-making process meant a greater demand for cotton. Cotton grew easily in the Southern states, but the cotton bolls contained numerous small seeds that were difficult and time-consuming to remove by hand. Unless a more efficient way could be found to separate the seeds from the bolls, there was little money to be made in growing cotton.

3   As a young man, Eli Whitney liked figuring out things. He studied machines and often found ways to improve them. Whitney began to think about the problem of removing seeds from cotton and decided that a machine could be built to do the job efficiently.

4   The machine Whitney designed was simple, but it worked like a charm. Cotton was fed into a machine with short wire teeth on a revolving cylinder. The thin cotton fibers were pulled through, leaving the seeds behind. Now, a single machine was capable of cleaning and processing up to fifty pounds of raw cotton daily.

5   The invention of the cotton gin brought about many changes. The most significant effect was that, at long last, growing cotton could be profitable. Cotton plantations sprang up in the South where once empty fields stood, and textile mills opened to make cloth. Thanks to Whitney's invention, the world was never the same again. Just as mechanization revolutionized life in England, the cotton gin gave the American South a new industry to call its own.

Hints

Which choice explains the problem that the cotton gin was invented to overcome?

Use the Hints on this page to help you answer the questions.

1 In America in 1792, growing cotton was not profitable. Which sentence from the text describes the problem as Eli Whitney understood it?

   A " . . . women and girls of the family generally did the spinning and weaving."

   B " . . . the process became mechanized, and new textile mills opened to meet the growing demand for cotton cloth."

   C " . . . the cotton bolls contained numerous small seeds that were difficult and time-consuming to remove by hand."

   D ". . . a single machine was capable of cleaning and processing up to fifty pounds of raw cotton daily."

Which choice shows the effect that the cotton gin had on history?

2 Based on evidence from the text, which statement best describes how the invention of the cotton gin influenced later events?

   A Eli Whitney made huge profits from the sale of cotton gins and became famous.

   B The easy removal of cotton seeds from cotton made life better for the workers.

   C Spinning wheels were no longer used due to the increase in cotton production.

   D The cotton gin led to the growth of cotton plantations and the textile industry.

How did Eli Whitney's cotton gin change people's ideas about growing cotton? What other changes came about as a result of the invention of the cotton gin?

3 The passage tells how the mechanization of cloth-making in England led to changes in America. Explain how the interactions between people, events, and ideas gave rise to a new industry in the South. Support your answer with at least two details from the text.

_____

_____

_____

_____

_____

_____

_____

Read the biography. Then answer the questions that follow.

Extraordinary People: Tim Berners-Lee

from HowStuffWorks online

1   Most people know that Thomas Edison invented the light bulb and that Alexander Graham Bell invented the telephone. But have you ever heard of Tim Berners-Lee?

2   Probably not, yet the work of Berners-Lee, the inventor of the World Wide Web, may have the most profound impact of all. Why is his name unknown to most of the world? The answer lies in the type of life he has chosen to lead and the role he has chosen to play in helping to guide this emerging technology.

3   If you were in a time machine and could travel back to 1960s London, you might find young Tim Berners-Lee busily constructing make-believe computers out of cardboard boxes or playing mathematical games with his parents at their kitchen table. Tim is fascinated by the world around him. His natural curiosity attracts him to a dusty Victorian-era encyclopedia he finds in his house; its mysterious title, *Enquire Within Upon Everything*, will stay with him for years to come.

4   Fast-forward to 2001. Over 250 million people are using the Internet, a system virtually unheard of 10 years earlier, and Tim Berners-Lee is largely responsible. How could one person make it all happen?

5   For some clues, let's go back to Tim's early adulthood. Tim was especially interested in two things: computers and how the human brain organizes and links information. He wondered how the mind can almost randomly connect so many different facts. For instance, how can a song or a scent mentally link or even transport someone to another time and place? Tim was so fascinated by computers that, before graduating from the University of Oxford, he built his very first one from a kit using a television and an early microprocessor.

6   In 1980, after graduating with a degree in physics, Tim went to work as a software engineer for an organization in Geneva, Switzerland. His job required a lot of research. He communicated with people all over the world and he was constantly answering the same questions over and over. He was frustrated by how poorly his mind could remember all of the reports and data he needed. He wished there were a way other people could simply access his data and he could access theirs via computer no matter where they were located.

7   Tim wrote a software program to help him keep track of important documents and, using a series of links (hypertext), he connected them together much like an index does in a book. He named the program Enquire after the book he loved as a child. In its original form, Enquire was capable of storing information and connecting documents electronically, but it could only access information on a single computer.

8   In 1989, Tim took a giant step towards his vision of a global system where documents could be linked via hypertext to the Internet, allowing people worldwide to easily share and link information. After much thought, he called his project the World Wide Web. Many people thought that connecting documents stored in individual computers around the world was impossible.

9   And even if it were possible, few of his fellow scientists thought it would ever become popular.

10   Tim was not discouraged. Working with a few colleagues who supported his vision, he developed the four critical foundations of the Web: The language for coding documents (HTML); the hypertext system for linking documents (HTTP); the system for locating documents on the Web (URL); the first graphical user interface (Internet browser). In 1991, the Web was launched and almost immediately, the Internet took off.

11   Although he has had many opportunities to do so, Tim has not profited from his creation. . . . [He] works for a non-profit organization located at M.I.T., a leading engineering university. Married with two children, Tim leads a good life, one that is full of professional challenges. He is pleased with the road he chose to follow. Today, he helps set standards and guides the Web's future, so he can be assured that it will remain open to all and not be splintered into many parts or dominated by one corporation. However, like Einstein, who was concerned with his role in the development of nuclear power, Tim believes that technology can be used for good or for evil. "At the end of the day," Tim says, "it is up to us: how we actually react, and how we teach our children, and the values we instill." To this day, Tim Berners-Lee works hard to see that the technology he invented remains accessible to all people around the globe. That, rather than instant wealth, is his reward.

Answer Form

1 (A) (B) (C) (D) **Number**   / 2
2 (A) (B) (C) (D) **Correct**

1 How did Tim Berners-Lee's work responsibilities in Switzerland influence his ideas about creating the Enquire program?

A He was looking for new ways to search for information beyond using encyclopedias.

B He wanted to use his knowledge of physics to do research and create more computer software for his company in Geneva.

C He spoke with people around the world and wished they would stop asking him the same questions over and over.

D He had trouble recalling facts he needed to do his job, and he longed for a way to connect and store data more easily.

2 Tim Berners-Lee imagined a system in which information could be exchanged between computers. How did this idea influence his life's work?

A It triggered his interest in building personal computers.

B It inspired him to develop the World Wide Web.

C It became the first step in building his own microprocessor.

D It encouraged him to publicly popularize his links to Enquire.

3 Based on the biography, explain how Tim Berners-Lee's early childhood interests influenced the path he chose as an adult. Use at least **two** details from the text to support your answer.

_____

_____

_____

_____

_____

4 Read these sentences from paragraph 5 of the biography.

> He wondered how the mind can almost randomly connect so many different facts. For instance, how can a song or a scent mentally link or even transport someone to another time and place?

Describe what influence this idea had on Tim Berners-Lee's approach to writing new programs that operate computers. Use at least **two** details from the biography to support your answer.

_____

_____

_____

_____

_____

_____

_____

_____

_____

_____

_____

✓ **Self Check** *Go back and see what you can check off on the Self Check on page 2.*

Read the article. Then answer the questions that follow.

The Bone Wars

by J. R. Hill

1   If you've spent any time in grocery checkout lines, you've probably seen magazines with pictures of celebrities behaving badly toward each other. You might believe that scientists would be above that sort of thing, but you'd be wrong. About 150 years ago, two scientists started a nasty feud that lasted for decades—and brought to light some of the most spectacular creatures that ever walked the earth.

2   Edward Cope and Othniel Marsh were paleontologists—scientists who study extinct life-forms, including dinosaurs. They met in 1864, when their careers were starting. Paleontology was a young science in the United States, and only a few dinosaurs had been discovered in North America.

Othniel Marsh   Edward Cope

3   Cope and Marsh were friendly at first, but their relationship quickly soured. In 1868, Cope and a team of hired men were digging up dinosaurs in New Jersey. Marsh journeyed there and stayed with Cope for a few weeks. Things seemed to go well, but after Marsh left, Cope learned that his guest and the team foreman had made a deal. In exchange for money, the foreman would send new fossils to Marsh instead of Cope. Marsh had fired the first shot in what scientists would come to call the "Bone Wars."

4   The war heated up fast. In 1869, Cope wrote an article describing a newly found extinct sea reptile he named *Elasmosaurus*. Cope included a drawing of the creature's skeleton. Another scientist soon pointed out that Cope had mistakenly stuck the beast's skull on its tail. Cope was humiliated, and Marsh crowed about the blunder to anyone who would listen. Shortly after, each man began publishing a string of scientific articles viciously attacking the other's ideas.

5   Cope and Marsh's thirst to outdo each other spilled into their fieldwork. Throughout the 1870s and 1880s, they led and sent teams into lawless regions of the western United States to hunt for dinosaur bones. The teams were told to slow and disrupt each other's work through bribery, stealing, and rock-throwing. The teams even used dynamite to blow up cliffs and bury fossils to keep discoveries from falling into each other's hands. To this day, scientists wonder what fantastic discoveries lay beneath tons of rubble.

6   In addition to sabotage, Cope and Marsh forced their teams to dig up and transport bones quickly. Such speed damaged many specimens, but each man wanted the credit of making the first discoveries of new species. Because they published their findings as quickly as possible, they made many mistakes. Marsh, for example, accidentally stuck the head of one dinosaur (*Camarasaurus*) on to the neck of another dinosaur (*Apatosaurus*) and thought he had discovered a new dinosaur—*Brontosaurus*. Unlike Cope's mistake with *Elasmosaurus*, paleontologists didn't discover and undo Marsh's *Brontosaurus* blunder for nearly 100 years.

7   Until the mid-1880s, only scientists knew about Cope and Marsh's fight. But when Cope ratted out Marsh to the *New York Herald*, their battle spilled out into the world at large. Cope and Marsh assaulted each other through letters published in the newspaper. For a time, they were as famous as any celebrities of today. And even when the public eventually stopped caring, the feud didn't cease. The two men of science took swipes at each other until Cope's death in 1897. Even in death, Cope kept up the attack. He donated his skull to science and asked that his brain size be compared with Marsh's. (Scientists of that time believed that a person with a large brain was smarter than a person with a small one.) For whatever reason, Marsh did not accept Cope's challenge.

8   The Bone Wars have a mixed legacy. On the one hand, American paleontology got a bad reputation from Cope and Marsh's cutthroat behavior. And the mistakes they made in their rush for glory slowed the progress of paleontology for many years. But the Bone Wars also produced a mountain of raw material. Cope and Marsh discovered more than 130 dinosaur species. Their teams dug up so many bones that scientists are still learning new things about them. And many of their most famous discoveries, including *Stegosaurus*, *Allosaurus*, *Diplodocus*, and *Triceratops*, fire the

imaginations of children (and more than a few adults) worldwide. Perhaps paleontology would have been worse off had the two men actually gotten along.

Answer the questions. Mark your answers to questions 1–7 on the Answer Form to the right.

Answer Form

1A Ⓐ Ⓑ Ⓒ Ⓓ	4 Ⓐ Ⓑ Ⓒ Ⓓ	
1B Ⓐ Ⓑ Ⓒ Ⓓ	5 Ⓐ Ⓑ Ⓒ Ⓓ	
2 Ⓐ Ⓑ Ⓒ Ⓓ	6 Ⓐ Ⓑ Ⓒ Ⓓ	**Number**
3 Ⓐ Ⓑ Ⓒ Ⓓ	7 Ⓐ Ⓑ Ⓒ Ⓓ	**Correct** /8

1 Answer Parts A and B below.

Part A

The article says that paleontology was a young science in the United States in the mid-1800s. How knowledgeable about the field were paleontologists of the time?

A They were more informed than those in other nations.

B They were the greatest experts of the field at the time.

C They were not very knowledgeable about their field.

D They were just as knowledgeable as any other scientists.

Part B

Which detail from the article **best** supports the answer to Part A?

A "Another scientist soon pointed out that Cope had mistakenly stuck the beast's skull on its tail."

B "Cope was humiliated, and Marsh crowed about the blunder to anyone who would listen."

C "Because they published their findings as quickly as possible, they made many mistakes."

D "Unlike Cope's mistake with *Elasmosaurus*, paleontologists didn't discover and undo Marsh's *Brontosaurus* blunder for nearly 100 years."

2 Marsh and Cope had a stormy relationship. Which event was the **most** important influence on this relationship?

A Marsh paid Cope's team foreman to send new fossils to him.

B Marsh claimed he was the first to discover a mistake by Cope.

C Groups of their workers threw rocks at each other.

D Cope and Marsh attacked each other in the newspapers.

3   Which sentence **best** describes how the two paleontologists influenced each other?

   A   Cope and Marsh would do almost anything to become public celebrities.

   B   The competition between Cope and Marsh pushed each man to make amazing discoveries.

   C   Cope and Marsh's mistakes destroyed their credibility as paleontologists.

   D   Cope and Marsh would have discovered even more dinosaur bones if they had worked together.

4   Each man thought he was better in his field than the other. Which evidence from the text **best** supports the inference that Cope also thought he was smarter than Marsh?

   A   Cope told the *New York Herald* about Marsh's actions.

   B   Cope described a newly found extinct sea reptile he named *Elasmosaurus*.

   C   Cope wanted his brain size to be compared with Marsh's after death.

   D   Cope published scientific articles viciously attacking Marsh's ideas.

5   A good summary includes only important details. Which of the following details is **not** important enough to include in a summary of the article?

   A   The rivalry between Cope and Marsh affected their fieldwork.

   B   Cope and Marsh brought to light some amazing discoveries.

   C   Each man's rush to claim glory caused mistakes to be made.

   D   The men gained fame due to their letters in the *New York Herald*.

6   The last paragraph says that the Bone Wars have a mixed legacy. How does the author develop this idea?

    A   by concentrating on the mistakes that Cope and Marsh made

    B   by presenting the pros and cons of Cope and Marsh's rivalry

    C   by giving the causes and effects of Cope and Marsh's rivalry

    D   by stating in sequence events detailing Cope and Marsh's rivalry

7   Which of the following lists only the **main topics** of "The Bone Wars" in the correct order?

    A   Cope and Marsh meet in 1864.
          Their feud begins in 1868.
          Cope publishes a mistake in 1869.
          The feud moves into fieldwork during the 1870s and 1880s.
          Cope dies in 1897, leaving Marsh the winner of the Bone Wars.

    B   Marsh begins the feud.
          The feud is fought through scientific articles.
          The fighting turns violent in fieldwork out West.
          Cope dies and wants his brain compared with Marsh's.
          The Bone Wars both helps and hurts the reputation of paleontology.

    C   The feud turns Cope and Marsh into celebrities.
          Marsh secretly tries to hire Cope's foreman.
          Cope publishes a mistake in a scientific journal.
          Cope and Marsh begin fighting the Bone Wars.
          Cope dies, so Marsh wins the Bone Wars.

    D   A feud begins between Cope and Marsh.
          Cope and Marsh compete in both articles and fieldwork.
          The fight leads to both mistakes and damaged specimens.
          The feud goes public and ends only with Cope's death.
          The Bone Wars slowed scientific progress but provided valuable fossils.

8 The last paragraph of the article states that "American paleontology got a bad reputation from Cope and Marsh's cutthroat behavior." Explain why this was true. Cite two pieces of text evidence to support your inference.

_____

_____

_____

_____

_____

9 Write a paragraph in which you analyze the positive influence Cope and Marsh's rivalry had on the field of paleontology, both in their own time and today. Support your analysis with details from the article.

_____

_____

_____

_____

_____

_____

_____

Performance Task—Extended Response

10   Think about how the author of "The Bone Wars" develops and explains the rivalry between Cope and Marsh over the course of the article. What are three central ideas about the rivalry? How is each idea developed and explained? What details support each one?

In your answer, be sure to
- identify three central ideas presented about the rivalry
- explain how the text develops and explains these ideas
- use details from the article in your answer

Check your writing for correct spelling, grammar, capitalization, and punctuation.

_____

_____

_____

_____

_____

_____

_____

_____

_____

_____

Unit 2
Key Ideas and Details in Literature

You are sitting in a darkened theater, waiting for a play to begin. Finally, the lights come on, the curtain rises, and the actors begin speaking their lines. As you watch, the story unfolds. From the **details** in the action and dialogue, you learn **key ideas** about the plot. The lighting, scenery, costumes, and makeup also contribute to the performance. Each part of the production adds to the audience's understanding of the plot. When you read a story, play, or poem, you are that text's audience. You understand key ideas by paying close attention to the author's descriptions and the characters' dialogue. Sometimes, you have to "read between the lines" and use the details in the text to figure out information that the author doesn't tell you directly.

In this unit, you will learn how to understand a literary work by reading closely and using evidence, or details, directly or by making inferences. You will learn to describe how a story's or play's plot unfolds and how aspects of the characters or setting affect what is happening in the plot. Finally, you will learn how to use all that information to summarize the text. Prepare to watch some fascinating stories from the past, present, and around the world. Let the curtain rise and the show begin!

✓ **Self Check**   **Fill out the Self Check on the next page.** ▶

Before starting this unit, check off the skills you know below. As you complete each lesson, see how many more you can check off!

✓ Self Check

I know how to:	Before this unit	After this unit
cite several pieces of evidence to support inferences about a literary text.	☐	☐
explain how setting, characters, or plot influence each other in a story or drama.	☐	☐
find a theme or central idea of a text and tell how it is developed.	☐	☐
summarize a text without giving personal opinions.	☐	☐

CCSS
RL.7.1: Cite several pieces of textual evidence to support analysis of what the text says explicitly as well as inferences drawn from the text.

Theme: *The Element of Surprise*

Have you ever looked at something that interested you, such as a hot air balloon or a telescope, and tried to figure out how it works? An **analysis** is an examination of how the different parts of something work together. When you read a story, you analyze how its parts—its characters, settings, and events—work together to create meaning.

Some story details are **explicit**, or clearly stated. "Jesse was excited about going to the museum" is an example of an explicit detail: You know that Jesse is excited and why. But story information can also be less direct. You might have to make an **inference**, or an educated guess based on details in the story and your own knowledge, to figure out what's going on.

> After his dad had gone upstairs, Pete clenched his fists and stomped out of the room to go get a bucket and fill it with soapy water. His dad had just told him they were having company that evening and that Pete had to help out by doing some extra chores. Pete had finished all of his homework in study hall that day and had planned on spending the afternoon reading his new comic book, not mopping floors and dusting shelves.

Using details from the text and your own knowledge, fill in the blanks in the chart below.

Evidence	+	Background Knowledge	=	Inference
• Pete "clenched his fists and _Stomped out of the room_." • Pete had "planned on spending the afternoon _reading his new comic book_, not _mopping floors & dusting shelves_"		When people clench their fists and stomp out of a room, these are signs that they _are angry_		Pete is angry about _his chores_.

When you're analyzing a story to make an inference, pay close attention to details in the text. Read closely to find evidence that you can cite, or give as proof, that the inference is reasonable. By making and supporting inferences, you'll be like an engineer looking at a machine you've never seen before, piecing together clues to figure out how it works.

Read this part of a short story about two criminals who kidnap a child and hold him for ransom.

Genre: **Short Story**

from "The Ransom of Red Chief" *by O. Henry*

We selected for our victim the only child of a prominent citizen named Ebenezer Dorset. . . . The kid was a boy of ten, with bas-relief freckles, and hair the colour of the cover of the magazine you buy at the news-stand when you want to catch a train. Bill and me figured that Ebenezer would melt down for a ransom of two thousand dollars to a cent. But wait till I tell you. . . .

The kid was in the street, throwing rocks at a kitten on the opposite fence.

"Hey, little boy!" says Bill, "would you like to have a bag of candy and a nice ride?"

The boy catches Bill neatly in the eye with a piece of brick.

"That will cost the old man an extra five hundred dollars," says Bill, climbing over the wheel.

That boy put up a fight like a welter-weight cinnamon bear; but, at last, we got him down in the bottom of the buggy and drove away. We took him up to the cave and I hitched the horse in the cedar brake. After dark I drove the buggy to the little village, three miles away, where we had hired it, and walked back to the mountain. . . .

(continued)

Explore how to answer this prompt: *"Use details from the passage to predict whether Sam and Bill's plot will succeed."*

A prediction is a type of inference. It is a reasonable guess that you need to support with evidence.

The chart below lists some details about the boy. Complete the chart with details from the text.

Evidence	+ Background Knowledge	= Inference
• "But wait till I tell you. . . ." • "The kid was in the street, ~~Throwing rocks at kittens~~ ." • "The boy catches Bill neatly ~~in the eye with a rock~~ ."	Throwing rocks at cats and people is mean. It suggests the boy is hard to deal with.	I predict that Sam and Bill's plot ~~will fail because the boy will be to hard to deal with.~~

After guarding the boy, Bill speaks with Sam before they write the ransom note. Continue reading, then answer the question that follows.

Close Reading

Underline at least two details that help you understand Bill's feelings about the boy.

(continued from page 46)

"You know, Sam," says Bill, "I've stood by you without batting an eye in earthquakes, fire and flood—in poker games, dynamite outrages, police raids, train robberies and cyclones. I never lost my nerve yet till we kidnapped that two-legged skyrocket of a kid. . . ."

"I'll be back some time this afternoon," says I. "You must keep the boy amused and quiet till I return. And now we'll write the letter to old Dorset."

Bill and I got paper and pencil and worked on the letter. . . . Bill begged me tearfully to make the ransom fifteen hundred dollars instead of two thousand.

"I ain't attempting," says he, "to decry the celebrated moral aspect of parental affection, but we're dealing with humans, and it ain't human for anybody to give up two thousand dollars for that forty-pound chunk of freckled wildcat. I'm willing to take a chance at fifteen hundred dollars. You can charge the difference up to me."

Hint

Look for text evidence suggesting that Bill thinks a two thousand dollar ransom is too much.

Circle the correct answer.

Why does Bill want to make the boy's ransom fifteen hundred dollars instead of two thousand?

A He knows the boy's father won't be able to afford a two-thousand-dollar ransom. *his father is rich*

B He believes it's morally wrong to ask for any ransom at all. *he wants the money*

C He thinks the boy is so difficult that his parents might not want to ~~spend~~ much money to get him back. *he good about*

D He worries that Sam will get nervous and back out of the plan if they ~~ask f~~or too much money. *is too late to back out.*

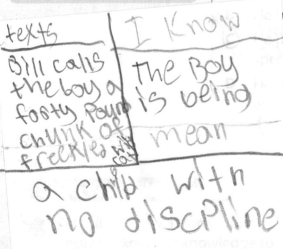

texts
Bill calls the boy a forty pound chunk of freckled w | *I know The boy is being mean*

a child with no discipline

...k of freckled wildcat." What does he mean? With a partner, ...ke an inference about the meaning of Bill's comment.

Read about the unexpected note Sam and Bill receive in response to their ransom request. Use the Study Buddy and Close Reading to guide your reading.

Will the boy's father agree to the terms of the ransom note? I'll underline sentences that tell what he thinks of the kidnappers' demands.

Close Reading

Find and **star** (*) the sentence in the letter that suggests how the boy's neighbors will feel about his return home.

Which phrases in paragraphs 4 and 5 are clues that tell you how the two kidnappers feel about Ebenezer Dorset's offer? **Circle** these words and phrases.

Genre: **Short Story**

from "The Ransom of Red Chief"

by O. Henry

1   *Gentlemen:* I received your letter to-day by post, in regard to the ransom you ask for the return of my son. I think <u>you are a little high in your demands,</u> and I hereby make you a counter-proposition, which I am inclined to believe you will accept. <u>You bring Johnny home and pay me two hundred and fifty dollars in cash,</u> and I agree to take him off your hands. You had better come at night, for the neighbours believe he is lost, and I couldn't be responsible for what they would do to anybody they saw bringing him back. Very respectfully, EBENEZER DORSET.

2   "Great pirates of Penzance!" says I; "of all the impudent—"

3   But I glanced at Bill, and hesitated. He had the most appealing look in his eyes I ever saw on the face of a dumb or a talking brute.

4   "Sam," says he, "what's two hundred and fifty dollars, after all? We've got the money. One more night of this kid will send me to a bed in Bedlam. Besides being a thorough gentleman, I think Mr. Dorset is a spendthrift for making us such a liberal offer. You ain't going to let the chance go, are you?"

5   "Tell you the truth, Bill," says I, "this little ewe lamb has somewhat got on my nerves too. We'll take him home, pay the ransom and make our get-away."

6   We took him home that night. We got him to go by telling him that his father had bought a silver-mounted rifle and a pair of moccasins for him, and we were going to hunt bears the next day.

7   It was just twelve o'clock when we knocked at Ebenezer's front door. Just at the moment when I should have been abstracting the fifteen hundred dollars from the box under the tree, according to the original proposition, Bill was counting out two hundred and fifty dollars into Dorset's hand.

Hints

> Think about Sam's immediate reaction to the counter-proposition. Then think about the conversation between Sam and Bill that follows.

1 Which statement best explains the reaction of the narrator, Sam, to Ebenezer Dorset's counter-proposition?

   A Sam thinks the counter-proposition is a joke and refuses to take it seriously.

   B Sam thinks the amount of money Ebenezer asks for is unfair and he convinces Bill that they should pay a lesser amount.

   C At first, Sam is happy about the counter-proposition, but then he gets angry again and asks for even more ransom money.

   D Sam is angry about the counter-proposition, but then Bill convinces him that it's a great offer since the boy is so horrible.

> Which sentence describes the offer Ebenezer Dorset makes to the kidnappers?

2 By the end of the story, the terms of the ransom have changed dramatically. Which sentence from the story best shows who sets the final terms of the ransom?

   A "I received your letter to-day by post, in regard to the ransom you ask for the return of my son."

   B "You bring Johnny home and pay me two hundred and fifty dollars in cash, and I agree to take him off your hands."

   C "Sam," says he, "what's two hundred and fifty dollars, after all?"

   D "Tell you the truth, Bill," says I, "this little ewe lamb has somewhat got on my nerves too."

> Does Ebenezer Dorset sound concerned about the safety of his son? What is the tone of his letter?

3 Sam and Bill initially wanted a two-thousand-dollar ransom for the boy. Explain why Ebenezer Dorset was able to convince the kidnappers to pay him two hundred and fifty dollars to take back his own son. Cite at least one direct quote from the story to support your explanation.

the son was sad and the letter was like mad they gave him the money to Dorset.

Read the story. Then answer the questions that follow.

from *Dusk*

by Saki

1   On the bench by Gortsby's side sat an elderly gentleman with a drooping air of defiance that was probably the remaining vestige of self-respect in an individual who had ceased to defy successfully anybody or anything.... As he rose to go Gortsby imagined him returning to a home circle where he was snubbed and of no account, or to some bleak lodging.... His retreating figure vanished slowly into the shadows, and his place on the bench was taken almost immediately by a young man, fairly well dressed but scarcely more cheerful of mien than his predecessor.

2   "You don't seem in a very good temper," said Gortsby.

3   "You wouldn't be in a good temper if you were in the fix I'm in," he said; "I've done the silliest thing I've ever done in my life."

4   "Yes?" said Gortsby dispassionately.

5   "Came up this afternoon, meaning to stay at the Patagonian Hotel in Berkshire Square," continued the young man; "when I got there I found it had been pulled down some weeks ago and a cinema theatre run up on the site. The taxi driver recommended me to another hotel some way off and I went there. I just sent a letter to my people, giving them the address, and then I went out to buy some soap—I'd forgotten to pack any and I hate using hotel soap. Then I strolled about a bit and looked at the shops, and when I came to turn my steps back to the hotel I suddenly realized that I didn't remember its name or even what street it was in.... I suppose you think I've spun you rather an impossible yarn," said the young man presently, with a suggestion of resentment in his voice.

6   "Not at all impossible," said Gortsby judicially; "I remember doing exactly the same thing once in a foreign capital."

7   The youth brightened at the reminiscence. "In a foreign city I wouldn't mind so much," he said; "one could go to one's Consul and get the requisite help from him. Unless I can find some decent chap to swallow my story and lend me some money I seem likely to spend the night on the Embankment."

8   "Of course," said Gortsby slowly, "the weak point of your story is that you can't produce the soap."

9   The young man sat forward hurriedly, felt rapidly in the pockets of his overcoat, and then jumped to his feet.

10   "I must have lost it," he muttered angrily.

11   "To lose a hotel and a cake of soap on one afternoon suggests willful carelessness," said Gortsby, but the young man scarcely waited to hear the end of the remark. He flitted away down the path, his head held high, with an air of somewhat jaded jauntiness.

12   "It was a pity," mused Gortsby; "the going out to get one's own soap was the one convincing touch in the whole story, and yet it was just that little detail that brought him to grief. If he had had the brilliant forethought to provide himself with a cake of soap."

13   With that reflection Gortsby rose to go; as he did so an exclamation of concern escaped him. Lying on the ground by the side of the bench was a small oval packet...It could be nothing else but a cake of soap, and it had evidently fallen out of the youth's overcoat pocket when he flung himself down on the seat. In another moment Gortsby was scudding along the dusk-shrouded path in anxious quest for a youthful figure in a light overcoat. He had nearly given up the search when he caught sight of the object of his pursuit standing irresolutely on the border of the carriage drive, evidently uncertain whether to strike across the Park or make for the bustling pavements of Knightsbridge. He turned round sharply with an air of defensive hostility when he found Gortsby hailing him.

14   "The important witness to the genuineness of your story has turned up," said Gortsby, holding out the cake of soap..."If the loan of a sovereign is any good to you—"

15   The young man hastily removed all doubt on the subject by pocketing the coin.

16   "Poor boy, he as nearly as possible broke down," said Gortsby to himself. "It's a lesson to me not to be too clever in judging by circumstances."

17   As Gortsby retraced his steps past the seat where the little drama had taken place he saw an elderly gentleman poking and peering beneath it and on all sides of it, and recognized his earlier fellow occupant.

18   "Have you lost anything, sir?" he asked.

19   "Yes, sir, a cake of soap."

Answer Form

1 Ⓐ Ⓑ Ⓒ Ⓓ
2 Ⓐ Ⓑ Ⓒ Ⓓ   **Number**
3 Ⓐ Ⓑ Ⓒ Ⓓ   **Correct** ╱ 3

1   Read these sentences from the story.

"'It was a pity," mused Gortsby; "the going out to get one's own soap was the one convincing touch in the whole story, and yet it was just that little detail that brought him to grief. If he had had the brilliant forethought to provide himself with a cake of soap.'"

Based on these sentences, with which statement would Gortsby **most likely** agree?

A   Fibbers will always make mistakes.

B   Travelers should always be aware of their surroundings.

C   People should carefully evaluate anything they are told.

D   Strangers should generously listen to each other's stories.

2 Which sentence from the story **best** supports the idea that Gortsby likes to judge others?

A "On the bench by Gortsby's side sat an elderly gentleman with a drooping air of defiance . . . "

B "'I remember doing exactly the same thing once in a foreign capital.'"

C "'To lose a hotel and a cake of soap on one afternoon suggests willful carelessness.'"

D "'It's a lesson to me not to be too clever in judging by circumstances.'"

3 Which sentence from the story shows that Gortsby doubts the young man's honesty?

A "'...I suddenly realized that I didn't remember its name or even what street it was in.'"

B "'Of course,'" said Gortsby slowly, "'the weak point of your story is that you can't produce the soap.'"

C Lying on the ground by the side of the bench was a small oval packet.

D "You don't seem in a very good temper," said Gortsby. . . .

4 Paragraph 13 of the story states that Gortsby uttered "an exclamation of concern." Explain why Gortsby was concerned. Quote at least **one** sentence from paragraph 14 to support your explanation.

_____

_____

_____

_____

_____

_____

_____

_____

✓ **Self Check** *Go back and see what you can check off on the Self Check on page 44.*

Analyzing the Interaction of Story Elements

CCSS

RL.7.3: Analyze how particular elements of a story or drama interact (e.g., how setting shapes the characters or plot).

Theme: *Imagination and Ingenuity*

A bicycle without wheels, pedals, and brakes wouldn't be complete or possible to ride. Similarly, a story wouldn't be complete or interesting to read without all of its parts working together. These parts, called **story elements,** include its characters, settings, and plot.

Analyzing a story means figuring out how its elements interact with each other. For example, you can analyze how the setting of a story shapes its plot. A story's plot includes a **conflict**, or a problem the characters must respond to, and a **resolution**, in which the problem is solved.

Look at the picture below. It shows the moment of conflict in an adventure story. Consider the importance of this setting to the story's conflict.

What is the setting? It is a river with rocks, whitewater rapids, and a waterfall.

What is the relationship between the setting and the story's conflict?

the setting causes the conflict. the problem the charactrs must face is a result change in setting

How do you think the characters will resolve the conflict? the can they to anchor to the rock.

Just as a bicycle can't move forward without all of its parts working together, stories don't go anywhere without the interactions of their characters, settings, and plots. By analyzing a story, you're figuring out how its parts relate to each other—and you might be learning a new way to enjoy the stories you read.

Read the first three paragraphs of this story.

Genre: **Historical Fiction**

Black Sunday   *by Taryn Trina*

It was April 14—one day before Cora's sixteenth birthday—and she felt the air change as she took the laundry down from the clothesline. The sky darkened over the Oklahoma plains and the wind threatened to blow the laundry away. Cora froze for a moment and then shouted "Dust storm!" loudly enough for everyone inside to hear.

Cora held the cellar door open for her mother and the younger children as they descended into the cool darkness. Cora's mother called for her to join them, but Cora was determined to find her father and brothers.

Cora saddled the old mare and rode across the fields, calling for her father until she finally spotted him. He was already riding back with her brothers, the storm creeping up the horizon nearly fast enough to overcome them. They tethered the animals in the barn stalls and sealed the doors to keep the precious livestock safe.

(continued)

Explore how to answer this question: *"What is the relationship between the setting and the conflict in this story?"*

Before you can analyze the relationship between setting and conflict, you need to be certain what the setting and conflict actually *are*. First, identify each of these elements on the lines below.

What is the setting of this story? _a ranch ok Plains_

What is the conflict in this story? _there is a dust storm_

Now that you've identified the setting and the conflict, start thinking about how they are related. Ask questions such as, "Does the conflict somehow change the setting?" Or, "Is the setting the cause of the conflict?" Asking these questions will help you analyze the relationship between story elements.

On the lines below, describe the relationship between the setting and the conflict in this story. Use details from the story to support your answer.

the setting in the cause of the conflict.

Continue reading "Black Sunday." Use the Close Reading and the Hint to help you answer the question.

Close Reading

Find and **underline** the sentence that best shows Cora taking charge to solve the problem.

(continued from page 54)

"What about your mother and the other children?" her father shouted over the increasing roar of the wind, clearly alarmed.

"They're already in the cellar," Cora answered. "Follow me, everyone. We can make it, but we have to move *now*!"

Soon they were all together, huddled around a lamp as the storm rattled the boards of the house overhead. That day would later become known as Black Sunday because of the epic storm that blew over the plains. But Cora would remember it best as the day before her sixteenth birthday, when she helped lead her family to safety.

Hint

Which choice shows Cora taking charge and suggests a happy ending to the story?

Circle the correct answer.

Which sentence from the passage best shows that Cora's ability to take charge in a dangerous situation will lead to a happy resolution?

A "Cora froze for a moment and then shouted 'Dust storm!' loudly enough for everyone inside to hear."

B "Cora held the cellar door open for her mother and the younger children as they descended into the cool darkness."

C "'Follow me, everyone. We can make it, but we have to move *now*!'"

D "That day would later be known as Black Sunday because of the epic storm that blew over the plains."

✎ Show Your Thinking

Explain how the sentence you chose demonstrates Cora taking charge and a happy ending.

_____

_____

_____

With a partner, discuss how Cora's actions and the plot events, including the resolution, help reveal her character.

Read the scene below, in which a beggar boy sets off a surprising chain of events at a London castle in the year 1547. Use the Study Buddy and the Close Reading to guide your reading.

As I read, I'm going to think about how the setting, characters, and plot interact. I'll note details that help me understand how the characters' actions move the plot forward.

Close Reading

What event causes the prince to behave as he does? **Draw a box** around details that explain his actions.

How is the setting of the guarded gate important to the events? **Underline** any details that show the importance of the setting to the events.

Genre: **Historical Fiction**

from *The Prince and the Pauper*

by Mark Twain

1   . . . . Poor little Tom, in his rags, approached, and was moving slowly and timidly past the guards, with a beating heart and a rising hope, when all at once he caught sight through the golden bars of a spectacle that almost made him shout for joy. Within was a comely boy, tanned and brown with sturdy outdoor sports and exercises, whose clothing was all of lovely silks and satins, shining with jewels; at his hip a little jewelled sword and dagger; dainty buskins on his feet, with red heels; and on his head a jaunty crimson cap, with drooping plumes. . . .

2   Tom's breath came quick and short with excitement, and his eyes grew big with wonder and delight. Everything gave way in his mind instantly to one desire: that was to get close to the prince, and have a good, devouring look at him. Before he knew what he was about, he had his face against the gate-bars. The next instant one of the soldiers snatched him rudely away, and sent him spinning among the gaping crowd of country gawks and London idlers. The soldier said,—"Mind thy manners, thou young beggar!"

3   The crowd jeered and laughed; but the young prince sprang to the gate with his face flushed, and his eyes flashing with indignation, and cried out,—

4   "How dar'st thou use a poor lad like that? How dar'st thou use the King my father's meanest subject so? Open the gates, and let him in!"

5   You should have seen that fickle crowd snatch off their hats then. You should have heard them cheer, and shout, "Long live the Prince of Wales!"

6   The soldiers presented arms with their halberds, opened the gates, and presented again as the little Prince of Poverty passed in, in his fluttering rags, to join hands with the Prince of Limitless Plenty.

Hints

Think about what Tom wants and how his attempt to achieve his goal causes trouble.

Use the Hints on this page to help you answer the questions.

1 Which sentence best shows how one character can set the events of a story in motion?

A "Tom's breath came quick and short with excitement, and his eyes grew big with wonder and delight."

B "Everything gave way in his mind instantly to one desire: that was to get close to the prince . . ."

C "The soldier said,—'Mind thy manners, thou young beggar!'"

D "Within was a comely boy, tanned and brown with sturdy outdoor sports and exercises . . ."

Which choice describes why a main character acts to change another's situation?

2 Which sentence best describes how story events influence a main character's actions?

A The prince sees Tom being mistreated by the soldier and takes pity on him.

B At first the crowd jeers and laughs, but then they snatch off their hats and begin to cheer for the prince.

C The soldiers make certain that Tom and the prince remain separated by the gate.

D The country gawkers and London idlers shame the prince into doing something to help Tom.

What problem does the guarded gate pose for Tom? What details show this problem? And how is the problem resolved?

3 In this passage, the setting of the guarded gate is an important cause of the main conflict. Write a paragraph supporting this idea. Use at least two details from the passage to support your response.

Because the gate is guarted, tom is trying to get passed the gate and the gate is makeing a lot of thinking with tom.

Read the story. Then answer the questions that follow.

Scarborough Fair Fantasy

by Stu Darnell

1   "Come on, Lacey, we're going to be late," said Eric, annoyed that his little sister kept stopping to look at the vendors' carts when he was due at the meadow to sing with his school chorus: The trip to Scarborough Renaissance Festival in Waxahachie, Texas, each April was a tradition at Eric's school. Families traveled to the fair to watch their children perform and to enjoy medieval food, entertainment, and crafts.

2   Eric looked over his shoulder just in time to see Lacey disappear into a tent unlike any he had ever seen. Most artisans had open stalls, but this was a tent with ornate walls fringed with gold tassels.

3   Sighing in frustration, Eric followed Lacey into the tent, where he found his sister sitting cross-legged on a pile of cushions, listening with rapt attention to a woman wearing the medieval costume of a merchant. He knew from his social studies class that most of the people who lived in the medieval times were peasants who wore patched clothing of rough cloth, while the nobility often wore fine clothes of silk or velvet richly embroidered with beads or jewels. This woman's dress was something in between the two—fine embroidered silk, but shabby. She probably had gotten it from the costume rack at the local thrift store just like me, Eric thought, glancing down at his long, silk-lined cape.

4   The mysterious woman held a book illustrated with richly detailed, ancient-looking illustrations as she told a story about a young silversmith's apprentice. Eric started to grab Lacey's arm but suddenly felt very weary. After all, he had risen at five in the morning for the long drive to Waxahachie, and he had just devoured a huge turkey leg. As he listened to the storyteller, Eric's eyes grew heavier and heavier.

5   Eric awoke with a start to find Lacey practically dragging him to his feet, whispering, "Come on, Eric—the Sheriff's after you!"

6   "What are you talking about?" asked Eric. As he emerged from the tent, he rubbed his eyes hard to make sure he was really awake. What was going on?

7   Before, the people at the fair had been wearing shorts and T-shirts, but now everyone seemed to be in full costume. Instead of pushing strollers, they were pushing crude carts and dodging farm animals in the square. And the air, which before had been filled with the scent of popcorn, now smelled of horses and smoke.

8   "Hear ye, hear ye!" boomed a loud voice.

9   Eric whirled around to see a man in a brown leather vest reading from a scroll: "Eric, a boy apprenticed to Randolph the silversmith, has fled from the neighboring town. He has stolen silver from his master. A reward is offered for his capture."

10   Eric felt two hands seize his arms from behind. "Here's the thief!" cried the burly owner of the hands.

11   "Wait, you're making a mistake!" cried Eric.

12   "Then what's this?" cried a woman in a green, woolen dress, snatching up the small, silver-colored MP3 player Eric had clipped to his costume. The player's ear buds flew out of Eric's ears, and the man holding his arms let go and started batting at the flying ear buds as if they were giant mosquitoes.

13   "Come on, Eric—run!" Lacey ran toward the largest building in the square, which Eric realized was a church. Close on his sister's heels, Eric rushed through its heavy doors and slammed them shut.

14   "Are you seeking sanctuary, a safe harbor, freedom from persecution, my children?" asked a man in a long, brown robe. Eric and Lacey nodded their heads, too stunned at first to speak.

15   "Are you going to turn me in?" stammered Eric fearfully.

16   The parish priest shook his head. "Anyone seeking sanctuary has protection in this church for forty days. Besides, the apprentice whom the constable seeks is here. He has already made his confession. Now, you wear the clothing of a noble, yet I can see that you are not."

17   "I'm just a kid!" Eric said, confused.

18   "You think you are the child of a goat? Poor boy. Even so, you will need peasants' clothing. You are violating the law by wearing the garb of the noble class." The man left and then came back with brown homespun leggings and a tunic. Eric bundled them under his arm.

19   "Um—thanks, but what are we going to do for forty days?" Before he got an answer, Eric yawned, feeling his eyes grow heavy again. He lay down on a bed of straw in the corner and watched sleepily while Lacey chased a mouse along the stone wall of the church.

20   When he awoke, Eric was back in the cozy tent. The storyteller was gone, but Lacey was curled up on a pillow next to him, snoring lightly. A pair of sneakers poked under the tent flap; it was their mother. "Eric, I've been looking everywhere—you'll be late for your performance!"

21   Eric got up groggily. Looking down, he noticed that he was still wearing his thrift-store costume, but later, when he patted his vest to feel for his MP3 player, it had disappeared.

---

1   Which sentence from the passage **best** shows how a change of setting leads to the main conflict?

Answer Form

1 Ⓐ Ⓑ Ⓒ Ⓓ
2 Ⓐ Ⓑ Ⓒ Ⓓ   **Number**
3 Ⓐ Ⓑ Ⓒ Ⓓ   **Correct**   /3

A   "'Come on, Lacey, we're going to be late,' said Eric, annoyed that his little sister kept stopping to look at the vendor's carts when he was due at the meadow to sing with his school chorus."

B   "Most artisans had open stalls, but this was a tent with ornate walls fringed with gold tassels."

C   "Eric whirled around to see a man in a brown leather vest reading from a scroll: 'Eric, a boy apprenticed to Randolph the silversmith, has fled from the neighboring town.'"

D   "Close on his sister's heels, Eric rushed through its heavy doors and slammed them shut."

2 Read the sentences from the story.

> "I'm just a kid!" Eric said, confused.
> "You think you are the child of a goat? Poor boy. Even so, you will need peasants' clothing. You are violating the law by wearing the garb of the noble class." The man left and then came back with brown homespun leggings and a tunic.

How does the setting of the story affect the events in the church?

A The priest knows that Eric is a time traveler from the future.

B The priest misinterprets Eric's modern language.

C The priest wrongly assumes that Eric is a thief because he has run to the church.

D The priest thinks Eric is a runaway apprentice.

3 Why do the townspeople think Eric is a thief?

A Randolph the silversmith has identified him.

B People think he is wearing a nobleman's stolen cape.

C Eric has an MP3 player which looks like it's made from silver.

D Eric is seen with silver that belongs to the silversmith.

4 Explain how the setting changes the first time Eric falls asleep. Describe how this change affects the series of events that follows. Use at least **two** details from the text in your response.

_____

_____

_____

_____

_____

_____

✓ **Self Check** *Go back and see what you can check off on the Self Check on page 44.*

Lesson 7 Part 1: Introduction

Determining Theme

CCSS

RL.7.2: Determine a theme or central idea of a text and analyze its development over the course of the text. . . .

Theme: *Setting a New Course*

Think back to your childhood. What life lesson did you learn from stories such as "Little Red Riding Hood" or "Snow White"? Here's a hint: They both have the same **theme**, or main message, which is "Good wins out over evil."

Study the image and headline below. Think about the theme they suggest.

Bobcat Bulletin

Issue 20

Daily Practice and Encouragement Transform Struggling Team into League Champions!

Circle the most important words in the headline. Then read the chart below to see how organizing details can help you figure out the message of the illustration.

	Events	Theme
Beginning of Season	The team struggles.	
End of Season	The team succeeds.	Hard work and the support of others leads to success.
Reason for Change from Beginning to End of Season	The coaches encouraged the team to practice more and work hard.	

Just as a winning team develops over time, an author develops a theme over the course of the story. As you read, note clues such as how characters change or how story events develop to help you identify the theme, or lesson about life, that the author is trying to share.

Read the first two paragraphs of a story about how a boy named Mick deals with a difficult situation.

Genre: **Realistic Fiction**

A Different Day *by Rachel O'Meara*

"Hand over your lunch money, kid!"

Mick stopped daydreaming and looked in the direction of the voice. In front of him was an all-too-familiar scene. Aaron was picking on Jake, just as he did every day at recess. But that was okay with Mick, because at least Aaron was not picking on him. It was also fine because everyone picked on Jake—that was just how things were around here, the accepted norm. In fact, every school Mick had ever attended had had a kid like Jake—someone who was an obvious target, easy to tease and bully.

Today was different, though, because Jake was standing tall, acting brave, and trying to stick up for himself. Aaron responded by getting nastier and louder as he hurled insults at Jake. He pushed forward, forcing Jake backwards and jabbing him in the chest. Jake looked terrified, and Mick could see that Jake's lips were stretched thin as he tried not to let anyone see he was close to yelling for help—or worse, sobbing. But to Mick's surprise, Jake still wasn't backing down.

(continued)

Explore how to answer this question: *"What theme is being developed in this part of the story?"*
Mick's feelings and observations about the other boys' actions offer clues about the theme.

Find story details that tell how Mick thinks and feels, some of which are shown in the chart below. Add details from the text, and complete the chart.

Point in Story	Important Events	Character's Words, Actions, and Feelings	Theme
Beginning	Aaron demands Jake's lunch money.	Mick watches Aaron pick on Jake. Mick feels that the situation is okay because everyone picks on Jake.	
Middle	Jake is standing up to Aaron.		

Close Reading

In the first part of the story, Mick only watches Aaron's interactions with Jake. In the second part of the story, Mick's feelings change. **Underline** the sentence that describes when Mick takes action.

Hint

Think about how Mick changes over the course of the story. Which choice best sums up the lesson you learn about life?

Continue reading the story. Use the Close Reading and the Hint to help you answer the question.

(continued from page 62)

As he watched from a few feet away, Mick slowly began to fill with anger toward Aaron and compassion for Jake. What was happening wasn't right, and somebody ought to do something. But, on the other hand, Aaron was a nasty character. And when dealing with someone like that, it might be best to lie low and not interfere.

"Hand it over! Now!" insisted Aaron impatiently.

Aaron faked a swipe at Jake, and then laughed loudly when Jake jumped back and cringed. The laughter was even crueler and more hurtful than the words. Today is different, thought Mick, and he forced his feet toward the conflict.

"Not today, Aaron," shouted Mick. "Leave Jake alone!"

Circle the correct answer.

Which statement best states a theme of the story?

A   Only someone who has been bullied can understand bullying.

B   It's best to stay out of trouble and never get involved.

C   It's important to take a stand against bullies.

D   Bullying will always be a problem that affects many teenagers.

✎ Show Your Thinking

Look at the answer you chose above. Tell which details in the story led you to choose that sentence as the theme.

_____

_____

With a partner, take turns summarizing the story. Then discuss which story events have the strongest impact on the story's theme.

Read the story. Use the Study Buddy and the Close Reading to guide your reading.

The author includes details to help me understand what kind of person Laila is. I'm going to underline clues that tell me something about her.

Close Reading

Laila has mixed emotions about the situation. **Underline** the sentence that explains why she feels the way she does.

How does Laila change at the end of the story? **Circle** the sentences that describe when Laila makes a decision to act differently.

Genre: **Realistic Fiction**

The Substitute   *by Bailey Sebastian*

1   When Laila walked into math class on Thursday, the room was in an uproar. Although the students usually took their seats immediately and opened their books quietly, today they were gathered in groups, chatting loudly, and laughing.

2   Laila stopped just inside the doorway, but then quickly spotted the reason for the change. Instead of Ms. Vasquez, a rather short, older gentleman with glasses perched crookedly on his nose stood at the front of the class. Laila did a double-take—the man was her neighbor, Mr. Marrero! She and her family had gone to pay their respects after his wife had passed away last year, and she remembered him telling an amazing story about surviving an emergency landing during a transcontinental flight.

3   "Hey, Laila, wasn't *Teen Idol* awesome last night?" yelled Jason.

4   "Y-yeah," stammered Laila. Jason didn't usually talk to Laila. The popular kids just wrote her off as "that quiet girl."

5   Laila bit her lip; she *wanted* to keep talking, but she felt bad for Mr. Marrero, and she was embarrassed by her class's behavior. Without realizing it, Laila reached over and flicked the light switch, just like Ms. Vasquez did when the class was unruly.

6   Suddenly silent, every classmate turned to stare at her, and Laila's cheeks burned bright red. But then she smiled at the substitute and said, "Hello, Mr. Marrero—"

7   Mr. Marrero focused, and then recognition dawned and he responded, "Oh, my neighbor . . . Laila, right?"

8   Laila heard someone snicker and knew it was time to blend back in or help Mr. Marrero. She took a deep breath. "Mr. Marrero, will you tell us about the time you were on a jet that crash-landed in the ocean?"

9   Thirty mouths gaped open, and sixty eyes looked with curiosity at Mr. Marrero, soon to be their new favorite substitute.

Hints

To help me answer the first question, I'm going to look back at the text I underlined in the story.

Only one claim is directly supported by details from the story.

Choose the details that best support the theme of the story.

Use the Hints on this page to help you answer the questions.

1 Which statement best describes Laila at the beginning of the story?

- **A** Laila is a quiet student who appreciates an orderly classroom.
- **B** Laila enjoys chatting with her friends before class.
- **C** Laila likes to be the focus of attention in all of her classes.
- **D** Laila dislikes the popular kids who ignore her.

2 Which sentence best states an important theme about human behavior as described in "The Substitute"?

- **A** Choosing to take action requires courage.
- **B** Older people often have wisdom to share.
- **C** A quiet person isn't necessarily a shy person.
- **D** Being popular isn't as important as being kind.

3 Select **two** pieces of evidence from "The Substitute" that support your answer to question 2.

- ☐ "him telling an amazing story about surviving an emergency landing"
- ☐ "The popular kids just wrote her off"
- ☐ "that quiet girl"
- ☐ "she wanted to keep talking, but she felt bad for Mr. Marrero"
- ☐ "every classmate turned to stare at her"
- ☐ "knew it was time to blend back in or help"
- ☐ "she took a deep breath"
- ☐ "tell us about a time when you were on a jet that crash-landed in the ocean"

Read the story. Then answer the questions that follow.

from *Little Women*

by Louisa May Alcott

While their father is serving in the Civil War, Meg, Jo, Beth, and Amy help their mother, Marmee, carry on with their daily lives. The family makes do with what little money they have. Then a telegram arrives. Father is ill, and Marmee needs to go to Washington.

1   How still the room was as they listened breathlessly and how suddenly the whole world seemed to change, as the girls gathered about their mother, feeling as if all the happiness and support of their lives was about to be taken from them.

2   Mrs. March read the message over, and stretched out her arms to her daughters, saying, in a tone they never forgot, "I shall go at once, but it may be too late. Oh, children, children, help me to bear it!"

3   For several minutes there was nothing but the sound of sobbing in the room, mingled with broken words of comfort, tender assurances of help, and hopeful whispers that died away in tears. Poor Hannah, their servant, was the first to recover, and with unconscious wisdom she set all the rest a good example . . . .

4   "I won't waste no time a-cryin', but git your things ready right away, mum," she said heartily, as she wiped her face on her apron . . . .

5   "She's right, there's no time for tears now. Be calm, girls, and let me think."

6   They tried to be calm, poor things, as their mother sat up, looking pale but steady, and put away her grief to think and plan for them.

7   "Where's Laurie?" she asked presently, when she had collected her thoughts and decided on the first duties to be done.

8   "Here, ma'am. Oh, let me do something!" cried the neighbor boy, hurrying from the next room . . . .

9   "Send a telegram saying I will come at once. The next train goes early in the morning. I'll take that."

10   "What else? The horses are ready. I can go anywhere, do anything," he said, looking ready to fly to the ends of the earth.

11   "Leave a note at Aunt March's. Jo, give me that pen and paper."

12   Jo drew the table before her mother, well knowing that money for the long, sad journey must be borrowed, and feeling as if she could do anything to add a little to the sum for her father.

13   "Jo, run to the rooms, and tell Mrs. King that I can't come. On the way get these things . . . . I must go prepared for nursing. Hospital stores are not always good . . . . Father shall have the best of everything. Amy, tell Hannah to get down the black trunk, and Meg, come and help me find my things, for I'm half bewildered."

The family rush off to help Marmee prepare. Beth runs to ask their neighbor, Mr. Laurence, for help. To the relief of the girls, he also makes plans to have his grandson's tutor escort Marmee to Washington.

14   Everything was arranged by the time Laurie returned with a note from Aunt March, enclosing the desired sum, and a few lines repeating . . . that she had always told them it was absurd for March to go into the army, always predicted that no good would come of it, and she hoped they would take her advice the next time. Mrs. March put the note in the fire, the money in her purse, and went on with her preparations . . . .

15   Jo came walking in with a very queer expression of countenance, for there was a mixture of fun and fear, satisfaction and regret in it, which puzzled the family as much as did the roll of bills she laid before her mother, saying with a little choke in her voice, "That's my contribution toward making Father comfortable and bringing him home!"

16   "My dear, where did you get it? Twenty-five dollars! Jo, I hope you haven't done anything rash?"

17   "No, it's mine honestly. I didn't beg, borrow, or steal it. I earned it, and I don't think you'll blame me, for I only sold what was my own."

18   As she spoke, Jo took off her bonnet, and a general outcry arose, for all her abundant hair was cut short.

19   "Your hair! Your beautiful hair!" "Oh, Jo, how could you? Your one beauty." "My dear girl, there was no need of this." "She doesn't look like my Jo any more, but I love her dearly for it!"

20   As everyone exclaimed, and Beth hugged the cropped head tenderly, Jo assumed an indifferent air, which did not deceive anyone a particle, and said, rumpling up the brown bush and trying to look as if she liked it, "It doesn't affect the fate of the nation, so don't wail, Beth. It will be good for my vanity, I was getting too proud of my wig. It will do my brains good to have that mop taken off. My head feels deliciously light and cool, and the barber said I could soon have a curly crop, which will be boyish, becoming, and easy to keep in order. I'm satisfied, so please take the money and let's have supper."

Answer the questions. Mark your answers to questions 1–3 on the Answer Form to the right.

Answer Form

1 Ⓐ Ⓑ Ⓒ Ⓓ
2 Ⓐ Ⓑ Ⓒ Ⓓ
3 Ⓐ Ⓑ Ⓒ Ⓓ   **Number Correct** / 3

---

1   What is an important theme of the story?

    A   Vanity and selfishness are stronger than generosity and kindness.

    B   In times of trouble, family and good friends support each other.

    C   Misfortune can overwhelm even the strongest people.

    D   The best way to deal with grief is to distract yourself with other tasks.

2   How does Aunt March's response to Marmee's note help to develop the theme?

     A   Despite the situation, Aunt March still wants to prove she was right.

     B   Aunt March gives only the amount of money she feels she is obligated to give.

     C   Even though she expressed her disapproval, Aunt March is still willing to help.

     D   Aunt March realizes that her early warnings were inappropriate and apologizes.

3   Which quote from the story **best** supports the story's theme?

     A   '"I won't waste no time a-cryin', but git your things ready right away, mum."'

     B   '"I earned it, and I don't think you'll blame me, for I only sold what was my own."'

     C   '"She's right, there's no time for tears now. Be calm, girls, and let me think."'

     D   '"That's my contribution toward making Father comfortable and bringing him home."'

4   Describe how the author uses the characters' actions to develop the theme over the course of this story. Cite at least **two** details from the text to support your response.

_____

_____

_____

_____

_____

_____

_____

_____

 **Self Check**   *Go back and see what you can check off on the Self Check on page 44.*

Lesson 8   Part 1: Introduction 👥

Summarizing Literary Texts

CCSS
RL.7.2: . . . provide an objective summary of the text.

Theme: *Myths and Legends*

Have you ever seen a movie that you couldn't wait to tell your friends about? You probably described it to them using just a few sentences. A **summary** is a brief retelling of a story that includes the main characters, setting, and important events, including the conflict and its resolution. When summarizing, be sure to tell events in the order they happen. Also be sure to tell it using **objective** statements that are free of opinions or judgments.

Read the story below. Make notes in the margins about the characters, setting, and events.

Read the chart below, noting how it only tells important details about the story.

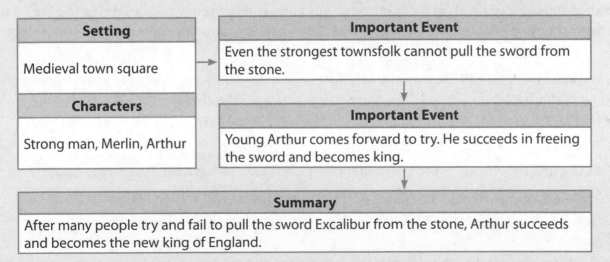

Setting	Important Event
Medieval town square	Even the strongest townsfolk cannot pull the sword from the stone.
Characters	**Important Event**
Strong man, Merlin, Arthur	Young Arthur comes forward to try. He succeeds in freeing the sword and becomes king.

Summary
After many people try and fail to pull the sword Excalibur from the stone, Arthur succeeds and becomes the new king of England.

Summaries retell important events and identify setting and characters in an objective fashion. Good readers summarize to check their understanding and remember important plot details.

Read the first three paragraphs of an Algonquin legend.

Genre: **Legend**

Glooskap and the Wasis   by Edgar Ingersoll

And so it was that Glooskap, the mightiest and most fearsome of all the Algonquin warriors, had traversed through the lands, defeating all his enemies. After many months, he returned to his village, where the people bowed their heads respectfully.

Upon arriving at his wigwam home, however, he glimpsed an odd creature sitting on the floor, sucking a piece of maple-sugar candy, troubling no one. Glooskap asked his wife what the creature was, to which she responded that it was the Wasis, a fierce being who was undefeated and would remain so until the end of time. She warned her husband that if he meddled with the Wasis, Glooskap would be plagued with suffering.

Glooskap was incensed that an enemy had infiltrated his home. He challenged the small creature to a test of strength, but the Wasis ignored him. Outraged, he ordered the Wasis to crawl to him and acknowledge him as its master, but the creature only laughed.

(continued)

Explore how to answer this question: *"What is the best way to summarize this part of the legend?"*

A summary includes characters, setting, and important events. Underline these elements in the text above.

Summaries should also be objective, or free of opinions and judgments. Read the following summary and cross out any opinion words or statements. Then check your work against the bullet points.

Glooskap is an ~~awesome~~ Algonquin warrior who comes home to his village after defeating his enemies. ~~I think it's funny~~ how he finds the Wasis sitting on the floor and thinks it's another enemy. He ~~foolishly~~ challenges and orders the Wasis around, but the little creature won't obey him.

- In the first sentence, "awesome" is an opinion, not a detail from the text. Cross it out.
- In the second sentence, "I think it's funny" is a judgment and should be crossed out.
- The word "foolishly" in sentence 3 is also an opinion. It should be crossed out, too.

With a partner, discuss another important event that should be added to the summary to make it more complete. Then take turns summarizing the text objectively and in your own words.

9.5/10

Close Reading

What are the most important events that occur in this part of the text? **Underline** two or more details that describe the ways the Wasis responds to Glooskap's actions.

Continue reading about Glooskap and the Wasis. Use the Close Reading and Hint to help you answer the question.

(continued from page 70)

In an uncontrollable fury, Glooskap screamed at the Wasis that he alone was the mightiest warrior! This time, the Wasis did respond: it opened its throat and let out a terrible, heartbroken wail.

Glooskap covered his ears, but the creature's howls split his skull. He asked it to stop crying, but it would not. He danced a funny dance, sang a song, and made a face, but it wasn't until Glooskap held the Wasis that the creature was finally appeased. Subdued, the baby cooed "goo" at his father—for son and father they were. And forever after, when a baby coos "goo goo" at his father, the Wasis remembers his victory over Glooskap.

Hint

Eliminate any choices that make a judgment, are inaccurate, or are vague.

Circle the correct answer.

Which of the following choices is the best summary of the story ending?

A Glooskap finally figures out that the Wasis is his son. He may have been a mighty warrior, but he wasn't very smart.

B The mighty Glooskap is unable to defeat the crying baby Wasis. This victory is remembered every time a baby coos at its father.

C The wife's warning that Glooskap would suffer proves to be wrong. Glooskap ends up enjoying the time he spends with his son.

D Although Glooskap asks the Wasis to stop crying, it refuses to do so. Even dancing, singing, and making a face doesn't work.

✏️ **Show Your Thinking**

Explain why one other answer choice is not a good summary of the story ending.

A is wrong becoues he is sad
C is wrong because thats not why he's sad.
D is wrong because nobody told him.

With a partner, take turns objectively summarizing the entire legend in your own words. Include characters, setting, and important events.

Read the myth. Use the Study Buddy and the Close Reading to guide your reading.

I know that a myth is a story set in a time and place unlike my own. Myths also often have fantastical characters. As I read, I'll think about how these elements might be included in a summary of the text.

Close Reading

Circle details that reveal the central conflict in this story and which characters are most affected.

What is the fate of the two main characters? **Underline** the most important events in the story's ending.

Genre: **Myth**

Beowulf and Grendel   *by Javier Moreno*

1   Long, long ago there lived a great king named Hrothgar who benevolently ruled over Denmark and its people. Every night the king hosted great feasts in Heorot Hall and joined in the merriment as songs were sung and stories were told.

2   Outside, lurking in the gloom, was a hideous monster named Grendel who hated the merry sounds that came from the hall. The sounds of song and laughter tortured him. Finally, late one night when the unsuspecting guests lay sleeping, Grendel entered the hall and killed thirty of Hrothgar's men. For the twelve long years that followed, no songs or laughter came from Heorot Hall. Even the bravest and strongest of Hrothgar's soldiers were powerless against the wrath of Grendel.

3   Finally, a hero appeared—Beowulf, who looked like a boy to Hrothgar's warriors. They gasped as he stood before the king of the Danes and declared, "I will kill this monster. I will leave behind my sword, and I shall destroy him with my bare hands."

4   The brave words of the youthful Beowulf filled King Hrothgar with hope. That night, there was feasting and merriment in Heorot Hall once more. When darkness fell over the land and each man went to take his rest, Beowulf alone stayed watchful and vigilant, waiting for the battle he knew was sure to transpire.

5   At last, Grendel entered Heorot Hall. Just as the monster was about to seize Beowulf, the youth caught Grendel by the arm, and man and monster wrestled until daylight. The battle was fierce and wild, but Beowulf emerged the victor. Fatally wounded, howling his song of death, Grendel fled the hall and ran until he reached the lake where he made his home. There, he plunged into the waters and quickly sank, never again to terrorize the Danes.

Hints

Which choice presents an objective statement that gives information about an important character and event?

Which choice gives an objective overview of the paragraph's important events?

As you write, think about where the story takes place, who it is about, and what happens to those characters from beginning to end.

Use the Hints on this page to help you answer the questions.

1 Which of the following statements would you most likely include in a summary of "Beowulf and Grendel"?

A Heorot Hall was once King Hrothgar's favorite place.

B Grendel preferred to live in dark, gloomy places.

C Hrothgar shows great weakness compared to the courageous Beowulf.

D Beowulf promises King Hrothgar that he will kill Grendel.

2 Which is the best summary of the last paragraph of the story?

A Beowulf and Grendel have a fierce and unrestrained battle.

B Beowulf defeats Grendel, who returns to his lake to die.

C Grendel howls a song of death while he flees the hall.

D Grendel gets what he deserves for terrorizing the Danes.

3 Write a summary of the story "Beowulf and Grendel" in your own words. Be sure to be objective and include at least three details about the main characters, setting, and important events.

The name of a person

In Hrothgar, its a lot of men. this is about grende. he walked to a hall with killed Hrothgar's men. he was the strongest soldiers. he was never again to terrorize the dance.

4/10 +3

we need to work on your sentence structure.

Read the myth. Then answer the questions that follow.

Gift from the Heavens

by Flora Diaz

1   At one time, the gods lived in the heavens while the mortals toiled on the earth. Zeus, king of all gods, did not look kindly on the mortals. Zeus believed that all heavenly powers belonged only to the gods and goddesses. Prometheus believed that these powers should be shared with the mortals.

2   Prometheus and Zeus were constantly getting into disputes. Once, Prometheus was asked to solve a conflict between the gods and mortal men. The men were going to sacrifice a bull during a festival and they had to decide which parts of the bull should be offered to the gods and which parts should be reserved for the men. Prometheus saw this as an opportunity to play a trick on Zeus. He butchered the bull and put the lean, tasty parts of the meat into a small serving bowl and then placed the gristle, bones, and fat into a much larger serving bowl. When Prometheus asked Zeus to select his meal, naturally he chose the larger portion.

3   When Zeus realized how he had been deceived, he was furious and immediately sought revenge. To punish both Prometheus and the mortals he cared about, Zeus snatched fire away from the men of earth, and kept it only for the gods.

4   During one bitterly cold winter, Prometheus watched the mortals huddle together like a pack of animals to keep warm. "They need to have fire returned to earth," he thought. So he decided to ignore Zeus' decree, no matter the risk. Prometheus lit a torch with the fire from the wheels of the chariot that carried the sun across the sky. He brought the flaming torch to earth and delivered fire to the mortals. As a result, life on earth was transformed. Not only did fire keep people warm, it also enabled them to cook food for the first time, as well as smoke the food and preserve it for later use. With the heat of the fire, they could even smelt metals and turn them into tools to use for farming.

5   The king of the gods was furious when he learned what Prometheus had done. He wanted to punish Prometheus and return the mortals to a life of pain and hardship. So Zeus came up with a plan. He asked the other goddesses to help him create a beautiful, mortal woman. His daughter Athena offered her assistance, and when the lovely creature was fully formed, Athena breathed life into her. Zeus named the woman Pandora, and she possessed unequalled beauty and charm. Zeus gave Pandora an ornate lidded box and sent her to Prometheus as a gift. He told Prometheus that Pandora would make a perfect bride.

6   Prometheus was suspicious of any gift from Zeus, despite the woman's incredible beauty. He suggested to his brother Epimetheus that he marry Pandora instead, which he willingly did. After they were wed, Epimetheus asked his bride what was inside the sealed box.

7   "I don't know," she replied. "I only know that Zeus gave me strict instructions never to open it."

8   "That is most unusual, but I would not trust Zeus. Perhaps we should bury the box," her husband responded.

9   Pandora had never given a thought to what was inside the box until her husband asked her about it. Now she was consumed with curiosity and she could think of nothing else. She wondered what it could be and

why Zeus was so determined to keep her from glancing inside. One night, while her husband was sleeping, Pandora pulled the box from its hiding place and cautiously opened the lid.

10   Immediately all manner of dreadful things were released from the box—disease, despair, malice, greed, death, hatred, violence, cruelty, and war. These torments traveled to earth, creating extreme discord and chaos for the mortals.

11   However, without Zeus' knowledge, his daughter Athena had put something else into the box, something that could help the mortals cope with all these miseries—hope. So hope also traveled to earth to serve as a balance to the woes that burden all mortals.

Answer the questions. Mark your answers to questions 1–3 on the Answer Form to the right.

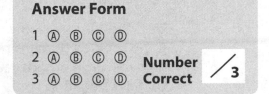

Answer Form

1 Ⓐ Ⓑ Ⓒ Ⓓ
2 Ⓐ Ⓑ Ⓒ Ⓓ   Number   /3
3 Ⓐ Ⓑ Ⓒ Ⓓ   Correct

1 Which of these is the **best** summary of paragraph 1?

   A Zeus cared only about the gods and had no compassion for mortals. Prometheus believed that the powers of the gods should be shared.

   B Zeus decreed that mortals would toil as his slaves on earth.

   C Prometheus thought that power should be shared among all the gods equally. Zeus wanted all of the power for himself.

   D Prometheus did not get along with Zeus. He turned all of his attention to taking care of the mortals.

2 Which sentence should be included in a summary of the story?

   A Epimetheus trusted Zeus more than he trusted his brother.

   B Prometheus made humans as powerful as gods.

   C Zeus gave Pandora the box but told her not to open it.

   D Pandora opened the box to rebel against Zeus.

because Zeus new what it is, and he want him to learn.

3 Which is the **best** summary of the key events of the story?

A Prometheus helped humans trick Zeus, so the king of all gods took fire away from humans. Prometheus lit a torch from the chariot that carries the sun and brought fire back to humans. Zeus saw how humans thrived with fire, so he had a beautiful woman created. She went to earth, married Prometheus' brother, and then released evil into the world.

B Prometheus helped humans trick Zeus by keeping the best part of a bull sacrifice for themselves. Zeus punished Prometheus and the humans by taking fire away from them. Prometheus felt pity for the suffering humans and brought fire back to them. Zeus took revenge by creating a woman who brought all the evil things to the world in a box.

C Zeus thought heavenly powers should not be shared with humans. Prometheus disagreed, so he showed humans how to trick Zeus. Zeus became angry and took fire away from humans. Prometheus saw how cold humans were, so he brought them back their fire. Humans began to cook, smoke food, and make farm equipment.

D Prometheus helped humans trick Zeus, so Zeus took fire away from humans. Prometheus, seeing how humans suffered, brought the fire back. Zeus then sent Pandora to Prometheus with a box she was not supposed to open. Prometheus' brother married Pandora. The curious Pandora then opened the box, letting out both evil and hope into the world.

4 Summarize in your own words how Prometheus helps humans. Support your answer with at least **three** details from the passage.

gods lived in the heavens while the mortals tolled on the earth, Zeus were constanly getting into disputes, when zeus realized how he had been deceived he was furious and immediately sought revenge.

Incomplete and not in your own words - Red

Read the story. Then answer the questions that follow.

Growing

by Jacob Henderson

1   Nate Brown leaned on his pointed stick to scan the fields. Far as the eye could see, potato fields stretched out: rows and rows of potato plants, representing hours and hours of work for him. His mother kept a small pumpkin patch, but the family depended on the potato for their own sustenance and for income. Nate sighed and bent down to coax another spud from the stony ground. Dusk was falling and soon the girls would be calling him in for supper.

2   The boy sighed deeply. Somewhere beyond these stingy New Hampshire fields, his brother Eben was marching gloriously with his regiment, defending the colonies against the British. That was work for a man! Nate closed his eyes and imagined himself with a musket in his calloused hands. It was the second year of the war, and he was no closer to the fighting.

3   "Nate!" A voice floated from the house, recalling the boy from his daydream.

4   He trudged toward the house, pausing to wash his hands at the pump and to remove his grimy boots before entering.

5   Around the table sat his sisters, Olive and Mary, along with his mother and father. A brief grace and a prayer for Eben were followed by the heaping of plates and the scraping of cutlery. There was little meat, but plenty of potatoes.

6   Father said, "Your cousin Abe has joined the militia—guess they finally thought he was old enough to be of use." He took a deep drink from his mug, ignoring Nate's open-mouthed stare.

7   While the girls helped Mother clear away the dishes, Nate stomped off to the pump to fill a bucket with water. The autumn sky was growing dark, and the high noises of the cicadas filled the air. A barn owl hooted. But there were other sounds drifting from beyond: the clink of metal, the tramp of boots, the hoarse voices of men limping from miles of steady marching. All of Nate's senses were alert now while the overflowing water bucket sat abandoned by the pump.

8   Then a few soldiers came into view, straggling through the thicket and emerging on the far side of the pumpkin patch. As they halted, waiting for the rest of the troops to catch up, the one who seemed to be the leader held up his hand in a gesture of greeting. He advanced toward the house, and Nate could see the lines of fatigue crossing his brow and the silver hair around his deeply tanned face.

9   "Boy," the soldier said, "My men need food and shelter for the night. Whereabouts would your Ma and Pa be?"

10   Wordlessly, Nate gestured toward the house, where Mother had lit a lantern against the falling darkness.

11   "Then maybe you could get your Pa to speak with me," the man said quietly, as if remembering discarded manners.

12   Father limped out of the doorway, leaning heavily on his cane. He had never completely recovered his balance after the accident several years before. The two men exchanged a glance of understanding, and then Father said, "You are all welcome to bed down in the barn. My daughters will give it a good sweeping and fix up some pallets for you."

13   "They haven't eaten, Father," Nate said hurriedly, staring over the field where perhaps a dozen men waited for their commander's orders. "I'll go to the root cellar and get some potatoes, and I'll roast them quick—and there's plenty of water," he added, turning again to the soldier. "Please tell the men to help themselves from the pump with this ladle."

14   He dashed inside and hollered to the women, who began rustling around the kitchen in preparation for feeding the troops. There was a buzz of excitement in the low-ceilinged room as Olive and Mary helped Mother reset the table with clean dishes.

15   Down in the root cellar, Nate picked over the potatoes, careful to select the best of their stores. Strangely, he found himself smiling: there was, after all, a way to help the American cause—by feeding the hungry troops, by offering hospitality to the weary soldiers.

16   As he lugged the heavy basket of potatoes up the steps, Nate became aware of the strength in his arms, of muscles that had been developing through the months of farm labor. He was growing, and someday soon he would be ready to do a man's job. But right now, he realized he had an important job of his own.

Answer the questions. Mark your answers to questions 1–5 on the Answer Form to the right.

Answer Form

1 Ⓐ Ⓑ Ⓒ Ⓓ
2A Ⓐ Ⓑ Ⓒ Ⓓ
3 Ⓐ Ⓑ Ⓒ Ⓓ
4 Ⓐ Ⓑ Ⓒ Ⓓ **Number**
5 Ⓐ Ⓑ Ⓒ Ⓓ **Correct** /5

1   Nate feels frustrated that he can't join his brother. Which of the following sentences from the story **best** supports this statement?

A   "Nate sighed and bent down to coax another spud from the stony ground."

B   "It was the second year of the war, and he was no closer to the fighting."

C   "He trudged toward the house, pausing to wash his hands at the pump and to remove his grimy boots before entering."

D   "Wordlessly, Nate gestured toward the house, where Mother had lit a lantern against the falling darkness."

2 Answer Parts A and B below.

Part A

Which of the following sentences **best** states an important theme about human behavior as described in "Growing"?

A There are many ways to serve a cause.

B There is danger and sorrow in wartime.

C There are family duties for each person.

D There are many things in life that are unfair.

Part B

Select **two** pieces of evidence from "Growing" that support the answer to Part A.

☐ "But right now, he realized he had an important job of his own."

☐ "'Your cousin Abe has joined the militia—guess they finally thought he was old enough to be of use.'"

☐ "But there were other sounds drifting from beyond: the clink of metal, the tramp of boots, the hoarse voices of men limping from miles of steady marching."

☐ "'They haven't eaten, Father,' Nate said hurriedly, staring over the field where perhaps a dozen men waited for their commander's orders."

☐ "'Please tell the men to help themselves from the pump with this ladle.'"

☐ "Strangely, he found himself smiling: there was, after all, a way to help the American cause—by feeding the hungry troops, by offering hospitality to the weary soldiers."

3　The setting of the story is a New Hampshire farm far away from the scenes of battle. How does the setting help to shape Nate's feelings?

   A　It makes him feel that he is alone.

   B　It makes him feel that his family is safe.

   C　It makes him feel that he is not useful.

   D　It makes him feel that his region is not patriotic.

4　The appearance of the tired commander makes a vivid impression on Nate. Which of the following sentences from the story **best** supports this statement?

   A　"As they halted, waiting for the rest of the troops to catch up, the one who seemed to be the leader held up his hand in a gesture of greeting."

   B　"He advanced toward the house, and Nate could see the lines of fatigue crossing his brow and the silver hair around his deeply tanned face."

   C　"'Boy,' the soldier said, 'My men need food and shelter for the night.'"

   D　"'Then maybe you could get your Pa to speak with me,' the man said quietly, as if remembering discarded manners."

5　What lesson does Nate learn in this story?

   A　Listen to your family and never complain.

   B　Never be jealous of what other people can accomplish.

   C　Soldiers are just like ordinary people.

   D　Everyone can contribute something in his or her own way.

6 Nate and his family play a role in the fight for American independence. Explain how the text supports the idea that Nate's family plays a role in the war. Cite evidence from the text to support your answer.

_____

_____

_____

_____

_____

_____

7 Summarize in your own words how Nate feels up until the point when he meets the commander. Support your answer with details from the story.

_____

_____

_____

_____

_____

8 Father has been injured and cannot participate in combat. How does this situation affect Father's meeting with the troop commander? Write a paragraph analyzing the meeting of the two men.

_____

_____

_____

_____

_____

_____

_____

_____

_____

_____

_____

_____

Performance Task—Extended Response

9 What conflict does Nate face at the beginning of the story? What events in the plot cause Nate to change and grow? Write an essay describing the conflict and how it is resolved. Explain how Nate changes as a result of events.

In your answer, be sure to
- identify the central conflict in the story and how it is resolved
- explain how Nate's situation and attitude change throughout the story
- use details from the story to support your answer

Check your writing for correct spelling, grammar, capitalization, and punctuation.

_____

_____

_____

_____

_____

_____

_____

_____

_____

_____

_____

Unit 3
Craft and Structure in Informational Text

Have you ever thought about the work that goes into taking a photograph? A photographer carefully adjusts the lighting and camera angles to capture exactly what he wants to appear in the photo. The photographer has a purpose in mind and carefully **crafts** the photo to achieve that purpose and to express his thoughts, or point of view, about the subject. An author of informational text also has a purpose in mind. The author chooses words, phrases, and sentences in the same way as the photographer chooses light and camera angles. These elements are carefully selected to fit into the overall **structure**, or framework, that the author has chosen for the text.

In this unit, you will learn to pay attention to the choices an author makes in crafting a text. You will figure out the meanings of words, including words used in unusual or very specific ways, and determine how the author's choice of words affects the meaning. You will also learn how the author chooses a structure, ensuring that all the sections fit together to develop the ideas. You will see how an author expresses a particular point of view to achieve his or her purpose. Look through your camera lens, focus carefully, and prepare to capture some fascinating information!

✔ **Self Check**   **Fill out the Self Check on the next page.** ▶

Before starting this unit, check off the skills you know below. As you complete each lesson, see how many more you can check off!

✓ Self Check

I know how to:	Before this unit	After this unit
explain the meanings of words and phrases in a text.	☐	☐
determine figurative, connotative, and technical meanings of words in a text.	☐	☐
explain how a specific word choice affects the meaning and tone of a text.	☐	☐
analyze the structure of an informational text, including how the sections fit together and develop the ideas.	☐	☐
explain an author's point of view and how the author makes his or her ideas stand out from others.	☐	☐

Analyzing Word Meanings

CCSS

RI.7.4: Determine the meaning of words and phrases as they are used in a text, including figurative, connotative, and technical meanings; analyze the impact of a specific word choice on meaning and tone.

Theme: *Little Creatures, Big Impact*

Why do authors choose the words they do? This question isn't as simple as it seems.

- Sometimes authors choose words to convey a **technical meaning**. Subject areas in science, math, and engineering express ideas using technical words and phrases.

- At other times, they select words for their **connotative meaning**. A word chosen for its connotation expresses not just an idea but also a feeling.

- And authors can use and combine words to produce a **figurative meaning**. These are words or phrases that express ideas in creative, unusual, or unexpected ways.

Underline words in the diagram below with technical, figurative, or connotative meanings.

The huge black eyes seem borrowed from the face of a space alien.

The wicked speed of the wings allows the wasp to snatch up its meal and dart away like a thief.

The female wasp's ovipositor, or egg-laying organ, is found in the abdomen. It also functions as a stinger to paralyze and kill prey.

The chart shows phrases from the diagram with each type of meaning. Complete the chart.

Example	Type of Meaning	Why the Author Uses It
"snatch up its meal"	connotative	to suggest that the wasp takes the meal suddenly, perhaps rudely
"ovipositor, or egg-laying organ, is found in the abdomen"		to communicate precisely which part of the wasp is being described
"eyes seem borrowed from the face of a space alien"		

Paying attention to the different types of meaning will help you understand how the author thinks and feels about a topic. For example, you might guess that the author of the diagram has some scientific knowledge about wasps—but also finds them rather unnerving!

Read the first three paragraphs of the following scientific account.

Genre: **Scientific Account**

Don't Let the Bedbugs Bite   *by Nick Marcus*

Bedbugs are a nuisance that spread quickly, so if you find bedbugs in your home, you owe it to yourself and others to take decisive and immediate action.

The scientific name for these tiny, bloodsucking insects is *Cimex lectularius*. They're called *bedbugs* because they mainly feed on blood at night while their hosts are asleep. They are like an army of minuscule vampires. Places like mattresses, couches, and chairs serve as luxurious havens in which thousands of them can live.

The bedbug inserts a syringe-like <u>proboscis</u> through the host's skin. It takes between three and ten minutes for the bug to drink its fill through this slender appendage. Its bite is small and painless, so the <u>victim</u> rarely wakes during this feeding time. Bedbugs are not known for disseminating disease, but the bumps they leave behind can become infected. Also, the saliva they release into the skin can make you itch so badly you'll want to <u>scratch your skin off</u>.

(continued)

Explore how to respond to this prompt: *"The underlined words and phrases in the passage express technical, connotative, and figurative meanings. Determine the meaning of each word or phrase as it is used in the passage."*

The technical word is *proboscis*. You can use context clues in the passage to figure out and describe what it means. Use the chart below to determine the meaning of *proboscis*.

Word	Context Clues	Meaning
Proboscis	"syringe-like," "through the host's skin," "drink its fill," "slender"	A proboscis is _____ _____.

Next, consider the connotative meaning of the word *victim*, which the author uses to describe the person being bitten. What does the word *victim* suggest about both the person and the bedbug?

The word *victim* suggests that _____.

Finally, the phrase "scratch your skin off" is figurative. What does this phrase help the reader understand about the itch caused by a bedbug's bite?

_____

_____

Continue reading the account about bedbugs. Use the Close Reading and Hint to help you answer the question.

Close Reading

Reread the paragraphs and **underline** any word or phrase that conveys a figurative meaning.

(continued from page 88)

Bedbug infestations can appear to be a blanket of crawling pinholes that cover the place where you rest. The teensy pests often hitch rides on suitcases left in hotel rooms and travel home with unwitting victims, so keep your luggage off the floor when you travel, and wash your clothes in hot water when you get home.

Use a flashlight and magnifying glass to scrutinize your mattress. If you find any evidence of bedbugs, destroy the mattress immediately and call a professional exterminator. You owe it to neighbors and fellow travelers not to spread the bedbug headache.

Hint

The **tone** of a text is its overall feeling—not just the information it communicates but also the feelings it expresses. Some texts can have more than one tone.

Circle the correct answer.

Which statement best describes the impact of the author's word choice on the overall tone of the account?

A Phrases like *teensy pests* and *hitch rides* give the whole account a humorous tone.

B Words like *rest*, *travel*, and *neighbors* give the account a comforting tone.

C The words *evidence* and *professional exterminator* are used to create a threatening tone.

D Words with technical meanings create an informative tone, but phrases like *crawling pinholes* add a note of disgust.

✎ Show Your Thinking

Explain which words and phrases helped you figure out the intended tone of the account.

_____

_____

_____

_____

💬 With a partner, discuss which words in this part of the account have connotative meanings and how they contribute to establishing the author's attitude toward bedbugs.

Read the scientific account. Use the Study Buddy and the Close Reading to guide your reading.

This science account will probably include many technical words. To be sure I understand the author's meaning, I'll circle words and phrases specifically related to insect biology. I'll also think about other types of word meanings as I read.

Close Reading

Authors often choose words for their strong connotations. Draw a **box** around words that were used instead of "cut," "stab," and "eat."

Underline words and phrases with figurative and connotative meanings that show what the author thinks about Goliath beetles.

Genre: **Scientific Account**

The Goliath Beetle   *by Eleanora Inez*

1   Named for the biblical giant Goliath, the Goliath beetle is the most colossal, brawniest, and heftiest kind of beetle in the world. Goliath beetles grow to a length of up to eight inches and may weigh as much as three and a half ounces. Most Goliath beetles are as large as a mouse. They have distinct vertical black bands, like the bars of a prison door, on the elytron that cover their wings. Some species may also have bright yellow, red, gray, or brown markings.

2   The Goliath beetle lives in flowers in the tropical rain forests of Africa. Goliath beetles have fearsome jaws that they use to slash, impale, and chomp food. Adult beetles primarily feed on sugary tree sap and fruit. Goliath beetles also have six powerful legs with sharp claws that can grip. The Goliath beetle uses its claws to gather food and to climb. In addition, the Goliath beetle has a pair of front and a pair of rear wings attached to its thorax. When it flies, it sounds like the whirl of a helicopter propeller.

3   Like other kinds of beetles, the Goliath beetle undergoes a metamorphosis—a four-stage process of change. This process takes place as the beetle develops. During the first stage, a female Goliath beetle lays its eggs in rotting wood or decaying plants. Once an egg hatches, the wormlike larva feeds on the wood or plant material until it is fully grown. The larva wraps itself in a cocoon like a suit of armor to protect itself. Then the pupa lives in the cocoon during the third stage. After several months, the cocoon breaks apart. An adult Goliath beetle steps forth to find a mate, and the four steps in the life cycle of a Goliath beetle are repeated.

4   Goliath beetles are truly the giants of the insect world, and their formidable presence leaves a lasting impression on those who view them.

Hints

Think about whether this word is used for its technical, figurative, or connotative meaning.

Use the Hints on this page to help you answer the questions.

1 Why has the author chosen to include the word *metamorphosis* in the text?

    A It highlights the comparison between the beetle and a helicopter.

    B It describes a biological process that the beetle undergoes.

    C It expresses the author's objectivity about an unusual insect.

    D It explains why scientists are impressed with the beetle's life cycle.

The best way to convey a violent connotation is by describing actions.

2 Which of the following is an example of the author using words that have a violent connotation?

    A She describes the vertical black bands on the elytron that cover Goliath beetles' wings.

    B She compares the Goliath beetle cocoons to suits of protective armor.

    C The author details the four stages of the Goliath beetle's life cycle.

    D She writes that Goliath beetles use their jaws to slash, impale, and chomp food.

What is the author's attitude toward the Goliath beetle itself?

3 Describe the overall tone of the account and the word choices the author uses to convey it. Cite at least three specific examples from the text to support your response.

_____

_____

_____

_____

_____

_____

_____

_____

_____

Read the article. Then answer the questions that follow.

from "Prime Time for Cicadas"

by Emily Sohn, Science News for Kids

1   If it hasn't happened yet, it could occur any day now.

2   The first signs are little holes in the ground in yards, orchards, and fields. Then, one warm evening, big, red-eyed bugs start crawling out of the holes.

3   The next morning, thousands upon thousands of these black, winged insects, known as cicadas, cover sidewalks, mailboxes, tree branches, and roofs across certain areas of the United States. The loud throb of their alien-sounding, high-pitched screeches fills the air. . . .

4   If you don't like bugs, watch out. For anyone who lives in the invasion area, the cicadas are impossible to ignore, says David Marshall. He's an evolutionary biologist and cicada expert. . . .

5   And, if you're caught by surprise, the experience can be pretty overwhelming. Some people find it downright creepy.

Puzzling cycles

6   Even if you don't get to witness the great cicada awakening, it's worth pondering the phenomenon. Despite years of research, the life cycles and habits of cicadas still present puzzles to modern science.

7   Researchers are especially interested in . . . periodical cicadas; these insects live only in this part of the world, and they appear just once every 17 years, on the dot. . . .

8   "This is a really special phenomenon that doesn't happen anywhere else in the world," Marshall says.

9   All cicada eggs hatch into juveniles underground, where they go through five stages of development before emerging as adults, mating, and starting the cycle all over again. Adult periodical cicadas are about 1.5 inches long. They can neither bite nor sting.

10   On average, a population of annual cicadas spends between 2 and 8 years underground before facing the light of day. Different populations stagger their maturation, though, so that a small number hatch each year. They usually appear in the summertime. You might see just a handful in your neighborhood every year. . . .

Prime time

11   One big mystery is why periodical cicadas wait such a long time and a particular number of years before emerging. The answer, some scientists now suggest, appears to involve weather and mathematics.

12   Periodical cicadas belong to a genus called *Magicicada,* which first appeared sometime around 1.8 million years ago. Back then, glaciers covered the land, and the climate of eastern North America was unpredictable. Sometimes summers were warm. Sometimes they were cold.

13   Juvenile *Magicicada* won't even crawl out of the earth until the soil reaches 64 degrees F., Marshall says. After that, they need consistently warm temperatures, usually above 68 degrees F., to survive.

14   By evolving to stay underground as long as possible, some experts say, cicadas reduced their chances of emerging during a particularly cold summer.

15   In one study, researchers from Tennessee and Arkansas looked at what would happen if there were one dangerously cold summer every 50 years for 1,500 years. Their mathematical model showed that cicadas with a life cycle of 7 years had only an 8-percent chance of surviving. With an 11-year cycle, survival jumped to 51 percent. At 17 years, cicadas had a 96-percent chance of living.

16   So, staying underground longer is better. In fact . . . cicadas live longer than almost any other insect.

Multiple breeding

17   Why do periodical cicadas live precisely 13 or 17 years?

18   Both 13 and 17 belong to a special class of numbers called primes. This means that the numbers can be evenly divided only by themselves or the number 1. The first few prime numbers are 2, 3, 5, 7, 11, 13, 17, 19.

19   Mathematicians spend a lot of time trying to understand prime numbers. Cicadas somehow understand primes instinctively. What's more, the insects seem to know how to count.

20   The fact that 17 and 13 are primes reduces the chances of interbreeding among different populations of 17- and 13-year cicadas, Marshall says.

21   Multiples of prime numbers are unlikely to overlap with multiples of other prime numbers. So, a cicada population that hatches every 2 or 5 or 7 years will hardly ever hatch at the same time as a population that hatches every 13 or 17 years. And the 13- and 17-year cicadas will emerge at the same time only once every 221 years.

22   If populations don't hatch at the same time, they can't mate with each other, so their genes remain distinct. That's important because genes help determine the length of the insect's life cycle. If a 5-year cicada were to mate with a 17-year cicada, for example, the length of the cycle would be different every generation. . . .

23   If all of this puzzles you, you're not alone. Scientists have lots of questions, too. "It's so difficult to explain this kind of thing," Marshall says. "It's such a remarkably complex species."

Answer Form

1 Ⓐ Ⓑ Ⓒ Ⓓ
2 Ⓐ Ⓑ Ⓒ Ⓓ   **Number** /3
3 Ⓐ Ⓑ Ⓒ Ⓓ   **Correct**

1   Read this sentence from paragraph 3.

> The loud throb of their alien-sounding, high-pitched screeches fills the air.

What does the author's word choice suggest about the sound that cicadas make?

A   It is so fascinating that everyone should hear it.

B   The sound is breathtakingly rhythmic and musical.

C   The noise is both awful and annoying.

D   The screeches are dangerous enough to lead to hearing loss.

2 Read this sentence from paragraph 7.

> Researchers are especially interested in . . . periodical cicadas; these insects live only in this part of the world, and they appear just once every 17 years, on the dot.

Why has the author chosen to use the figurative phrase *on the dot*?

A to describe the small holes made by cicadas as they hatch

B to highlight their specific and extraordinary life cycles

C to identify the precise location where they may be seen

D to suggest the amazing regularity of when they will emerge

3 Why do you think the author chose to use the words *prime time* in the title?

A to reveal her knowledge about prime numbers and cicada instincts

B to focus on the importance of the insect's well-timed life cycle

C to highlight how researchers solved a puzzling mystery about the insect

D to emphasize that cicadas must emerge in the evening in order to survive

4 Describe the tone of the article and how the author's choice of words creates it. Cite at least **two** specific words and phrases chosen by the author to support your answer.

_____

_____

_____

_____

_____

_____

_____

✓ **Self Check** *Go back and see what you can check off on the Self Check on page 86.*

Determining Point of View

CCSS
RI.7.6: Determine an author's point of view or purpose in a text and analyze how the author distinguishes his or her position from that of others.

Theme: *Catastrophes*

Look at a photo or a picture of an event, and you can usually figure out the feelings and attitudes of the people involved. Actions, body language, and other clues give away each person's **point of view** about what's happening.

Can you figure out the feelings of the people watching the parade in the picture below? Circle clues that help you figure out their points of view.

Read the chart below, which provides details that suggest different points of view about the parade scene.

Topic	Evidence	Positive (+) or Negative (–) Attitude	Point of View
Parade	The woman is smiling. The man in the baseball cap is waving a flag.	+	The man and woman are excited and happy to be watching the parade.
	The child is frowning and holding his ears.	–	The child dislikes the noise from the parade.

When you're reading a book or magazine, you must use different clues to help you determine the author's point of view. Notice the content and language choices; they'll help you infer an author's position on a topic. Also look for clues that reflect an author's **purpose**, or main reason for writing, and the tone being adopted. Analyze facts an author includes and leaves out, the opinions expressed, and word choices. All of these details help reveal the author's point of view—where he or she stands—on a particular topic.

Read the following scientific account about the eruption of Mount St. Helens.

Genre: **Scientific Account**

Rising from the Ashes　*by Lee McLoughlin*

It was a disaster, the stuff of nightmares, and yet it began in broad daylight. On the morning of Sunday May 18, 1980, Mount St. Helens erupted with a horrendous blast that blew 1,300 feet off the top of the mountain. Within minutes, an ash cloud shot 15 miles into the sky. People up to 200 miles away could hear the roar of the volcano. And people as far away as Spokane, Washington, 350 miles from the mountain, watched in amazement as ash from the black sky turned their world a powdery grey.

That morning, Craig Reddinger of Richmond, Washington, was sunbathing with his wife. Reddinger witnessed the ash cloud blot out all daylight and, terrified, thought it was the end of the world. To some it was. The terrible blast knocked down nearly 150 square miles of forest, felling trees like matchsticks. The dreadful eruption lasted 9 hours, but Mt. St. Helens and the surrounding wilderness were forever changed within moments.

(continued)

Explore how to answer this question: *"What is the author's point of view about the eruption?"*

Point of view is what authors think, feel, or believe about a topic based on their interests and values. Complete the chart below to help you determine the author's point of view.

Topic	Evidence from the Text	Positive (+) or Negative (–) Attitude	Author's Point of View
Eruption of Mount St. Helens	It was a disaster, the stuff of nightmares	(–)	
	a horrendous blast		

With a partner, take turns rereading the first two paragraphs of the account. Identify all of the negative words and phrases used to describe the eruption of Mount St. Helens.

Continue reading the account about Mount St. Helens. Then answer the question that follows.

Close Reading

Think about the author's point of view on page 104. Then **circle** the phrase that signals a shift in attitude in this part of the account. Think about why the author may have made this kind of shift.

(continued from page 104)

From a scientific perspective, however, the eruption was an exciting event. Ecologist Charlie Crisafulli points out that the volcanic devastation at Mount St. Helens provides insight into the reawakening of ecosystems. "It's the most thoroughly studied large-forest disturbance in the world," claims Crisafulli.

The blast zone, once barren and uninhabitable, is gradually becoming fertile ground for growing numbers of plant and animal life. Like the mythical phoenix, the blast zone is rising from the ashes, reborn and very much alive. The spectacular event shocked and amazed many. Nature's ability to heal herself, however, is even more awe-inspiring.

Hint

The different attitudes expressed in the account support the author's purpose for writing. Which answer choice best explains why the author presents different points of view?

Circle the correct answer.

Which sentence most accurately describes the author's purpose for writing this account?

A The author's purpose is to persuade readers to agree that the Mount St. Helens eruption was a horrible disaster.

B The author's purpose is to tell the frightening yet exciting story of the Mount St. Helens eruption.

C The author's purpose is to show readers that even this terrifying natural disaster has had some benefits.

D The author's purpose is to convince readers to research the Mount St. Helens eruption.

✎ **Show Your Thinking**

Using text evidence, explain the author's point of view about the Mount St. Helens eruption.

_____

_____

💬 With a partner, discuss the different viewpoints in the account and explain which view is strongest.

Read the editorial below about the Gulf Oil Spill. Then answer the questions that follow.

One way to identify an author's point of view is to find words or phrases in the text that communicate a strong opinion or feeling. I will look for describing words that give me clues about the author's opinions.

Close Reading

Underline sentences in paragraphs 2 and 3 that present the point of view of the BP executives. Think about why the author might have included those details.

What position does the author take on BP and the oil spill? **Circle** words and phrases in the first and fourth paragraphs that express the author's viewpoint.

Genre: Editorial

The BP Oil Spill   *by Kate Jackson*

1   In April of 2010, a British Petroleum oil rig exploded. The blast caused a horrific oil spill in the Gulf of Mexico. Known to many as the "Disaster in the Gulf," this tragic event killed not only workers, but innocent wildlife as well. It also assaulted the environment. BP knew an event like this was possible, but the reckless company refused to take the threat seriously.

2   Months before the explosion, BP's David Rainey had assured members of the U.S. Senate that deep-water oil drilling was safe. Rainey had also remarked that drilling had "been going on for the last 50 years . . . in a way that is both safe and protective of the environment."

3   The spill leaked millions of barrels of oil into the ocean. It then took five months for the company to seal the underwater well properly. Doug Suttles, a BP executive, claimed that the company worked "around the clock to stop the flow of oil, protect the shore, clean up the damage, and restore the Gulf Coast. We also want to ensure that a tragedy like this never happens again."

4   Those five months took a terrible toll on beaches, animals, and the fishing industry. Although the words of Suttles sounded noble, BP did not act quickly or thoughtfully to control the disaster. Experts also feel that an ounce of prevention could have avoided the disastrous spill altogether. Furthermore, there is evidence suggesting that the oil industry was aware of drilling dangers but carelessly dismissed them.

5   Many reports had also warned of the difficulty of capping a deep water spill. BP ignored these warnings and continued to drill as planned. Robert Bea, an expert in offshore engineering, called BP's practices a "recipe for disaster," but BP willfully refused to listen. At least we know they're listening now.

Hints

How does the author describe BP? Look for words that describe the company's actions.

Use the Hints on this page to help you answer the questions.

1 Which sentence most accurately summarizes the author's point of view in the editorial?

   A The explosion leaked millions of barrels of oil into the Gulf Coast, but BP responded quickly and responsibly.

   B The oil spill disaster was a result of BP's thoughtless actions and its refusal to listen to experts.

   C The rig explosion is a tragedy, but events like this are a problem that the oil industry can learn how to control.

   D BP has been drilling safely in the Gulf of Mexico for over fifty years, and one accident should not be held against the company.

Look for quotes in the text that describe the BP executives' position on deep-water drilling. How well do their statements reflect what actually happened?

2 Why does the author of the editorial include statements made by the BP oil executives?

   A to show the contrast between the evidence and the company's official position

   B to emphasize that the oil company executives are truthful but unimaginative

   C to explain why BP's actions were understandable

   D to defend the company's actions both before and after the deep water oil spill

Look back at the words and phrases you circled in the editorial that show the author's strong feelings and beliefs.

3 Think about the author's attitude toward the oil spill. Then explain the author's purpose, or reason for writing this editorial. Use at least two details from the text to support your answer.

_____

_____

_____

_____

_____

_____

_____

_____

Read the scientific article. Then answer the questions that follow.

from "A Dire Shortage of Water"

by Emily Sohn, Science News for Kids

Causes

1   Scientists are just beginning to understand the conditions that lead to droughts. They're finding that small changes in the flow of wind and water can have a huge effect on climate around the globe.

2   Strangely enough, much of the story depends on the temperature of water in the oceans.

3   Normally, winds blow west across the tropical Pacific Ocean, away from Central and South America. As wind-driven warm water moves over the ocean, it piles up in Indonesia and elsewhere in the western Pacific. Warm air rises offshore, causing rain to fall. Meanwhile, cold water comes up from the bottom off the coast of South America. This flow allows a richness of life to flourish near the coast, and it helps maintain predictable weather patterns from season to season.

4   Every 5 to 10 years or so, though, the wind dies down. As a result, the surface of the Pacific Ocean gets warmer. Rainfall then tends to fall further to the east. Such a change in weather causes, among other things, floods in Peru and droughts in Australia and Indonesia. This new weather pattern is known as El Niño.

5   An opposite cascade of events happens during the weather pattern called La Niña, when Pacific surface temperatures cool down. Both El Niño and La Niña, when they happen, usually last for 2 to 4 years.

6   The current drought in the West could last much longer than that. In fact, historical records show that droughts typically go on for 10 to 50 years.

7   And it's not just El Niño and La Niña at work. In the last few years, scientists from the U.S. Geological Survey (USGS) have begun to link precipitation on the Colorado Plateau to temperature shifts both in the Pacific Ocean and in the Atlantic Ocean.

Atlantic Effects

8   A recent statistical study by USGS researchers found that less moisture falls on the United States when surface temperatures in the North Atlantic are warmer than normal. These conditions prevailed during a number of droughts over the past century.

9   The study also found a correlation between warm water in the central North Pacific and drought in the southwestern and northern plains of the United States. When water is warm in both the North Atlantic and the North Pacific at the same time, conditions can get mighty dry in the American West.

10   This explains at least a part of what's going on right now in the Colorado River Basin, geologist John Dohrenwend says.

11   Records show that the basin's annual flow volume has been dropping for more than a century. But the drought has grown much worse since the year 2000. Compared to measurements taken in 1922, water flow has dropped to one-third of its original rate.

People Problems

12   Oceans can't take all of the blame for the impact of today's drought, Dohrenwend says.

13   Although ocean temperatures may be an important factor in starting a drought, people are making the problem of water shortages much worse. Dohrenwend notes that cities are growing faster in the southwest than anywhere else in the country. And people keep pouring in.

14   "Many of these people are retired persons who lived in the northeast or northwest and want to get out of the cold," Dohrenwend says. It's hard for them to adjust to using less water than they're used to, he adds, and they don't want to let go of their golf courses, green lawns, or long showers.

15   "Over time, more and more water has to be allocated to people moving in and less goes to everything else," Dohrenwend says.

16   Ironically, as the drought continues, the cycle feeds on itself. Ranchers go out of business because they don't have enough water to grow alfalfa for their cattle. Then developers arrive and build more homes. As more people move in, the demand for water continues to grow—even as the supply of water rapidly dwindles.

How Long?

17   It's impossible to know how long this drought will last, and some scientists are beginning to fear the worst.

Answer Form

1 Ⓐ Ⓑ Ⓒ Ⓓ
2 Ⓐ Ⓑ Ⓒ Ⓓ   **Number**
3 Ⓐ Ⓑ Ⓒ Ⓓ   **Correct** /3

1 Read these two sentences.

> Some people believe that droughts are the fault of nature, which we can't control. These people say that Earth has always experienced water shortages and that we do not need to worry about the issue.

How does the author of "A Dire Shortage of Water" reveal a point of view that differs from the statement above?

A   She mentions recent scientific discoveries about ocean temperatures, global climate, and drought.

B   She refers to historical records of droughts in the western part of the United States.

C   She explains that ocean temperatures cause drought, but human settlements make the problem worse.

D   She reports that the rate of water flow in the Colorado River Basin has decreased to about one-third of its original rate.

2   Which sentence from the text **best** shows the author's intent to describe how both human and natural factors contribute to drought?

     A   "Such a change in weather causes, among other things, floods in Peru and droughts in Australia and Indonesia."

     B   "When water is warm in both the North Atlantic and the North Pacific at the same time, conditions can get mighty dry in the American West."

     C   "Although ocean temperatures may be an important factor in starting a drought, people are making the problem of water shortages much worse."

     D   "As more people move in, the demand for water continues to grow—even as the supply of water rapidly dwindles."

3   How does the content of the passage reflect the author's point of view?

     A   It shows that the author approves of ongoing scientific research.

     B   It provides facts and statistics showing that the problem of water shortages is growing.

     C   It shows that the author feels hopeless about the fate of our planet.

     D   It shows that the author dislikes the fact that cities are growing faster in the southwest than elsewhere.

4   In your own words, describe the author's point of view about the water shortage and tell how you determined it. Use at least **two** details from the article to support your answer.

_____

_____

_____

_____

_____

_____

✓ **Self Check**   *Go back and see what you can check off on the Self Check on page 86.*

Read the article. Then answer the questions that follow.

"Goldilocks" and Life on Other Planets: Just Right or a Lot of Hype?

by Lindsay Manez

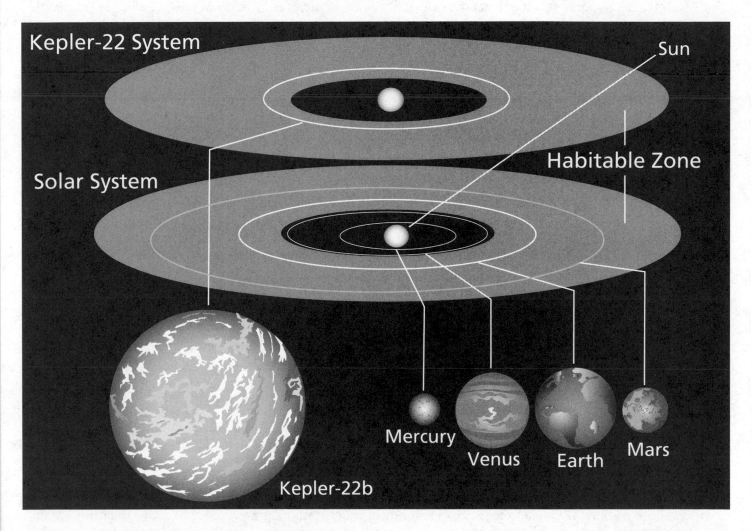

1   Most children and adults are familiar with the classic story "Goldilocks and the Three Bears." In the story, a very particular little girl slips into an empty house looking for the perfect bowl of porridge. She wants one that is neither too hot nor too cold but instead is "just right." Scientists in the National Aeronautics and Space Administration (NASA) are also searching for "just right" perfection. Their focus is on planets located in habitable zones, which they call "Goldilocks zones." These are regions in the space around a star where temperatures are neither too hot nor too cold for water to exist on the planet's surface. Scientists think that planets located in these zones may be "just right" for supporting life.

2   The Kepler space mission is tasked with finding such planets. The team of NASA scientists monitors the findings of the Kepler spacecraft, with its unblinking eye in the sky. The astronomical telescope observes, from a fixed position, more than 100,000 sun-like stars at the same time. Launched in March 2009, the Kepler detects transits, or occasions when a planet crosses in front of a star and causes the star's brightness to dim. By interpreting information about a transit, NASA scientists on Earth can calculate a lot of data. Some of this data includes the period of a planet's orbit around its star, the mass of the star, the size of the star, the size of the planet, the temperature of the star, and the likely temperature of the planet.

3   Interpreting data from transits provides a limited amount of information, however. For example, the mass and density of the planets cannot be determined until scientists conduct further research using instruments on Earth. Nonetheless, the Kepler mission has uncovered hundreds of possible planets. One in particular has many NASA scientists talking.

4   In December 2011, the Kepler space mission announced the discovery of Kepler-22b. This planet is at the center of the habitable zone of the star around which it orbits. The planet shares many characteristics with Earth, including a star that some at NASA have called the "twin" of our sun. Located about 600 light years from Earth, Kepler-22b is double the size of Earth but smaller than Neptune. Its 290-day year—the amount of time it takes to completely circle its star one time—is similar to Earth's 365-day orbit around the sun. Most remarkable, however, is the planet's perfect Earth-like temperature: 72° Fahrenheit (22° Celsius). Further studies from the ground will be necessary before scientists can determine whether Kepler-22b has an atmosphere or even a solid surface. However, Kepler-22b's ideal location in a Goldilocks zone and its perfect temperature for the presence of water have many scientists considering the idea that, like Earth, this planet may be able to support life . . . and perhaps already does!

5   Some think that the idea of discovering life on other planets is thrilling. Imagine humanlike creatures who can communicate with each other, build cities, care for families, and make discoveries—beings who are as curious about us as we are about them. I think it is vital to consider the scientific definition of life, however, and to take the recent excitement with a grain of salt. In science, "life" is considered ANY organism that can take in nutrients and use them to make energy, grow, react to events in the outside world, and reproduce. Humans, along with animals and plants, are forms of life. However, a single microscopic bacterium is also a form of life. It can perform these very same complex processes. Therefore, while Kepler-22b may be located in an ideal Goldilocks zone with the perfect temperatures to sustain life, that life may be nothing more than some bacteria.

6   At present, the Kepler spacecraft can determine only whether other planets exist, not whether life exists on those planets. Because Kepler-22b is trillions of miles from Earth, evidence to prove the presence of any form of life on the new planet is unlikely to arise in this lifetime—if ever. NASA's discovery of a new planet is certainly cause for excitement, but I believe that theorizing about the existence of life on newly discovered planets should be left to the writers of science fiction. Scientific researchers should be more concerned with scientific facts. NASA and the Kepler mission can continue the pursuit of life on other planets in habitable zones. I, however, will remain like the choosy Goldilocks of children's fiction and reserve my enthusiasm until the time is "just right"—upon the discovery of a planet that can sustain human life.

Answer Form

1	Ⓐ	Ⓑ	Ⓒ	Ⓓ	5	Ⓐ	Ⓑ	Ⓒ	Ⓓ
2	Ⓐ	Ⓓ	Ⓒ	Ⓓ	6	Ⓐ	Ⓓ	Ⓒ	Ⓓ
3	Ⓐ	Ⓑ	Ⓒ	Ⓓ	7A	Ⓐ	Ⓑ	Ⓒ	Ⓓ
4	Ⓐ	Ⓑ	Ⓒ	Ⓓ	7B	Ⓐ	Ⓑ	Ⓒ	Ⓓ

Number Correct ⁄8

Answer the questions. Mark your answers to questions 1–7 on the Answer Form to the right.

1 Read these sentences from the article.

> The team of NASA scientists monitors the findings of the Kepler spacecraft, with its unblinking eye in the sky. The astronomical telescope observes, from a fixed position, more than 100,000 sun-like stars at the same time.

The word "fixed" in this sentence **most** closely means

A influenced

B mended

C ready

D stationary

2 Which sentence from the text **best** shows the author's intent to describe the type of information the Kepler mission is gathering?

A "The astronomical telescope observes, from a fixed position, more than 100,000 sun-like stars at the same time."

B "Some of this data includes the period of a planet's orbit around its star, the mass of the star, the size of the star, the size of the planet. . . ."

C "Interpreting data from transits provides a limited amount of information, however."

D "For example, the mass and density of the planets cannot be determined until scientists conduct further research. . . ."

3 How does the information in the fourth paragraph help to develop the article?

A It explains what scientists hope to learn about Kepler-22b.

B It provides a comparison between Kepler-22b and Earth.

C It emphasizes events that led to the discovery of Kepler-22b.

D It identifies challenges in researching Kepler-22b from Earth.

4 Read this sentence from the article.

> Imagine humanlike creatures who can communicate with each other, build cities, care for families, and make discoveries—beings who are as curious about us as we are about them.

Why does the author **most likely** include this sentence in the article?

A to challenge a common opinion about life on other planets

B to highlight the impossibility of finding life on other planets

C to describe how many people think of life on other planets

D to suggest why people are interested in life on other planets

5 With which statement would the author of this article **most likely** agree?

A NASA scientists should focus on interpreting the data they have collected about newly discovered planets.

B NASA scientists should develop technology that can determine whether life is present in habitable zones.

C NASA scientists should conduct more research on the conditions that are suitable for life on other planets.

D NASA scientists should consider classifying more planets in the solar system as part of the habitable zone of the sun.

6 Which statement **best** describes how the illustration contributes to the content of the article?

A It depicts what a habitable zone is.

B It shows how the Kepler spacecraft works.

C It maps the exact location of planet Kepler-22b.

D It illustrates the data the Kepler mission has produced.

7 Answer Parts A and B below.

Part A

What does the word "particular" mean in this sentence from paragraph 1 of the passage?

In the story, a very particular little girl slips into an empty house looking for the perfect bowl of porridge.

A specific

B unusual

C special

D choosy

Part B

Which phrase from paragraph 1 of the passage **best** helps the reader understand the meaning of "particular"?

A "neither too hot nor too cold"

B "focus is on planets"

C "regions in the space around a star"

D "planets located in these zones"

8 Read this sentence from the article.

I think it is vital to consider the scientific definition of life, however, and to take the recent excitement with a grain of salt.

Explain the meaning of the phrase "with a grain of salt" as it is used in the sentence. Use details from the article to support your answer.

_____

_____

_____

9 What are the differences between the author's opinion on the possibility of life on other planets and the opinions of NASA scientists? Write a paragraph explaining your answer. Use details from the article to support your answer.

_____

_____

_____

_____

_____

_____

_____

_____

_____

_____

_____

_____

Performance Task—Extended Response

10   The author makes several references to Goldilocks throughout the article. To whom or what does the author compare Goldilocks? How do these comparisons contribute to the development of the article as a whole? Write an essay of three to four paragraphs explaining your answer.

In your answer, be sure to
- explain to whom or what the author compares Goldilocks
- explain how these comparisons contribute to the development of the article as a whole
- use details and examples from the article in your answer

Check your writing for correct spelling, grammar, capitalization, and punctuation.

_____

_____

_____

_____

_____

_____

_____

_____

_____

_____

_____

_____

_____

_____

_____

_____

_____

_____

_____

_____

_____

_____

Unit 4
Craft and Structure in Literature

An artist is at work on a painting. She mixes the colors to get just the right tone, adding highlights and shadows to the canvas. Through the painting, the artist expresses her viewpoint about a subject. Like a painter, an author **crafts** a text, using words and phrases like brushstrokes on the page. The author carefully chooses words and phrases and creates rhymes or repeating sounds, as the artist chooses colors, to craft the **structure** of the text. Through the narrator or characters in a story or the speaker in a poem, the author expresses a point of view or perspective. This adds color and texture to the work, just like in a painting.

In this unit, you will learn how poets and writers of stories and plays make deliberate choices about the language they use to create tone and meaning. In a similar way, they choose a form and structure that best suit their purpose and express their point of view. Writers are artists, so look for the pictures they have painted with their words as you read a variety of poems, stories, and dramas in this unit!

✓ **Self Check** **Fill out the Self Check on the next page.** ▶

Before starting this unit, check off the skills you know below. As you complete each lesson, see how many more you can check off!

✔ Self Check

I know how to:	Before this unit	After this unit
explain the meanings of words and phrases in a text, including figurative meanings and connotations.	☐	☐
analyze how the author's use of rhyme or other repetitions of sound affect a poem, play, or story.	☐	☐
analyze different poetic forms or structures.	☐	☐
explain how a play's structure contributes to the meaning.	☐	☐
describe how the author develops and contrasts the points of view of the narrator or other characters in a text.	☐	☐

Lesson 12   Part 1: Introduction 👥
Determining Word Meanings

CCSS

RL.7.4: Determine the meaning of words and phrases as they are used in a text, including figurative and connotative meanings . . . .

Theme: *The City and the Country*

Here's a question you've probably asked: "What does that word mean?" You can usually answer it by looking up the word in a dictionary. But words and phrases have meanings beyond their dictionary definitions—specifically, connotative and figurative meanings.

The **connotative meaning** of a word or phrase is the feeling it tends to produce. Think about three words people often use to describe big cities: *lively, crammed,* and *busy.* A *lively* city sounds like a fun place to be. A *crammed* city sounds like it might be uncomfortable. And a *busy* city doesn't sound either fun or uncomfortable—it just sounds like a city, nothing more. *Lively* has a good connotation, *crammed* a bad one, and *busy* a neutral one.

Authors also use **figurative language** to express ideas or experiences vividly. A common type of figurative language involves making an imaginative comparison—finding an unusual way that two different things seem to be alike. You can understand most figurative language by identifying what is compared and thinking about the effect of the comparison.

Read the passage. As you do, notice any imaginative comparisons the author makes.

As I stood atop the mighty skyscraper, a gentle breeze wrapped its arms around me. Down below, the people were as small as ants, and the cars were toys making their way through a miniature city. Muffled sounds floated up like balloons, the wind murmured softly, and a bird called from somewhere in the distance.

The chart below contains examples of figurative language from the passage. Study the first row, then complete the empty sections.

Example	What Is Compared	Effect of Comparison
"a gentle breeze wrapped its arms around me"	a breeze and a person's arms	to make the breeze seem calming and pleasant, like a hug
"the cars were toys"	cars and toys	
"muffled sounds floated up like balloons"		

So the question "What does that word mean?" is a little more interesting than it might seem. Reading becomes richer when you pay attention to these other, "extra" meanings.

Read the beginning of a poem that describes the speaker's view of London as viewed from a bridge.

Genre: **Lyric Poem**

Composed Upon Westminster Bridge   *by William Wordsworth*

Earth has not anything to show more fair:
Dull would he be of soul who could pass by
A sight so touching in its majesty:
This City now doth, like a garment, wear
The beauty of the morning; silent, bare,
Ships, towers, domes, theatres, and temples lie
Open unto the fields, and to the sky;
All bright and glittering in the smokeless air.

(continued)

Explore how to answer this question: *"How does the speaker use figurative language to make comparisons, and what is the effect?"*

Think about what connection the speaker makes between a garment (a piece of clothing) and the beauty of the morning. What do these two unlike things have in common? Also think about how the speaker personifies the city, or gives it human-like qualities.

Use what you know about figurative language to complete the chart below.

Example	What Is Compared	Effect of Comparison
"This City now doth, like a garment, wear The beauty of the morning;"		

On the lines below, explain what the speaker's use of language tells you about his feelings for the city. Support your ideas with specific details from the poem.

_____

_____

_____

_____

Close Reading

Circle the words in the poem with positive connotations. How do they build on the positive feelings created in the first stanza?

Hint

Look back at the words you circled. What do they suggest about the speaker's feelings?

Continue reading the poem. Use the Close Reading and the Hint to help you answer the question

(continued from page 122)

Never did sun more beautifully steep
In his first splendour, valley, rock, or hill;
Ne'er saw I, never felt, a calm so deep!
The river glideth at his own sweet will:
Dear God! the very houses seem asleep;
And all that mighty heart is lying still!

Circle the correct answer.

Based on the connotations of words such as *splendour, calm,* and *sweet,* what is the speaker's attitude toward the view of London in the morning?

A He admires the peace and beauty of the city scene.

B He prefers city sights to the valleys and hills of the country.

C He wishes that the river would flow quietly through the city.

D He hopes that the heart of the city will remain still and silent.

Show Your Thinking

Explain how the speaker's description of the houses conveys his feelings about the city scene.

_____

_____

_____

_____

With a partner, discuss the final two lines of the poem. What might the speaker mean by using the phrase "mighty heart"?

Read the following poem excerpt. Use the Study Buddy and Close Reading to guide your reading.

As I read, I'm going to think about how the speaker uses language in creative ways to convey thoughts and feelings about city and country life. I'll look for examples of figurative language and words with connotations, such as "weather–wise."

Close Reading

What words does the speaker use to describe life in the country? **Underline** these terms and write a **plus** or **minus** sign next to them to show whether they have positive or negative connotations.

Does the speaker prefer city or country life? Draw a **box** around descriptive words and phrases that indicate his feelings about the city.

Genre: **Lyric Poem**

from "At Loafing–Holt"
by Paul Laurence Dunbar

Since I left the city's heat
For this sylvan, cool retreat,
High upon the hill–side here
Where the air is clean and clear,
5 I have lost the urban ways.
Mine are calm and tranquil days,
Sloping lawns of green are mine,
Clustered treasures of the vine;
Long forgotten plants I know,
10 Where the best wild berries grow,
Where the greens and grasses sprout,
When the elders blossom out.
Now I am grown weather–wise
With the lore of winds and skies.
15 Mine the song whose soft refrain
Is the sigh of summer rain.
Seek you where the woods are cool,
Would you know the shady pool
Where, throughout the lazy day,
20 Speckled beauties drowse or play?
Would you find in rest or peace
Sorrow's permanent release?—
Leave the city, grim and gray,
Come with me, ah, come away.
25 Do you fear the winter chill,
Deeps of snow upon the hill?
'Tis a mantle, kind and warm,
Shielding tender shoots from harm.
Do you dread the ice–clad streams,—
30 They are mirrors for your dreams.

Have you ever seen the high buildings of Manhattan,
   near sundown, on a cold, gray day?
Ah, then, you have missed something.
35   Let me tell you how it is.
Walk down Lexington Avenue Towards 57th Street,
And look to the west.
Look up and see
The Great tall buildings,
40   The cold stone buildings,
High against the sky.
Look! The great stone buildings are pink!
The setting sun is making them rosy!
They are solid and rosy,
45   And give forth light.
The gray sky is confused and scurrying;
It is rosy too, in spite of itself.
The proud gorgeous buildings
Love the light
50   They love the sun for making them rosy,
Showing what they can be.
Busy people go about their business,
Eyes on the ground,
While the proud gorgeous buildings say with the
55   wheat fields:
"See what nature and man can do!
See what nature and man can do!
Be happy,
We are the rosy buildings and the wheat."

---

1   Which sentence from the poem signals the connection between New York and Kansas?

   A   "And I remember the wheat fields there."

   B   "See what nature and man can do!"

   C   "The setting sun is making them rosy."

   D   "Let me tell you how it was."

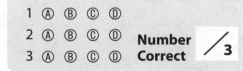

Answer Form

1 Ⓐ Ⓑ Ⓒ Ⓓ

2 Ⓐ Ⓑ Ⓒ Ⓓ   **Number**

3 Ⓐ Ⓑ Ⓒ Ⓓ   **Correct**   /3

2   Read lines 46–47 from the poem.

> The gray sky is confused and scurrying;
> It is rosy in spite of itself.

What is the meaning of the figurative language used in these lines?

A   The gray sky moves quickly back and forth in a very confused way.

B   The gray sky seems to be hiding behind buildings so people can no longer see it.

C   The gray sky reveals a developing a storm system that will soon bring rain.

D   The gray sky has clouds moving across it, reflecting light from the setting sun.

3   Read lines 48–49 from the poem.

> The proud gorgeous buildings
> Love the light

Based on the connotations of the words in these lines, what is the speaker's attitude toward the buildings?

A   The speaker admires the buildings' beauty and power.

B   The speaker sees the buildings as cold stone structures.

C   The speaker prefers natural creations like waves of wheat.

D   The speaker feels that they, like humans, enjoy sunlight.

4   Explain how the speaker uses both connotative and figurative language to express her feelings about how people and nature work together. Include at least **two** examples from the poem to support your response.

_____

_____

_____

_____

_____

_____

✓ **Self Check** *Go back and see what you can check off on the Self Check on page 120.*

Analyzing Rhyme and Repetition

CCSS
RL.7.4: . . . analyze the impact of rhymes and other repetitions of sounds (e.g., alliteration) on a specific verse or stanza of a poem or section of a story or drama.

Theme: *Honoring Heroes*

Did you know that a song is a poem in disguise? Like songwriters, poets and other authors revel in the musical quality of language. They use words, sounds, and rhythm in creative ways.

Repetition—the repeated use of a sound, word, phrase, or line—is one way in which authors produce an effect that adds meaning. An example of this is **alliteration**, or the repetition of consonant sounds at the beginnings of words. **Rhyme**, or the repetition of sounds at the ends of words, gives poems a musical quality and creates unity between ideas.

Read this poem. Look for the ways in which the poet uses rhyme and alliteration.

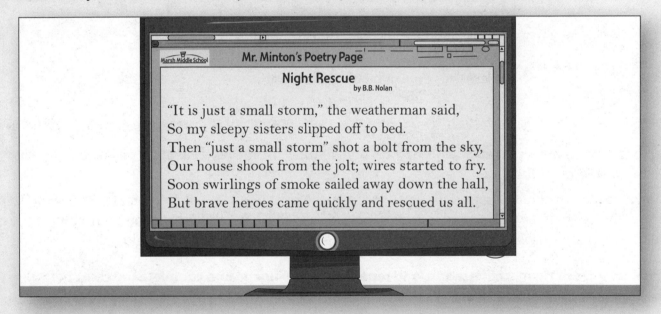

Mr. Minton's Poetry Page

Night Rescue
by B.B. Nolan

"It is just a small storm," the weatherman said,
So my sleepy sisters slipped off to bed.
Then "just a small storm" shot a bolt from the sky,
Our house shook from the jolt; wires started to fry.
Soon swirlings of smoke sailed away down the hall,
But brave heroes came quickly and rescued us all.

Draw arrows to connect pairs of rhyming words, and circle the alliterations. Think of how the poet's word choice affects the poem. Then compare your thoughts to the chart below.

Sound Device	Examples	Impact on Meaning
Rhyming words	said, bed; bolt, jolt; sky, fry; hall, all	They connect ideas and create unity and structure.
Alliteration	small storm sleepy sisters slipped soon swirlings, smoke sailed	Using the same sound calls attention to those words.

All authors choose words to convey meaning. But some authors—especially poets—arrange words to make the best use of their sounds. Being aware of sound devices such as alliteration and rhyme will help you "hear" how words can flow in a way that's music to your ears.

Read the first two stanzas of a poem about Harriet Tubman.

Genre: **Lyric Poem**

Harriet Tubman   *by Eloise Greenfield*

Harriet Tubman didn't take no stuff
Wasn't scared of nothing neither
Didn't come in this world to be no slave
And wasn't going to stay one either

"Farewell!" she sang to her friends one night
She was mighty sad to leave 'em
But she ran away that dark, hot night
Ran looking for her freedom
She ran to the woods and she ran through the woods
With the slave catchers right behind her
And she kept on going till she got to the North
Where those mean men couldn't find her

(continued)

Explore how to answer this question: *"How does the poet use rhyme, alliteration, and repetition in her description of Harriet Tubman?"*

Analyzing the effect of the sound devices chosen by the poet will help you interpret her message. Think of how the poet's choices emphasize important ideas and make her thoughts clearer. Also think of how the meaning of the poem would change without the rhyme, alliteration, and repetition.

Find examples of rhyme, alliteration, and repetition in the poem, and complete the chart below. Describe how they affect the poem's overall message or the meaning of a particular stanza.

Sound Device	Examples	Impact on Meaning
Rhyming Words	neither, either behind her, find her	
Alliteration	nothing neither	
Repetition		

With a partner, analyze the line "She ran to the woods and she ran through the woods" to determine the effect of the poet's use of repetition. How would the meaning of the line be different without it?

Continue reading the poem about Harriet Tubman. Use the Close Reading and the Hint to help you answer the question.

Close Reading

What sound devices does the poet use in this stanza? **Circle** examples of rhyming words and **underline** lines or phrases that are repeated.

(continued from page 130)

Nineteen times she went back South
To get three hundred others
She ran for her freedom nineteen times
To save Black sisters and brothers
Harriet Tubman didn't take no stuff
Wasn't scared of nothing neither
Didn't come in this world to be no slave
And didn't stay one either

And didn't stay one either

Hint

What did you think about Harriet when you read that she made the journey nineteen times?

Circle the correct answer.

Which choice best states the impact that the repeated phrase "nineteen times" has on the poet's message?

A The repetition of the phrase creates a musical rhythm in the first few lines of the stanza.

B The repetition emphasizes how frequently Tubman traveled back to the South.

C The repetition helps readers understand that "nineteen times" is the most important idea.

D The repetition of the phrase highlights Tubman's determination and courage.

Show Your Thinking

Explain how the sound devices helped you interpret the poet's feelings about Harriet Tubman.

_____

_____

_____

_____

With a partner, discuss how repetition of the line "And didn't stay one either" added to your understanding of the poem. What phrase does it echo from the first stanza?

Read the drama, which quotes from John Greenleaf Whittier's "Barbara Frietchie" and Alfred Lord Tennyson's "The Charge of the Light Brigade." Use the Study Buddy and Close Reading to guide you.

So far, the poems I've read use sound devices to add meaning to the lines. I wonder how they'll add meaning in this drama. As I read, I'll look for examples and think about how their use can help me understand what happens in this scene.

Close Reading

Underline examples of alliteration and words that rhyme. What effect do they create?

Circle words and phrases that are repeated in the dialogue. What impact do they have on the characters?

Genre: **Drama**

To Honor   *by Jayna Taylor*

1   *Scene II, in which three students discuss their group project*

2   TIA: Mr. Claypool said we have to find "a unique way to honor a hero" in our Veteran's Day presentation. People have been honoring heroes forever; so how can we possibly be unique?

3   JEROME: Yeah, like way back in Roman times when conquering generals were given a parade with chariots, cheering crowds, tons of trumpets—

4   ALICIA: That gives me an idea. We can create a unique version of an old way of honoring a hero by using poetry somehow. People have been writing poems about heroes forever.

5   JEROME: Poetry? Really? Poems are about flowers and fluff!

6   ALICIA: No way! What about this poem from the Civil War? It's about a woman who stood up to the Southern soldiers by hanging up the Union flag after they took it down.

   Up rose old Barbara Frietchie then,
   Bowed with her fourscore years and ten;
   Bravest of all in Frederick town,
   She took up the flag the men hauled down;

7   JEROME: Hmm, bravest of all . . . that's neat. Do you know others?

8   TIA: Well, there's a famous poem about a battle in 1854 when British soldiers bravely charged a hill while cannons thundered all around them. It goes, "Cannon to right of them/Cannon to left of them, . . ."

9   JEROME: Yeah, poems about soldiers, . . . bravest of all. Wait! There's got to be poems about bravery and courage, and lots of veterans have proved they're brave. We can find poems that describe the bravest of all!

10   TIA: That's *it*, Jerome! We'll put together a slide show using poems about bravery—and music, too. Jerome, you're a genius!

Hints

> How does the poet create a sense of unity in the Barbara Frietchie poem?

1 Which of the following describes the effect of a sound device that the poet uses in the Barbara Frietchie poem (paragraph 6)?

A The repetition of the sound at the end of *bravest* and the beginning of *town* stresses the importance of these words.

B The rhyming words at the end of each pair of lines tie the lines together and cause the lines to flow in a musical way.

C The repetition of the word *up* in the first and fourth lines shows that Barbara Frietchie's bravery made the town look up to her.

D The similar sounds in the words *Frietchie* and *flag* call attention to the connection between Barbara Frietchie and her heroic deed.

> What phrase does Jerome repeat several times?

2 Which phrase is used to highlight Jerome's gradual change in attitude?

A "chariots, cheering crowds, tons of trumpets"

B "flowers and fluff"

C "bravest of all"

D "poems about soldiers"

> What happens before, during, and after each student says the phrase "bravest of all"?

3 Read the statement below. Then answer the question that follows.

The author repeats the phrase "bravest of all" to emphasize how the students build on each other's ideas as they plan their presentation.

Write a paragraph explaining how you can tell that the above statement is true. Use at least two details from the passage to support your response.

_____

_____

_____

_____

_____

_____

_____

Read the story. Then answer the questions that follow.

Welcome Home

by Joyce Mallery

1   As far back as I could recall, basketball has been my passion. My father had set up a basketball hoop in our backyard, and my older brother Andy had started showing me how to play basketball from the time I was small. As I grew older, playing basketball became the focus of my life.

2   In most situations, I tend to be a shy and timid person, but I become someone completely different when I'm on the basketball court. It's almost like a switch turns on inside of me, and I can shut out everything else. When I'm playing basketball, my brother calls me Fast and Furious Fi. *Fi* rhymes with *see*, and Fi is short for Fiona. When I'm playing basketball, the spectators love to chant rhymes during the game: "What do you see, Fi?" "Score one for me, Fi!" and even "Hey Fi, make it three!!"

3   My brother has always been my best friend. While we did all the things that kids generally do to annoy each other, we always seemed to know what was in each other's hearts. But the past year has been so hard for me because my brother enlisted in the Air Force, and shortly after, he was deployed to the Middle East. My heart still thumps when I think back to the night before he left—the night we sat together and silently stared at the stars. "I don't know what I'll do without you," I blurted out, despite my feeble attempt to put on a brave face.

4   Andy was quiet, which is totally unlike him. "I'm scared to leave," he admitted quietly. "But it will be easier for me to be away if I know you're okay, and we can always text and email. I just have to know that you're going to be all right while I'm gone, Fiona—that you're going to be the star of your basketball team and work to get good grades."

5   I hugged him and I couldn't stop crying. My passion is basketball, and I'll work hard to get good grades because I know those things are important to my brother. "Hang in there, Fast and Furious," he whispered, trying his best to reassure me. But instead of fast and furious, I felt lost and lonely.

6   My life just wasn't the same after Andy left. My friends didn't seem to comprehend how I felt now that my brother was not around and how I worried about him. "I'd love to have my brother leave for awhile," my best friend Chloe once said. It took all the strength I had not to start crying, and I could tell that Chloe immediately regretted her remark. "I guess that was a thoughtless thing to say," she mumbled apologetically. "I know how much you love Andy."

7   The following week, Chloe and I were at the library when she called me over to her computer and pointed to a website. "Fiona, look at this," she said excitedly. "My mom told me about this: Troop Greeters official website. People assemble at the airport and greet the troops that pass through." We read the mission statement together: The mission of Troop Greeters is to express the nation's gratitude and appreciation to the troops, for those going overseas and for those heroes coming home.

8   The website said we could contact the group for additional information. "Let's go outside and call," Chloe suggested. I grabbed my cell phone and dialed the number. A woman answered, and she explained it all to us. "We'll let you know when flights are arriving, " she said. "Have at least one parent accompany you. The welcome means so much to our returning and departing military personnel."

9   That night I discussed it with my parents. "This sounds like a wonderful idea," Mom said. "And we'll bring Chloe, too, since it was her idea."

10   Then, the night before we were scheduled for our first meet-and-greet, I started to get really nervous about talking to strangers. Finally, I called Chloe. "I can't do this. I'll have no idea what to say!" I moaned.

11   "Wait a minute—you can't back out now!" Chloe snapped. "What happened to 'Fast and Furious Fi' of the basketball court? You're acting more like a foolish and flighty fan in the bleachers!" Then, in a softer voice, she added , "I've got an idea. Why don't you bring your basketball with you. That way the troops will know something about you right from the start, and you'll have something to talk about. "

12   The next morning we stood in line with the other troop greeters. Suddenly, there was a rush of footsteps and uniforms, and we could feel an electric buzz of excitement and energy. The first man in line looked at me, smiled, and shook my hand. "Thank you for coming," he said. "And you're a basketball player! Can I borrow this?" He grabbed the ball and started dribbling and laughing. Then he passed it to his friend.

13   I took a deep breath and forced myself to ask, "Did you play basketball in high school? I play for my varsity team." That remark brought a grin to several faces.

14   After that, it was easy for me to talk to the troops. Each one said hello and asked about my basketball. And every time I said, "Welcome home!" I knew in my heart that someday soon I would be uttering those words to my own hometown hero—my brother.

Answer the questions. Mark your answers to questions 1–3 on the Answer Form to the right.

Answer Form

1 Ⓐ Ⓑ Ⓒ Ⓓ
2 Ⓐ Ⓑ Ⓒ Ⓓ   **Number**   /3
3 Ⓐ Ⓑ Ⓒ Ⓓ   **Correct**

---

1   What effect does the author's use of rhyme have in paragraph 2?

A   The spectators' rhymes reflect the excitement at Fi's basketball games.

B   The spectators' rhymes add a musical quality to the paragraph.

C   The spectators' rhymes foreshadow which team will win the next game.

D   The spectators' rhymes reinforce Fiona's strong bond with her brother.

2　Why has the author chosen to use phrases such as "silently stared at the stars" and "lost and lonely" in the scene that took place the night before Andy left?

　A　to highlight similarities between the feelings of the brother and sister

　B　to build up the mood of stillness and sadness

　C　to create suspense about what will happen after Andy leaves

　D　to emphasize the close relationship between Fiona and her brother

3　How does Chloe's use of the phrase "Fast and Furious Fi" help Fiona to rethink her feelings about meeting strangers?

　A　It helps Fiona see the differences between basketball players and the arriving troops.

　B　It suggests that Fiona should remember what Andy said the night before he left.

　C　It emphasizes that Fiona should think up rhymes to chant for the soldiers.

　D　It reminds Fiona to draw on the confidence she gained from playing basketball.

4　A student made this claim: The author uses repetition and alliteration to draw the reader's attention to Fiona's feelings at different points in the story. Write a paragraph explaining how you can tell that the claim is true. Use at least **two** details from the passage to support your response.

_____

_____

_____

_____

_____

_____

_____

✓ **Self Check**　*Go back and see what you can check off on the Self Check on page 120.*

Analyzing the Structure of a Poem

CCSS
RL.7.5: . . . Analyze how a . . . poem's form or structure (e.g., . . . sonnet) contributes to its meaning.

Theme: *A Family Scrapbook*

Poetry is writing that uses words, sound, and structure in special ways to express meaning. Sometimes, poets arrange their thoughts in **stanzas**, or groups of lines. Stanzas may have a particular pattern of rhyming words. Sometimes poets write in **free verse**. In free verse, the arrangement of lines is irregular, and there may be no **rhyme scheme**, or pattern of rhyme, at all. Poets may also repeat certain sounds, words, or patterns to call attention to them, or create a rhythm.

Read the poem excerpt below, which describes the tasks a mother must do each day. Notice the rhyme scheme, which is based on the last sound of each line. When two lines have the same rhyming sound, they are assigned the same letter. Also, look for the groups of verbs at the end of each line, and circle them.

from "Song of the Old Mother"	Rhyme Scheme
by William Butler Yeats	
I rise in the dawn, and I kneel and blow	A
Till the seed of the fire flicker and glow;	A
And then I must scrub and bake and sweep	B
Till stars are beginning to blink and peep	B

Read the chart to learn how the structural elements in this poem contribute to its meaning.

Structural Element	What It Adds to the Poem
Rhyme scheme	The AABB rhyme scheme helps tie together the parts of each idea—starting the fire, and cleaning all day.
Repeated pattern	Ending each line with a group of verbs suggests the day-in and day-out nature of the woman's work.
Poem's Meaning: The work of a mother is ongoing and difficult.	

Listen closely the next time you read or hear a poem read aloud. Ask yourself these questions to better understand the poem's meaning: how is the poem organized? Does it rhyme, or is it free verse? Does the poet use repetition? If so, what effect does it create? Understanding poetry can be difficult, but asking questions like these can make it easier.

Read the poem below, which is about a child woken in the night by a hooting owl.

Genre: **Lyric Poem**

A Barred Owl   *by Richard Wilbur*

The warping night air having brought the boom
Of an owl's voice into her darkened room,
We tell the wakened child that all she heard
Was an odd question from a forest bird,
5   Asking of us, if rightly listened to,
"Who cooks for you?" and then "Who cooks for you?"

Words, which can make our terrors bravely clear
Can also thus domesticate a fear,
And send a small child back to sleep at night
10   Not listening for the sound of stealthy flight
Or dreaming of some small thing in a claw
Borne up to some dark branch and eaten raw.

Explore how to answer this question: *"How does the structure of the poem contribute to its meaning?"*

"A Barred Owl" is a lyric poem, or a poem that expresses the speaker's feelings. In this poem, parents want to comfort their frightened child, even though they realize the owl may not be as innocent as they tell her it is.

In the poem above, number the stanzas and think about the meaning in each one. Mark the rhyme scheme and underline any instances of repetition. Then, complete the following chart.

Structural Element	What It Adds to the Poem
Stanzas	
Rhyme scheme	The AABB rhyme scheme is similar to a lullaby used to help a child fall asleep.
Repetition	
Poem's Meaning:	

With a partner, take turns discussing how you interpreted the poem's meaning. Citing evidence from the text, explain how the different structural elements helped you come to that conclusion.

Read the poem, then use the Close Reading and Hint to help you answer the question.

Close Reading

This is a sonnet, a lyric poem with 14 lines. Think about how the phrase "count the ways" in the first line relates to phrases in other lines. **Underline** the phrase that is repeated throughout the poem.

Genre: **Sonnet**

How Do I Love Thee?   *by Elizabeth Barrett Browning*

How do I love thee? Let me count the ways.
I love thee to the depth and breadth and height
My soul can reach, when feeling out of sight
For the ends of Being and ideal Grace.
5   I love thee to the level of everyday's
Most quiet need, by sun and candle–light.
I love thee freely, as men strive for Right;
I love thee purely, as they turn from Praise.
I love thee with a passion put to use
10   In my old griefs, and with my childhood's faith.
I love thee with a love I seemed to lose
With my lost saints,—I love thee with the breath,
Smiles, tears, of all my life!—and, if God choose,
I shall but love thee better after death.

Hint

Look closely at the repeated phrases that you underlined. How do they connect to the poem's title?

Reread the poem. Then explain how the poet has used repetition to express the speaker's feelings.

_____

_____

_____

_____

✎ Show Your Thinking

Citing evidence from the poem, explain how the poem's structure helps you understand the speaker's feelings.

_____

_____

 With a partner, list and discuss the ways in which the speaker answers the question "How Do I Love Thee?"

Read the poem. Use the Study Buddy and Close Reading to guide your reading.

An ode is a type of lyric poem that celebrates something. I will keep this in mind as I read to see what the poem celebrates.

Close Reading

The speaker mentions mistakes in some photos. **Underline** instances of all the things that are wrong with the photos.

The speaker starts by flipping through a book of photos. Does he keep doing so to the end? What changes, and how do the lines and stanzas help show that change?

Genre: **Ode**

Ode to Family Photographs
by Gary Soto

This is the pond and these are my feet,
This is the rooster, and this is more of my feet.

Mama was never good at pictures.

This is the statue of a famous general who lost an arm,
5   And this is me with my head cut off.

This is a trash can chained to a gate,
This is my father with his eyes half–closed.

This is a photograph of my sister
And a giraffe looking over her shoulder.

10   This is our car's front bumper.
This is a bird with a pretzel in its beak.
This is my brother Pedro standing on one leg on a rock,
With a smear of chocolate on his face.

Mama sneezed when she looked
15   Behind the camera: the snapshots are blurry,
The angles dizzy as a spin on a merry–go–round.

But we had fun when Mama picked up the camera.
How can I tell?
Each of us laughed hard.
20   Can you see? I have candy in my mouth.

Hints

Eliminate answer choices that misinterpret the poet's use of structure.

1 How does the structure the poet uses help add meaning to the text?

 A The use of the rooster imagery suggests the speaker lives on a farm.

 B The free–form lines mirror the speaker's fun and lighthearted tone.

 C The italicized sentence shows the speaker's anger at the mother.

 D The rhyme scheme mirrors the turning of pages in a photo album.

How is this ode a celebration?

2 How do the speaker's feelings become clearer in the last stanza of this poem?

 A The speaker wishes his mother had been a better photographer.

 B The speaker regrets how he described the photographs.

 C The speaker reveals that he likes his mother's photography.

 D The speaker is upset that the photographs had mistakes.

Think about how the speaker's actions and feelings are communicated not just through his words but also through the repetition of phrases and the lengths of stanzas.

3 This poem explores a relationship between photographs and memories. Write a paragraph that describes how the structure of the poem helps to explore this relationship. Use at least three details from the text to support your response.

_____

_____

_____

_____

_____

_____

_____

_____

_____

_____

_____

Read the poem. Then answer the questions that follow.

A Boy and His Dad

by Edgar Guest

A boy and his dad on a fishing–trip—
There is a glorious fellowship!
Father and son and the open sky
And the white clouds lazily drifting by,
5 And the laughing stream as it runs along
With the clicking reel like a martial song,
And the father teaching the youngster gay
How to land a fish in the sportsman's way.

I fancy I hear them talking there
10 In an open boat, and the speech is fair.
And the boy is learning the ways of men
From the finest man in his youthful ken.
Kings, to the youngster, cannot compare
With the gentle father who's with him there.
15 And the greatest mind of the human race
Not for one minute could take his place.

Which is happier, man or boy?
The soul of the father is steeped in joy,
For he's finding out, to his heart's delight,
20 That his son is fit for the future fight.
He is learning the glorious depths of him,
And the thoughts he thinks and his every whim;
And he shall discover, when night comes on,
How close he has grown to his little son.

25 A boy and his dad on a fishing–trip—
Builders of life's companionship!
Oh, I envy them, as I see them there
Under the sky in the open air,
For out of the old, old long–ago
30 Come the summer days that I used to know,
When I learned life's truths from my father's lips
As I shared the joy of his fishing–trips.

Answer the questions. Mark your answers to
questions 1–3 on the Answer Form to the right.

Answer Form

1 Ⓐ Ⓑ Ⓒ Ⓓ

2 Ⓐ Ⓑ Ⓒ Ⓓ

3 Ⓐ Ⓑ Ⓒ Ⓓ

**Number
Correct** /3

1   Which statement **best** describes the structure of the poem?

   A   The poem has three stanzas, and each stanza uses repetition.

   B   The poem has four stanzas, and each stanza uses a rhyme scheme.

   C   The poem has four stanzas that use repetition in alternating stanzas.

   D   The poem has five stanzas that use rhyme and repetition.

2   How does the question at the beginning of the third stanza help to develop the central idea of the poem?

   A   The speaker realizes that the father and son's time together is more important than fishing.

   B   The speaker understands that the son will soon be ready to face the challenges of life.

   C   The speaker envies the relationship the father and son reveal during the fishing trips.

   D   The speaker imagines what the father and son are learning about fishing.

3   How do the speaker's feelings become clear in the last stanza of this poem?

   A   The speaker wants all fathers and sons to go on fishing trips.

   B   The speaker hopes that sons will learn lessons about life from their fathers.

   C   The speaker wants to go on fishing trips with his grandfather.

   D   The speaker fondly remembers his own experiences as a young boy.

4   The central idea of this poem is that a man and his son happily bond while on a fishing trip. Write a paragraph that describes how the structure of the poem helps to express this central idea. Use at least **three** details from the text to support your response.

_____

_____

_____

_____

_____

_____

_____

_____

_____

_____

_____

_____

_____

_____

_____

_____

_____

_____

✓ **Self Check**   _Go back and see what you can check off on the Self Check on page 120._

Analyzing the Structure of Drama

CCSS
RL.7.5: Analyze how a drama's . . . form or structure (e.g., soliloquy . . .) contributes to its meaning.

Theme: Anne Frank: Diary to Drama

There are many ways to tell a story. For example, a story can be told in a book, in a movie, or through a play. All of these forms contain characters, setting, and plot, but a play has some special characteristics. First of all, a play, or drama, relies on **dialogue**, the characters' words, to move the plot forward. Dramas also contain **stage directions**, which describe the setting and explain what the actors should do or how they should speak or behave. Dramas are organized into **scenes**, which are like chapters in a book, and scenes are grouped into **acts**.

Read the beginning of *The Diary of Anne Frank* by Frances Goodrich and Albert Hackett. The play is based on a young Jewish girl's diary, which details struggles endured by her family and friends when they had to go into hiding in an attic in Amsterdam during World War II.

Act 1, Scene 1

The curtain rises on an empty stage. It is late afternoon November, 1945. The rooms are dusty, the curtains in rags. Chairs and tables are overturned.

*The door at the foot of the small stairwell swings open. M*R. F*RANK comes up the steps into view. He stands looking slowly around, making a supreme effort at self-control. He is weak, ill. His eye is caught by something lying on the floor. It is a woman's white glove. He holds it in his hand and suddenly all of his self-control is gone. He breaks down, crying.*

*We hear footsteps on the stairs. M*IEP G*IES comes up, looking for M*R. F*RANK. M*IEP *is a Dutch girl of about twenty-two. She is pregnant. Her attitude toward M*R. F*RANK *is protective, compassionate.*

M*IEP: Are you all right, M*R. F*RANK?

M*R. F*RANK: *(Quickly controlling himself.)* Yes, Miep, yes . . . .

Underline details in the stage directions and dialogue that tell you something about the setting and characters. Compare what you learned to the information in the chart.

Setting	Characters	Plot
• November, 1945 • No one has lived in the rooms for a long time.	• Mr. Frank: ill, sad • Miep: pregnant Dutch woman who is protective of Mr. Frank	• Finding the glove makes Mr. Frank cry. Something tragic must have happened here.

When you read a play, imagine it is being performed with actors on a stage. If you are not actually watching a play, the stage directions and the dialogue help you visualize what's going on, so be sure to read them both very carefully.

Read the beginning of Act 1, Scene 2, which introduces the Van Daan family.

Genre: **Drama**

The Diary of Anne Frank, Act 1, Scene 2

by Frances Goodrich and Albert Hackett

It is early morning, July, 1942. The rooms are bare, as before, but they are now clean and orderly.

MR. VAN DAAN, a tall, portly man in his late forties, is in the main room, pacing up and down, nervous. . . . His clothes and overcoat are expensive and well cut.

MRS. VAN DAAN sits on the couch, clutching her possessions, a hatbox, bags, etc. She is a pretty woman in her early forties. She wears a fur coat over her other clothes.

PETER VAN DAAN is standing at the window of the room on the right, looking down at the street below. He is a shy, awkward boy of sixteen. At his feet is a black case, a carrier for his cat. The yellow Star of David is conspicuous on all of their clothes.

(continued)

Explore how to answer this question: *"What do these stage directions tell you about the setting and characters in the play?"*

The stage directions introduce new characters and give information about a change to the setting. Note that Scene 2 is set at an earlier time than Scene 1.

Think about what the stage directions tell you about the setting and characters. Study the chart below and fill in the missing information.

Describe the Setting	Describe the Characters
• July 1942, during World War II • The rooms:	• Mr. Van Daan: tall, portly, nervous • Mrs. Van Daan: • Peter:

Compare your notes about setting and characters with a partner. Discuss any differences in the meaning you identified from details revealed by the stage directions.

Continue reading Act 1, Scene 2. Use the Close Reading and the Hint to answer the question.

Close Reading

Underline details in the dialogue and stage directions on this page that tell you what is happening at this point in the play. How does this scene create a feeling of tension?

(continued from page 146)

MRS. VAN DAAN: (*Rising, nervous, excited.*) Something's happened to them! I know it! MR. FRANK said they'd be here at seven o'clock. He said . . .

MR. VAN DAAN: They have two miles to walk. You can't expect . . .

MRS. VAN DAAN: They've been picked up. That's what's happened. They've been taken . . .

(MR. VAN DAAN *indicates that he hears someone coming.*)

MR. VAN DAAN: You see?

Hint

Note the characters' words and actions. What tells you this is not an everyday situation?

Circle the correct answer.

Which statement best describes this plot event based on the dialogue and stage directions in this scene?

A   People the Van Daans know may be in danger.

B   Mrs. Van Daan is a nervous and excitable person.

C   The Van Daans are waiting to have dinner with friends.

D   Mr. Frank called to say he would be running late.

Show Your Thinking

Look back at the answers you did not choose. Which ones do not fit the details in the scene? Which one tells about a character instead of a plot event?

_____

_____

_____

_____

Discuss with a partner other details that tell you about the characters of Mr. and Mrs. Van Daan.

Read part of Act 1, Scene 2 below. Use the Study Buddy and the Close Reading to guide your reading.

Sometimes people's actions tell as much about them as what they say. As I read, I'm going to look for examples of stage directions that tell me more about the play's characters.

Close Reading

What does Anne's reaction to her father's monologue, or speech, reveal about her character? **Circle** the stage directions that answer the question.

Underline the benefits of being in hiding that Mr. Frank lists in his monologue. Then draw a **box** around earlier stage directions that show he knows his family is in danger despite his reassurances.

Genre: **Drama**

The Diary of Anne Frank, Act 1, Scene 2

by Frances Goodrich and Albert Hackett

MR. FRANK: Annele, there's a box there. Will you open it? (*He indicates a carton on the couch. Anne brings it to the center table.*)

ANNE: (*pulling out a pasteboard-bound book*). A diary! (*She throws her arms around her father.*) I've never had a diary. And I've always longed for one. (*She looks around the room.*) Pencil, pencil, pencil, pencil. (*She starts down the stairs.*) I'm going down to the office to get a pencil.

MR. FRANK: Anne! No! (*He goes after her, catching her by the arm and pulling her back.*)

ANNE: (*Startled.*) But there's no one in the building now.

MR. FRANK: It doesn't matter. I don't want you ever to go beyond that door.

ANNE: (*Sobered.*) Never . . . ? Not even at nighttime, when everyone is gone? Or on Sundays? Can't I go down to listen to the radio?

MR. FRANK: Never. I am sorry, Anneke. It isn't safe. No, you must never go beyond that door.

(*For the first time* ANNE *realizes what "going into hiding" means.*)

ANNE: I see.

MR. FRANK: It'll be hard, I know. But always remember this, Anneke. There are no walls, there are no bolts, no locks that anyone can put on your mind. Miep will bring us books. We will read history, poetry, mythology. (*With his arm about her, they go over to the couch, sitting down side by side.*) As a matter of fact, between us, Anne, being here has certain advantages for you. For instance, you remember the battle you had with your mother the other day on the subject of overshoes? You said you'd rather die than wear overshoes. But in the end you had to wear them? Well now, you see, for as long as we are here you will never have to wear overshoes! Isn't that good? And the piano! You won't have to practice on the piano. I tell you, this is going to be a fine life for you! (ANNE's *panic is gone.*)

Hints

Which stage direction appears after the father's monologue?

1 Which stage direction shows that Mr. Frank's speech has calmed his daughter?

    A   "(She starts down the stairs.)"

    B   "(. . . ANNE realizes what 'going into hiding' means.)"

    C   "(She throws her arms around her father.)"

    D   "(ANNE'S panic is gone.)"

How does Anne react when she opens the carton?

2 What can you tell about Anne's relationship with her father from the dialogue and stage directions?

    A   She is angry at her father for grabbing her arm.

    B   She has a close relationship with her father.

    C   She doesn't respect her father's decisions.

    D   She wishes her father would treat her like an adult.

How do the stage directions in the middle of Mr. Frank's monologue differ from those before his speech?

3 Explain how Mr. Frank's actions and words show that he wants to comfort his daughter but is also afraid for her. Use at least three details from the text to support your answer.

_____

_____

_____

_____

_____

_____

_____

_____

_____

_____

Read part of Act 2, Scene 4. Then answer the questions that follow.

The Diary of Anne Frank, Act 2, Scene 4

by Frances Goodrich and Albert Hackett

From 1942–1944, Anne kept a detailed diary of her life. Her family continued to hide, fearing the real possibility of being caught and removed to a Nazi concentration camp. Anne's words are a testimony to the courage of families like hers and the brave citizens who risked their safety to protect innocent lives.

ANNE: *(Looking up through skylight.)* Look, Peter, the sky. What a lovely day. Aren't the clouds beautiful? You know what I do when it seems as if I couldn't stand being cooped up for one more minute? I think myself out. I think myself on a walk in the park where I used to go with Pim. Where the daffodils and the crocus and the violets grow down the slopes. You know the most wonderful thing about *thinking* yourself out? You can have it any way you like. You can have roses and violets and chrysanthemums all blooming at the same time. . . . It's funny . . . I used to take it all for granted . . . and now I've gone crazy about everything to do with nature. Haven't you?

PETER: *(Barely lifting his face.)* I've just gone crazy. I think if something doesn't happen soon . . . if we don't get out of here . . . I can't stand much more of it!

ANNE: *(Softly.)* I wish you had a religion, Peter.

PETER: *(Bitterly, as he rolls over.)* No, thanks. Not me.

ANNE: Oh, I don't mean you have to be Orthodox . . . or believe in heaven and hell and purgatory and things . . . I just mean some religion . . . it doesn't matter what. Just to believe in something! When I think of all that's out there . . . the trees . . . and flowers . . . and seagulls . . . when I think of the dearness of you, Peter . . . and the goodness of the people we know . . . Mr. Kraler, Miep, Dirk, the vegetable man, all risking their lives for us every day . . . When I think of these good things, I'm not afraid any more . . . . I find myself, and God, and I . . .

PETER: *(Impatiently, as he gets to his feet.)* That's fine! But when I begin to think, I get mad! Look at us, hiding out for two years. Not able to move! Caught here like . . . waiting for them to come and get us . . . and all for what?

ANNE: *(Rises and goes to him.)* We're not the only people that've had to suffer. There've always been people that've had to . . . sometimes one race . . . sometimes another . . . and yet . . .

PETER: *(Sitting on upstage end of bed.)* That doesn't make me feel any better!

ANNE: I know it's terrible, trying to have any faith . . . when people are doing such horrible . . . *(Gently lifting his face.)* but you know what I sometimes think? I think the world may be going through a phase, the way I was with Mother. It'll pass, maybe not for hundreds of years, but some day . . . I will believe, in spite of everything, that people are really good at heart.

PETER: *(Rising, going to the windowseat.)* I want to see something now . . . Not a thousand years from now.

ANNE: *(As she comes to him.)* But, Peter, if you'd only look at it as part of a great pattern . . . that we're just a little minute in life . . . *(She breaks off.)* Listen to us, going at each other like a couple of stupid grownups! *(She holds out her hand to him. He takes it.)* Look at the sky now. Isn't it lovely? *(Sits as PETER puts his hands on ANNE'S shoulders. PETER rises, stands behind her with arms around her. They look out at the sky.)* Someday, when we're outside again I'm going to . . . *(She breaks off as she hears the sound of a car outside, its brakes squealing as it comes to a sudden stop. The people in the other rooms also become aware of the sound. They listen tensely. Another car outside comes to a sudden stop.)*

Answer the questions. Mark your answers to questions 1–3 on the Answer Form to the right.

Answer Form

1 Ⓐ Ⓑ Ⓒ Ⓓ
2 Ⓐ Ⓑ Ⓒ Ⓓ   **Number** ╱
3 Ⓐ Ⓑ Ⓒ Ⓓ   **Correct** ╱3

1 What does the dialogue between Anne and Peter at the beginning of the scene reveal?

A Peter thinks Anne is courageous.

B Anne thinks Peter is unreasonable.

C Peter's situation is much worse than Anne's.

D Anne's imagination is more vivid than Peter's.

2 What does Anne's monologue, beginning with "I know it's terrible . . .", contribute to the meaning of the play?

A It expresses Anne's innocence about the world she lives in.

B It allows Anne to speak to the audience about her mother.

C It conveys the playwrights' beliefs about people during wartime.

D It provides background information about the story itself.

3 What do the final stage directions **most likely** indicate about the setting of the play?

    A   The war in Europe has suddenly ended.

    B   The people in the attic have been rescued.

    C   The house in Amsterdam has been bombed.

    D   The hiding place in the attic has been discovered.

4 Write a paragraph explaining how Anne's statement that "people are really good at heart" creates irony in the scene. Use at least **two** details from the text to support your response.

_____

_____

_____

_____

_____

_____

_____

_____

_____

_____

_____

_____

_____

_____

✓ **Self Check** *Go back and see what you can check off on the Self Check on page 120.*

Analyzing Point of View

CCSS

RL.7.6: Analyze how an author develops and contrasts the point of view of different characters or narrators in a text.

Theme: *Perspectives*

Roller coasters aren't for everyone. You might love the thrills, but your friend keeps her eyes closed the whole time! Each of you has your own perspective, or **point of view**, about the experience.

Stories contain different points of view, too. Sometimes you'll get the point of view of the narrator, or the voice telling the story. At other times you'll get the point of view of one or more characters. By revealing their words, thoughts, feelings, and actions, the author gives you insight into the characters' attitudes about the events and people around them.

Who are the main characters in the scene below? How would the description of the same event differ if it were told from each character's point of view?

Read the chart below. Note how the evidence shows why a contrast exists between the acrobat's point of view about the situation and the audience member's perspective.

Character	Evidence	Point of View
Acrobat	says next trick will be tough; walking a high tightrope	The routine is very dangerous, and he could fall at any minute.
Audience Member	smiling, eyes wide, says acrobat makes it look easy	The acrobat seems very talented, and he's in no danger.

The characters in the scene are having two different experiences and would tell different versions of the same story. In other words, *how* an event is described is directly affected by *who* is describing it. So by carefully choosing or describing points of view, the author is able to advance the plot and help readers understand the characters' actions and motivations.

Read this story about Ramon and Blanca's trip to an art museum.

Genre: **Realistic Fiction**

Places of Disinterest   by Rowena Jackson

Another Inez family Saturday afternoon outing was drawing to a close, and for Blanca and Ramon's parents, the car ride home from the art museum couldn't be over fast enough. Blanca stared stonily out the car window, while Ramon beamed.

"That is the absolute last time you get to pick where we go," Blanca exclaimed and scowled at her older brother. "The entire exhibit was filled with paintings that looked like someone ran around splashing buckets of paint randomly all over the canvas."

"That's called *expressionism*," Ramon eagerly explained, "Each painting is meant to evoke a feeling. What were some of the emotions you experienced in the exhibit?"

"I felt quite frustrated and exhausted," Blanca sighed dramatically, and then she exclaimed, "And I didn't appreciate that security guard being so rude to me!"

"You sat on a priceless metal sculpture! He was just doing his job."

(continued)

Explore how to answer this question: *"How does the author contrast the points of view of the different characters?"*

To figure out each character's point of view, identify words and phrases that reveal his or her thoughts, feelings, and attitudes toward story events. Underline text evidence that suggests how Blanca feels about the afternoon at the art museum. Circle the evidence that suggests how Ramon feels about the same experience. Then complete the chart below, and compare the characters' points of view.

Character	Evidence	Point of View
Blanca	stares stonily out window, doesn't want Ramon to pick an activity again, disliked the paintings, sat on a sculpture	
Ramon		enjoyed his time at the museum because he understands and appreciates fine art

Blanca and Ramon have contrasting perspectives about their experience at the museum. How do the characters' interests and feelings affect their points of view?

_____

_____

Continue reading about the visit to the art museum. Use the Close Reading and the Hint to help you answer the question.

Close Reading

How do Blanca's and Ramon's points of view differ about the still–life paintings? **Underline** the words and phrases that show the contrast.

(continued from page 154)

After a few moments, Ramon tried again. "Those still–life pieces were so remarkable. Did you notice how the artists captured the interplay of light and shadow across even such ordinary objects?"

Blanca checked her text messages for the billionth time and muttered angrily, "Sure, I always pay attention to boring stuff like light and shadow when I'm looking at a bowl of fruit."

"Well, was there anything at the museum that you enjoyed?"

Blanca thought carefully for a moment before flashing her wrist—"I did enjoy the gift shop, because I got this cool watch."

Hint

How does Ramon react to Blanca's complaints?

Circle the correct answer.

Based on evidence from the story, which statement best describes Ramon's point of view about his sister?

A He thinks Blanca could be a painter if she paid attention to details.

B He believes she should admit to knowing that the art is valuable.

C He hopes to convince her that she can appreciate fine art.

D He's not sure that Blanca will ever appreciate expressionism.

Show Your Thinking

Citing evidence from the text, describe how the author contrasts Blanca's point of view from that of her brother.

_____

_____

_____

_____

 With a partner, discuss how the contrasting points of view help readers understand the characters' relationships with one another.

The following is a retelling of an ancient Zen tale called a *koan*, which is meant to teach a moral or lesson. Read the tale and use the Study Buddy and the Close Reading to guide your reading.

Genre: **Allegory**

Authors often reveal their characters' thoughts and feelings through dialogue. As I read, I'll pay close attention to what the characters say.

Close Reading

How does Sakura feel about Gessen? **Underline** any evidence in the text that explains her point of view.

What do the last two paragraphs reveal about Gessen's motives? **Star (*)** any details that help explain how his actions reflect his point of view.

"The Stingy Artist"   *retold by Keisha Walker*

This is the tale of Gessen, a Tibetan monk who became a famous artist. Recognized for his amazing talent, Gessen would always demand payment in advance before ever picking up a paintbrush.

1   A wealthy and proud noblewoman named Sakura heard of a wonderfully skilled artist named Gessen. She quickly summoned him to her palace to paint a scene of her three prized dogs.

2   "How much can you pay?" Gessen inquired sternly.

3   "It is shameful to speak of money so early in the discussion," the noblewoman replied, barely hiding her contempt.

4   "Perhaps," replied Gessen, unmoved. "But I must know now!"

5   Sakura sneered at the artist, but she finally named a price. Gessen demanded more. Finally, the two agreed on the fee, the highest sum ever paid for a painting anywhere in the land. Gessen was paid in advance, and the piece was unveiled at a grand feast in honor of the noblewoman's prized dogs.

6   "It is the grandest painting in my collection, to be sure," the noblewoman told Gessen over dinner. "But you taint its beauty with your stinginess and petty desire for money. You would no doubt ask me for a year's wages to sketch upon my napkin. Your outrageous greed means you will never paint anything of worth."

7   "A year's wages I will take, if that is what you will pay." Gessen bore the scorn of all at the table, especially from she who would hold a lavish feast for pampered canines while people starved.

8   For you see, unbeknownst to Sakura or her guests, Gessen's village was suffering from a terrible famine. He had used every bit of his earnings to fill a warehouse with grain, to repair the roads leading to the National Shrine, and to build his people a new temple. And when all had been accomplished, he gave his paintings away for free, never again asking for a single coin.

Hints

As you fill out the graphic organizer, think about how the author reveals the characters' thoughts and feelings through dialogue and narration.

1 For each character, identify two or more details from the text that support your analysis of each character's point of view.

Character	Evidence	Point of View
Gessen		
Sakura		

Which answer choice helps explain why Gessen charges such high prices?

2 Which statement best describes Gessen's attitude toward money?

   A   Gessen thinks people should spend money any way they wish.

   B   Gessen believes art is more important than money.

   C   Gessen thinks that money is more important than beauty.

   D   Gessen feels money should be used to help others, not wasted.

As you write, think about how Sakura's ignorance of Gessen's motives colors her point of view.

3 Citing at least two specific details from the text and the chart above, contrast the points of view of Gessen and Sakura from *The Stingy Artist*.

_____

_____

_____

_____

_____

_____

_____

_____

Read this excerpt from *The Good Earth*, a novel written by Pearl S. Buck. Then answer the questions that follow.

Pearl Sydenstricker Buck was born in 1892 in West Virginia but soon moved back to Zhenjiang, China, with her missionary parents. Raised by a Chinese nanny, Pearl learned Chinese tales and myths and could speak and write both English and Chinese by the age of four. Her daily interactions with the people of Zhenjiang taught Pearl a great deal about Chinese life and customs.

While Pearl traveled back to the United States for brief time periods, she spent most of the first forty years of her life in China. In 1917, Pearl and her husband John moved to a poor rural community in the Chinese province of Anhui. There Pearl observed the challenges and hardships faced by impoverished peasant–farmers. Later, during her writing career, Pearl was able to draw from a wealth of memories about China and its people.

from *The Good Earth*

by Pearl S. Buck

A hard-working peasant named Wang Lung labors long hours in his fields to feed his growing family. After years of fruitful harvests, however, a severe drought cripples the countryside, and all its inhabitants suffer as the crops wither and perish. Ultimately, the family's food stores are exhausted, the family ox is consumed, and they are starving. All that remains of Wang Lung's inheritance is his land, now just bleak, hardened fields. In this scene, Wang Lung senses the hopelessness building inside him; then he sees his uncle and two men come up to his house. How well-fed they look! Wang Lung all but accuses his uncle of being heartless enough to feed himself while his relatives are starving.

1   "I have thought of nothing but of you and of your father, who is my brother," retorted his uncle briskly, "and now I prove it to you. As soon as I could, I borrowed from these good men in the town a little food on the promise that with the strength it gave me I would help them to buy some of the land about our village. And then I thought of your good land first of all, you, the son of my brother. They have come to buy your land and to give you money—food—life!" His uncle, having said these words, stepped back and folded his arms with a flourish of his dirty and ragged robes.

2   Wang Lung did not move. He did not rise nor in any way recognize the men who had come. But he lifted his head to look at them and he saw that they were indeed men from the town dressed in long robes of soiled silk. Their hands were soft and their nails long. They looked as though they had eaten and blood still ran rapidly in their veins. He suddenly hated them with an immense hatred. Here were these men from the town, having eaten and drunk, standing beside him whose children were starving and eating the very earth from his fields; here they were, come to squeeze his land from him in his extremity. He looked up at them sullenly, his eyes deep and enormous in his bony, skull–like face.

3   "I will not sell my land," he said.

4   His uncle stepped forward. At this instant the younger of Wang Lung's two sons came creeping to the doorway upon his hands and knees. Since he had so little strength in these latter days the child at times had gone back to crawling as he used in his babyhood. . . .

5   "What is your price?" Wang Lung whispered at last. Well, there were these three children to be fed—the children and the old man. He and his wife could dig themselves graves in the land and lie down in them and sleep. Well, but here were these.

6   And then one of the men from the city spoke, a man with one eye blind and sunken in his face, and unctuously he said, "My poor man, we will give you a better price than could be got in these times anywhere for the sake of the boy who is starving. We will give you . . ." he paused and then he said harshly, "we will give you a string of a hundred pence for an acre!"

7   Wang Lung laughed bitterly. "Why, that," he cried, "that is taking my land for a gift. Why, I pay twenty times that when I buy land!"

8   "Ah, but not when you buy it from men who are starving," said the other man from the city. He was a small, slight fellow with a high thin nose, but his voice came out of him unexpectedly large and coarse and hard.

9   Wang Lung looked at the three of them. They were sure of him, these men! What will not a man give for his starving children and his old father! The weakness of surrender in him melted into an anger such as he had never known in his life before. He sprang up and at the men as a dog springs at an enemy.

10   "I shall never sell the land!" he shrieked at them. . . . "I will dig up the fields and feed the earth itself to the children and when they die I will bury them in the land, and I and my wife and my old father, even he, we will die on the land that has given us birth!"

Answer Form

1 Ⓐ Ⓑ Ⓒ Ⓓ
2 Ⓐ Ⓑ Ⓒ Ⓓ   **Number** ⟋ 3
3 Ⓐ Ⓑ Ⓒ Ⓓ   **Correct**

1   Look at the chart below.

CHARACTER	POINT OF VIEW	EVIDENCE
Wang Lung	upset that he is forced to choose between feeding his family and selling his land	

Which sentence from the text **best** completes the chart?

A   "He did not rise nor in any way recognize the men who had come."

B   "They looked as though they had eaten and blood still ran in their veins."

C   "Well, there were these three children to be fed—the children and the old man."

D   ". . . here they were, come to squeeze his land from him in his extremity."

2   Based on the text evidence, which statement **best** reflects the contrast between Wang Lung's point of view and the city men's?

   A   Wang Lung thinks his uncle is heartless, but the men are sure that his uncle really does have Wang Lung's best interests in mind.

   B   Wang Lung thinks the men are taking advantage of him, but the men believe a starving man has no choice but to sell.

   C   Wang Lung thinks that the men from the city are soft, but they are convinced that peasants can be easily fooled.

   D   Wang Lung believes that his uncle's proposal is unreasonable, but the men believe that Wang Lung is uncertain and slow to make decisions.

3   Based on story details and the characters' attitudes, which sentence **best** reveals an important value in Chinese culture?

   A   "'I have thought of nothing but of you and of your father . . . .'"

   B   ". . . they were indeed men from the town dressed in long robes . . . ."

   C   "I will not sell my land . . . ."

   D   ". . . we will give you a better price than could be got in these times . . . ."

4   Explain how the author's background is reflected in Wang Lung's response to the city men. Use at least **three** details from the text to support your answer.

   _____

   _____

   _____

   _____

   _____

   _____

   _____

   _____

   _____

✓ **Self Check**   *Go back and see what you can check off on the Self Check on page 120.*

Read the poem and the drama. Then answer the questions that follow.

The Sky Is Low

by Emily Dickinson

The sky is low, the clouds are mean,

A traveling flake of snow

Across a barn or through a rut

Debates if it will go.

5   A narrow wind complains all day

How some one treated him;

Nature, like us, is sometimes caught

Without her diadem.[1]

[1] **diadem:** a crown

Not a Cloud in the Sky

by Martine Nowak

The setting is the front lawn of a small house on a dead end lane. The yard is littered with the castoffs of a family: two old bicycles with training wheels, a stack of board games, and numerous packs of trading cards. There are also items such as a toaster and an old cooking grill displayed on top of a picnic table. The time is late morning, the month is July. A strong sun beats down on the heads of Thomas, fourteen years old, and his brother, Alec, twelve years old.

THOMAS: (*pacing up and down by the picnic table*) Where is everyone, anyhow? It certainly isn't the weather that's keeping people away from our yard sale. There isn't a cloud in the sky! (*He pushes his baseball cap back on his head and looks around, squinting in the sunlight. There are still no customers approaching.*)

ALEC: (*staring down at the grass, where a cabbage butterfly has just alighted on a patch of clover*) Maybe no one will buy this old stuff, Tom—there's rust on both of the bikes. Who really wants a bunch of board games all strapped together with string and rubber bands?

From within the house, we overhear the thumping sounds of heavy objects being moved across the floor, and the voices of the boys' parents engaged in packing.

THOMAS: I can't wait to sell everything and jump in that van. I've always wanted to live in the city, and it's finally going to happen. (*He glances over at a swing set in the corner of the yard.*) This place was great when we were little kids, but there's nothing much to do here now. You have to admit, the city is much more exciting, and we'll meet new people and everything. Right? And you'll get to visit as many museums as you like, whenever you like, and bring your sketch pad. And when you're ready for high school there are schools that specialize in art. Mom told me all about it; she says it's a "huge selling point."

ALEC: (*in a dull, flat voice*) Yeah, I guess so, miles of museums in the city.

THOMAS: Hey! Here come a couple of little kids. That little girl looks just the right size for your old two-wheeler. Hi, kids! Come on over! Look at all the things you might want to buy—or have your parents buy, I mean. Here's a set of baseball cards I've been collecting for years, but you can have them for just two bucks.

LITTLE GIRL: Those are boys' bikes, huh? Do you have any bikes for a girl?

ALEC: Sorry. (*He bends down to look into the child's eyes.*) You ought to ask your Mom and Dad for a real nice bike, made for a girl, with white streamers on the handles. You'd like that, wouldn't you? Betsy, right?

LITTLE GIRL: (*Scowling*) My name is Miriam. My brother is Mark but he's only two and a half.

THOMAS: (*positioning himself between Alec and the children and displaying a broad grin*) We have some incredible stuff here for kids just your ages. We've got a basket stocked with great toys—toys we'd keep for ourselves if we weren't moving to a small apartment in the city.

ALEC loses all interest in the proceedings. He wanders over to the rock garden that boasts a scattering of small purple flowers. He begins to speak, even though no one seems to be listening.

It took us weeks to get this garden the way Mom wanted it to look. We must have made half a dozen trips to the gardening center. I helped her to design it. I think I still have the sketches I did before we started working on it. And over there is where I first met Janine—she just wandered over from her new house and asked if she could swing on our swing set. Boy, I never thought we would become such great friends. And camping out on the lawn in Dad's old army tent—the noises of the crickets and the shadow the bats made and how scared I was when Tommy crept out of the tent at midnight and starting growling like a bear until Dad came out with a flashlight and told us to settle down or come on back in the house. (*Sighs*) I don't know what it will be like not to live here anymore. This is where I've been my whole life, and Tom too, even though he doesn't seem to care about it—not the way I do, anyhow.

ALEC stands with his back to his brother and the jumble of the yard sale, hands in his pockets. From what seems to be a blue sky, a light rain begins to fall, watering the rock garden and sending the little customers shrieking across the lawn, heading back home.

Answer the questions. Mark your answers to questions 1–5 on the Answer Form to the right.

Answer Form

1	Ⓐ	Ⓑ	Ⓒ	Ⓓ
2	Ⓐ	Ⓑ	Ⓒ	Ⓓ
3	Ⓐ	Ⓑ	Ⓒ	Ⓓ
4A	Ⓐ	Ⓑ	Ⓒ	Ⓓ
4B	Ⓐ	Ⓑ	Ⓒ	Ⓓ
5	Ⓐ	Ⓑ	Ⓒ	Ⓓ

Number Correct /5

1 How does the speaker use figurative language to describe the flake of snow in the first stanza of the poem?

   A   The speaker explains the sound it makes.

   B   The speaker exaggerates the way it travels.

   C   The speaker describes how it thinks.

   D   The speaker compares it to the sky and the clouds.

2 What is the connotation of the word "debates" in line 4 of the poem?

   A   The snowflake seems uncertain and hesitant.

   B   The snowflake seems angry and quarrelsome.

   C   The snowflake appears to be speaking to someone.

   D   The snowflake appears to be playing with someone.

3 What impact does the use of rhyme have on the poem?

   A   The rhyme creates a powerful emotional effect.

   B   The rhyme creates a drowsy, monotonous effect.

   C   The rhyme creates a musical effect, as in a song.

   D   The rhyme creates a conversational effect, as in dialogue.

4 Answer Parts A and B below.

Part A

Based on the play "Not a Cloud in the Sky," which statement **best** describes Thomas's point of view about moving to the city?

A   He doesn't understand why Alec is so excited to move.

B   He is afraid to move but is making the best of the situation.

C   He thinks the move to the city will be a very good thing.

D   He is sorry to leave the old home with all of its memories.

Part B

Which sentence from the play **best** supports the answer to Part A?

A   "You have to admit, the city is much more exciting, and we'll meet new people and everything."

B   "It certainly isn't the weather that's keeping people away from our yard sale."

C   "Yeah, I guess so, miles of museums in the city."

D   "Here's a set of baseball cards I've been collecting for years, but you can have them for just two bucks."

5 Which phrase signals a major change in the focus of the poem?

A   "A traveling flake of snow"

B   "Debates if it will go."

C   "A narrow wind complains all day"

D   "Nature, like us, is sometimes caught"

6 The central image of this poem is a bleak winter's day. Write a paragraph that describes how the structure of the poem helps to communicate this central image. Cite at least two details from the poem to support your response.

_____

_____

_____

_____

7 The footnote to the poem defines "diadem" as a crown. How does the connotation of the word "diadem" show the speaker's feelings about nature? Use details from the poem to support your answer.

_____

_____

_____

_____

8 How does the author use dialogue to reveal the different point of view of Tom and Alec? Use details from the play to support your answer.

_____

_____

_____

_____

9 Read the statement below.

In the play, the setting helps to reveal how each brother feels about moving.

Write a paragraph supporting this statement. Cite at least two pieces of evidence from the story to support your response.

_____

_____

_____

_____

_____

_____

_____

_____

_____

_____

_____

Performance Task—Extended Response

10   Think about how Alec's monologue contributes to the meaning of the play. What details in this speech help you better understand Alec's feelings? Be sure to include details from the play in your answer.

In your answer, be sure to
- explain how the monologue expresses Alec's feelings about moving away from his home
- identify language in the monologue that reveal aspects of Alec's character
- use details from the play in your answer

Check your writing for correct spelling, grammar, capitalization, and punctuation.

_____

_____

_____

_____

_____

_____

_____

_____

_____

_____

_____

_____

_____

_____

_____

Unit 5
Integration of Knowledge and Ideas in Informational Text

Have you ever heard a speech given by a candidate running for office? Candidates make claims about how the country should be run or how to improve their communities. Smart voters try to learn all they can about the candidates before they cast their votes. They listen to the candidates' speeches, read articles expressing different viewpoints, and follow reports in the media. Only after **integrating** all of that information do they decide how to vote. A smart reader, like a smart voter, collects **knowledge** and **ideas** from a variety of sources and integrates it, or puts it together, to thoroughly understand a topic. Then the reader, like a voter, can make an informed choice about what to believe.

In this unit, you will learn to evaluate information from a variety of sources and to compare the print version of a text with an audio, video, or multimedia version. You will look for an author's claims in a text and decide whether they make sense and are well supported by reasons. You will read different texts on the same subject, looking at how each author emphasizes different pieces of evidence to present a different viewpoint. Let's see which authors get your votes!

✔ **Self Check**   **Fill out the Self Check on the next page.** ▶

Before starting this unit, check off the skills you know below. As you complete each lesson, see how many more you can check off!

✓ Self Check

I know how to:	Before this unit	After this unit
follow the argument an author makes and evaluate its claims.	☐	☐
tell whether an author's claims make sense and are supported by enough good reasons.	☐	☐
explain how authors present different interpretations of information on the same topic.	☐	☐
compare and contrast the experience of reading a text to hearing an audio version or watching a video of that text.	☐	☐

Lesson 17   Part 1: Introduction 👥

Evaluating an Argument

CCSS

RI.7.8: Trace and evaluate the argument and specific claims in a text, assessing whether the reasoning is sound and the evidence is relevant and sufficient to support the claims.

Theme: *Energy and Our Future*

When you hear the word *argument*, do you picture people involved in some kind of shouting match? That may be what some arguments look like, but in writing, an **argument** is a text that explains why an author's position on an issue is valid.

When building an argument, a writer makes one or more **claims**, or statements he or she believes to be true. Then the writer backs up each claim with **evidence**, or information that supports the claim. Part of figuring out the strength of an argument is determining whether there is enough evidence to support the claim—and also whether the evidence does, in fact, act as support at all.

Read the following from an argument about solar-powered cars. First, circle the claim. Next, underline evidence. Finally, cross out any information that does not support the claim.

> Dedicating research money to the development of affordable solar-powered cars would be a wise investment. First, solar cars would help end our dependence on fossil fuels like oil and coal, which contribute to the pollution of our atmosphere. In addition, solar power is a renewable resource; unlike fossil fuels, it will never run out. Solar cars would also help the consumer save money. Panels attached to cars can collect sunlight and turn it into electricity, so no one would ever need to buy another tank of gas. Finally, solar-powered cars would also come in all the same colors as gas-powered cars.

Read the chart below to see how the author constructed the argument.

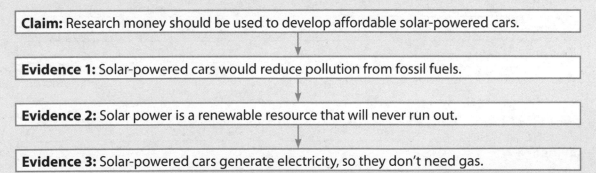

Claim: Research money should be used to develop affordable solar-powered cars.

Evidence 1: Solar-powered cars would reduce pollution from fossil fuels.

Evidence 2: Solar power is a renewable resource that will never run out.

Evidence 3: Solar-powered cars generate electricity, so they don't need gas.

To trace the reasoning behind an argument, identify the author's claims and evidence. Then judge whether the author provides enough evidence and whether it is relevant, or actually supports each claim. If the ideas have a sound basis in logic, then the argument is valid.

The following excerpt is from a speech about meeting the energy needs of the United States.

Genre: **Speech**

from "A Generational Challenge to Repower America" *by Al Gore*

What if we could use fuels that are not expensive, don't cause pollution, and are abundantly available right here at home?

We have such fuels. Scientists have confirmed that enough solar energy falls on the surface of the earth every 40 minutes to meet 100 percent of the entire world's energy needs for a full year. Tapping just a small portion of this solar energy could provide all of the electricity America uses.

And enough wind power blows through the Midwest corridor every day to also meet 100 percent of U.S. electricity demand. Geothermal energy, similarly, is capable of providing enormous supplies of electricity for America.

(continued)

Explore how to answer this question: *"This excerpt follows a section of the speech in which Gore makes claims about the dangers of relying on expensive foreign oil. What is Gore's claim in this part of the speech?"*

Here it's important to identify or infer the speaker's claim about other energy-generating options. In this case, the claim is made in the form of a question.

Underline facts in the text that relate directly to the claim. Then complete the graphic organizer.

Claim: We should use fuels that are cheaper, cleaner, and more easily accessible than foreign oil.

Evidence 1:

Evidence 2:

With a partner, discuss whether or not Al Gore has presented enough relevant evidence to support his claim.

Continue reading the excerpt from Al Gore's speech. Use the Close Reading and the Hint to help you answer the question.

Close Reading

In this section, Gore introduces a new claim, recommending a way to begin using renewable energy. What evidence does Gore provide to support this claim? **Underline** details that support his claim.

(continued from page 172)

The quickest, cheapest, and best way to start using all this renewable energy is in the production of electricity. In fact, we can start right now using solar power, wind power, and geothermal power to make electricity for our homes and businesses.

But to make this exciting potential a reality, and truly solve our nation's problems, we need a new start.

That's why I'm proposing today a strategic initiative designed to free us from the crises that are holding us down and to regain control of our own destiny. It's not the only thing we need to do. But this strategic challenge is the lynchpin of a bold new strategy needed to re-power America.

Hint

In a valid argument, the evidence must be sufficient to prove the claims. Does Gore provide enough evidence?

Circle the correct answer.

How well does the author support his claim that the best way to begin using solar, wind, and geothermal power is to make electricity?

A   He supports it well because the energy crisis is holding us back.

B   He supports it well because he proposes a new energy strategy.

C   He supports it poorly because he does not say why this way is best.

D   He supports it poorly because these energy sources are not actually forms of renewable energy.

✏️ **Show Your Thinking**

Look at the answer that you chose above. Citing text evidence, explain why you chose this answer.

_____

_____

💬 Consider both parts of the speech together. With a partner, evaluate the validity of the argument and claims made in favor of developing alternative energy sources.

Read the article. Use the Study Buddy and the Close Reading to guide your reading.

Sometimes an author's position and claims are not stated. As I read the article, I'm going to infer the author's claims from the supporting evidence that's given.

Close Reading

What is the author's claim about the Advanced Clean Cars Program? **Circle** the sentences that reveal what the author believes to be true.

How does the data in the bullets help to support the author's claims? **Underline** the supporting evidence.

Genre: **Economic Article**

from "Clean Cars for California"

from Energy Independence Now

1   On January 28, 2012, the California Air Resources Board unanimously voted to adopt the Advanced Clean Cars Program, which represents the most comprehensive effort in the world to set society on path to end our dependence on oil. It's a tremendous victory for California residents and consumers, with national and global benefits and implications. By 2025 in California:

2   • One in seven new cars sold will be zero-emission (battery electric or hydrogen fuel cell electric) or plug-in hybrid vehicles, and approximately 1.4 million of these vehicles will be on the road;

3   • Greenhouse gases will be reduced by 52 million tons, the equivalent of taking 10 million cars off the road;

4   • Tailpipe emissions of soot- and smog-forming emissions will be cut by 75%;

5   • California drivers will save $5 billion in operating costs, with average consumers seeing nearly $6,000 in fuel cost savings over the life of the advanced car (compared to added upfront costs of approximately $2,000); and

6   • 21,000 jobs will be added in California, rising to 37,000 in 2030.

7   The program rightly focuses industry efforts on both incremental and transformative change. On the incremental side, the Low Emission Vehicle (LEV) regulations set targets for automakers to improve the efficiency and emissions systems associated with internal combustion engines, which are likely to be at least part of our transportation portfolio well into the future.

Hints

Identify the answer choice that best summarizes the lines you circled on the previous page

Use the Hints on this page to help you answer the questions.

1 Which statement best expresses the author's claim?

A It is important to reduce fuel costs for California drivers so that they can save money each year.

B By requiring cleaner, more efficient engine and emission systems, the Advanced Clean Cars Program benefits everyone.

C Requiring that one in seven cars be a zero-emission or plug-in vehicle is the only way to significantly reduce greenhouse gases.

D The greatest achievement of the Advanced Clean Cars Program is that it will create 21,000 jobs now and more in the future.

Eliminate answer choices that do not specifically support the author's claim.

2 What evidence does the author provide to support this claim?

A The author explains that the cars will still play an important role in our future system of transportation.

B The author describes how the California Clean Air Resources Board adopted the Advanced Clean Cars Program.

C The author points out how dependence on oil harms both the nation and the world.

D The author provides details about how the Advanced Clean Cars Program will reduce car emissions and benefit consumers.

Is all of the evidence relevant, or actually related to the claim? Is there enough evidence to fully support the claim?

3 Decide how successful the author's argument about the Advanced Clean Cars Program is. Write a paragraph evaluating the soundness of the author's claims and the evidence used to support it. Cite at least two details from the passage to support your response.

_____

_____

_____

_____

_____

_____

Read the persuasive essay about wind power. Then answer the questions that follow.

The Case for Wind Power

by Scott Shears

1   As the world's population grows, so does the need for energy resources. The fossil fuels we have long relied on are both destructive and finite. Burning coal, oil, and natural gas releases carbon into the air, trapping more of the sun's heat in our atmosphere. And mining of these resources is becoming more costly Already it is becoming harder to reach the remaining resources, and eventually even those will run out. When the world's energy needs rise while its access to fuel falls, there will be a crisis, one only made worse by the effects of climate change. The most practical solution is to replace the harmful, limited fuels with ones that are safe and limitless. That is why the U.S. government should fund the research and development of wind power, a clean and renewable resource. And these efforts should begin now.

2   The vast majority of the electricity we use comes from power plants that run on fossil fuels. Burning these fuels turns the massive turbines that generate electricity. It also releases greenhouse gases into the air. These gases are considered to be a major contributor to global warming. The steady rise in the average atmospheric temperature of the planet will eventually result in the melting of glacial ice, the rise of ocean levels, and the shifting of climates.

3   Wind power, in contrast, produces electricity without pollution. Wind turbines look and act like a common pinwheel—only on a much larger scale. They can be as tall as a 20-story building and have blades 200 feet long. The blades catch the wind, which turns a generator that produces electricity. This type of energy production burns no fuel, generates no emissions, and causes no harm to the environment. Additionally, wind power is a renewable resource that will never run out. Wind farms can stretch for hundreds of square miles and contain hundreds of individual turbines. A vast plain dotted with these elegant white machines is an impressive sight to behold. With additional government funding for research, turbine technology will become more efficient, producing more electricity with less wind power.

4   Critics of wind power maintain that the infrastructure it requires is not feasible. Wind blows strongest in open areas where tall buildings cannot block the currents. So wind farms must be built far away from the urban areas that need the power most. Hundreds of miles of costly new transmission lines would be required to connect the wind farms to existing electrical storage facilities. Critics say this expense, in addition to building the farms in the first place, is too great for the government to support.

5   But not every city needs to draw its wind power from so far away. In recent years, coastal cities such as Los Angeles, San Francisco, and New York City have considered constructing offshore wind farms. These cities require massive electrical resources, making wind power an attractive possibility. Winds blow harder offshore, which can translate into more power. Also, offshore winds blow strongly during the afternoon hours when energy consumption is at its peak. Constructing offshore wind farms and new transmission lines will be expensive, but this investment will surely pay off in the long run. Over time, drilling and mining for oil and coal will become more costly, but wind power is always free.

6   Another charge critics level is that wind power is unreliable. As they point out, the weather is unpredictable. Winds do not blow at consistent speeds, and sometimes they do not blow at all. In order to prevent power outages, backup power plants burning fossil fuels must be ready to kick in when the air is still. But backup power plants would only operate occasionally, contributing far less pollution than the ones in use today. And the development of storage batteries, to build up power reserves to be used when winds are low, would further reduce the use of fossil fuels. One such a battery will be part of a new wind power installation in Hawaii. Officials there plan to generate 70 percent of their state's power needs from renewable sources.

7   Wind power is the most practical solution to our nation's power needs. It draws on the endless blowing of the wind, so it will never run out. It creates no pollution, so it will not foul the air or contribute to global warming. And as it replaces fossil fuel power, it will reduce greenhouse gas emissions. Our government can make this change happen more quickly by investing in wind power. It is time for America to face the future and the undeniable part wind power will need to play.

Answer Form

1 Ⓐ Ⓑ Ⓒ Ⓓ
2 Ⓐ Ⓑ Ⓒ Ⓓ   **Number** ⟋3
3 Ⓐ Ⓑ Ⓒ Ⓓ   **Correct**

1   Which statement **best** expresses the author's claim about wind power?

A   Climate change can be reversed by switching from fossil fuels to wind power.

B   Wind power is superior to fossil fuels because it is cheaper than drilling or mining.

C   Wind power will be expensive to adopt and will not be a reliable energy source.

D   The government should invest in wind power because it is clean and renewable.

2   Which sentence from the essay **best** supports the author's claim that wind power will reduce the release of greenhouse gases?

A   "Wind farms can stretch for hundreds of square miles and contain hundreds of individual turbines."

B   "This type of energy production burns no fuel, generates no emissions, and causes no harm to the environment."

C   "Over time, drilling and mining for oil and coal will become more costly, but wind power is always free."

D   "But backup power plants would only operate occasionally, contributing far less pollution than the ones in use today."

3 Which piece of evidence from the text is **not** relevant to the author's claim?

A "Wind power, in contrast, produces electricity without pollution."

B "In addition, wind power is a renewable resource that will never run out."

C "A vast plain dotted with these elegant white machines is an impressive sight to behold."

D "Constructing offshore wind farms and new transmission lines will be expensive, but it is an investment that will surely pay off in the long run."

4 Below are three claims that one could make based on the essay "The Case for Wind Power."

CLAIMS

	Wind power is reliable.
	Wind power is affordable.
	Wind power is ecological.

Part A

Put an "X" by the claim that is supported by the most relevant and sufficient facts in "The Case for Wind Power."

Part B

Write a short paragraph with at least **three** details to show how the claim you chose in Part A is supported by relevant and sufficient facts in the essay.

_____

_____

_____

_____

_____

_____

 **Self Check** *Go back and see what you can check off on the Self Check on page 170.*

Comparing and Contrasting Texts

CCSS

RI.7.9: Analyze how two or more authors writing about the same topic shape their presentations of key information by emphasizing different evidence or advancing different interpretations of facts.

Theme: *Facing the Challenges*

Imagine that two artists use the same paints to paint a mountain scene. One creates a dark, scary landscape, and the other paints a bright, peaceful place. Even though the artists use the same materials and paint the same subject, their results depend on the effects they want to achieve and the colors they choose to create those effects. In the same way, authors may write about the same topic, but, depending on their purpose, they may choose to focus on different details and evidence. As a result, they produce very different products.

Look at the cartoon below and think about how the characters are reacting to the poster. What if they both decided to write reports about global warming? How might each of them approach the topic?

Read the information in this chart. Which facts do you think each of the two characters would emphasize when writing about global warming?

General Facts	Causes of the Problem	Effects on Wildlife
• Earth's average temperatures are increasing. • Rising temperatures result in melting of the polar ice caps. • Polar ice melt causes sea levels to rise.	• Fossil-fuel emissions release heat-trapping gases into the atmosphere. • The additional heat raises local temperatures and, in turn, impacts Earth's climates.	• Loss of habitat due to ice melt results in decreasing animal populations. • Changes in feeding and migration patterns put animals at risk.

While both students would probably use the information in the first column, the girl probably would also use the evidence in the second column, while the boy would focus on facts from the third one. Always keep in mind that an author's purpose for writing shapes the way he or she presents key information as well as which facts and evidence are emphasized.

Read the following scientific account about global warming.

Genre: **Scientific Account**

Global Warming: Why? *by Rex Woodbury*

Scientists who study climate models and climate patterns are concerned that the Earth's average temperatures seem to be increasing. They also report that a warm-up of even a few degrees will have far-reaching effects on climate, wildlife, human food production, and fresh water supplies. Why is this happening?

To understand global warming, imagine that our planet is wrapped in a blanket. The blanket is made up of carbon dioxide and other gases that collect and trap the sun's heat in the Earth's atmosphere. It's important to understand that this blanket serves as protection from the intensity of the sun and its dangerous rays. The burning of fossil fuels and other human activities, however, have changed the make-up of this protective covering. In simple terms, by adding more gases, we've added more layers, and the blanket traps more heat than it should, heat that changes our environment.

Explore how to answer this question: *"How does the author's purpose shape the focus of the account and the key information he presents?"*

In the first paragraph, the author points out the problem caused by increasing temperatures and then asks a question. In the second paragraph, he answers that question by explaining more about the process of global warming.

In the chart below, write the focus of this account. After you read the account on the next page, fill in columns 2 and 3. Then compare and contrast the ideas you wrote.

Focus of Account 1	Focus of Account 2	Ideas in Both Accounts
Its talking about climate models and climate patterns	It talking about the global warming.	they both about the heat,

Read another account about global warming. Use the Close Reading and the Hint to help you complete the chart and then answer the question.

Genre: **Scientific Account**

The Side Effects of Warming *by Di Garza*

Global warming widely impacts both Earth's climate and the environment as a whole. The Arctic regions, in particular, are suffering due to climate change. Glacial ice is melting at an alarming rate. The amount of ice lost in recent years equals the combined area of Alaska, Texas, and Washington. This change to the Arctic landscape endangers many of the creatures living there. Polar bears, for example, depend on glacial ice. It allows them to travel far from land to open water to find their favorite prey, seals. A decrease in this ice limits the bears' ability to reach their prey, thus reducing their chance of survival. Only by changing human habits that contribute to climate change, such as the use of fossil fuels, can we stop the harmful effects of global warming on wildlife.

Close Reading

The accounts here and on page 180 both tell about global warming, but they use key information differently. **Underline** any facts in this account that are similar to those in the first one. **Star (*)** any unique details. Use this information to complete the chart on the previous page.

Hint

What is the main point that the author of this account wants you to know? How is it different from the first account?

Circle the correct answer.

How does the focus of this account differ from the account on page 180?

A Instead of telling the cause of global warming, it explains an effect.

B Instead of describing one solution, it tells about many possibilities.

C Instead of talking about glacial ice, it describes polar bear habits.

D Instead of naming climate changes, it warns of future problems.

✎ Show Your Thinking

Compare and contrast the key information presented in the two passages. What evidence, if any, do both include? Why has it been presented differently?

_____

_____

_____

_____

With a partner, summarize how the author's purpose in each passage shapes the presentation.

Read the following passages about desalination, or the removal of salt from water. Use the Study Buddies and Close Readings to guide your reading.

As I read this passage, I'll think about the author's purpose, and I'll note the way it determines how the key information is presented.

Close Reading

Circle one piece of key information in each paragraph that helps you understand the author's most important ideas.

What kind of information does the author include about desalination? **Underline** details about this process that help you understand it.

Genre: **Report**

Some Simple Water Science
by Grace Carter-Hamm

1   If 70 percent of Earth's surface is covered in water, then why do news headlines warn us that water is scarce and that we're running out of it? The problem is that most of this water is salt water, which cannot be used by humans, most land animals, or plants. Only 2.5 percent is fresh water that can actually be drunk or used to water crops.

2   With all that salt water just floating around, it's natural to wonder if there's a way to remove the salt and make it usable. Well, there is, and the answer came from seabirds. A special membrane in the birds' throats will stop salt molecules but allow water molecules to pass through it. After years of studying this membrane, scientists have figured out how to copy this desalination technique using a process called *reverse osmosis*.

3   To understand reverse osmosis, you must first understand osmosis itself. Picture a bowl with two compartments. Separating the two is a semipermeable membrane—a barrier that allows some molecules to pass through it but not others. One compartment holds fresh water and the other sugar water. Checking the bowl hours later, you discover that the sugar solution is less sweet than it had been. Osmosis has occurred: molecules of water have traveled from the fresh water side (an area of no sugar concentration) to the sugar side (an area of high concentration), making the concentrations more equal.

4   In reverse osmosis, the process is reversed. It maximizes areas of concentration instead of equalizing them. The process forces salt molecules in seawater, for example, to separate away from the water molecules rather than allowing them to mix together. Thus, fresh water is born.

5   Today, special desalination plants work to remove salt from seawater, creating potable drinking water. Thanks to seabirds, these plants can help to solve the world's water problems.

This next passage also deals with desalination. I wonder how the focus of this one will differ. I'll look for key information as I read.

Close Reading

Underline any information in this passage that is the same as or similar to facts presented in "Some Simple Water Science."

How is the discussion of desalination different in this passage? **Star (*)** any facts about desalination that were not present in the previous text.

Genre: **Persuasive Essay**

Water for the World   *by Lee Epstein*

1   The essential ingredients for life are food, water, and shelter. Water, of course, is especially important. Not only do we need to drink it to survive, but we also need it to water our crops and take care of livestock, both of which are primary food sources. Without a ready supply of clean, fresh water, however, these needs cannot be met. As the number of people in our world continues to grow, meeting everyone's water requirements becomes more and more challenging. How can this be, though, if most of Earth's surface is water?

2   Although 70 percent of Earth is covered in water, only a small fraction of that total is fresh water safe for human use. This amount appears even smaller when considering that the population has tripled over the last hundred years or so and our water use has increased six-fold. Not only are there more people, but they are using more water than in the past. In some areas, the supply is dwindling while the demand continues to grow.

3   Given our limited fresh water resources and increased water needs, we must turn to other means of providing adequate water supplies to the 1.1 billion people who currently do not have access to clean, safe water. One popular solution for some areas experiencing water stress or an imbalance between water use and resources is *desalination*. The process "manufactures" fresh water from seawater.

4   Desalination, or the removal of salt from salt water through reverse osmosis, is not a new idea. The Greeks and Romans were doing it thousands of years ago, one potful of water at a time. Luckily, technology has made the task easier: As of 2009, there were more than 1,400 desalination plants around the world, producing more than 15 billion gallons of usable water per day.

5   Despite our progress in making desalination a viable solution to the water crisis, we still have a long road ahead. Countries must continue to work toward building more desalination plants to keep up with the growing need for fresh water. Only then will our water resources become as limitless as the sea.

183

Hints

What point was the author of each passage trying to make about desalination?

Use the Hints on this page to help you answer the questions.

1 Which sentence best sums up how the focus of the first passage differs from the second passage?

  A The first passage describes the growing demand for fresh water, while the second describes the current limits to water resources.

  B The first passage stresses the scarcity of fresh water, while the second explains how salt can be removed from seawater.

  C The first passage presents the pros and cons of desalination, while the second argues that desalination is the solution to water problems.

  D The first passage describes the desalination process, while the second discusses how desalination can help solve the water crisis.

Look back at the information you underlined to see which facts are featured in both passages.

2 Which of the following explains how the two authors shape their presentations by using similar key information in a different way?

  A Both authors talk about how people need water to survive, but the second explains what will happen if water needs aren't met.

  B Both authors name reverse osmosis as a key part of desalination, but the first explains the science principles used in the process.

  C Both authors explain that 1.1 billion people don't have clean, salt-free water, but the second uses the fact to support desalination.

  D Both authors say that only a small percent of Earth's water is fresh, but the first discusses the challenges of finding water resources.

Why do you think the authors chose to include the facts they did?

3 Compare the presentations about desalination in the two passages. Explain how they are alike and different. Describe how the authors use similar and different facts to achieve their unique purposes. Use at least two details from the texts in your response.

_____

_____

_____

_____

_____

_____

Read both scientific articles about endangered fish. Then answer the questions that follow.

from "Big Fish in Troubled Waters"

by Stephen Ornes, Science News for Kids

1   You may have heard the popular saying "there are always more fish in the sea." But as a number of new studies show, the truth of that statement depends on the kind of fish. Fish populations are changing, and not necessarily for the better.

2   Consider the case of big, predatory fish. These giants, like sharks and cod, devour other, smaller fish. Big fish are an important part of the marine ecosystem—which includes the ocean and all the things living in it—because they keep down the numbers of smaller fish. Without fish that eat other fish, populations of smaller swimmers could swell. More of these smaller fish would devour more plants, leaving less vegetation for other organisms—or for future fish.

3   As fierce and ferocious as predators can be, they're no match for fishing technology. Many people love to eat predatory fish like sharks, cod and tuna. According to two new, large studies, these giant predators are becoming scarce. One study shows how the populations are decreasing; the other shows how fishing hauls, or the amount of fish caught, have changed. Together, the studies suggest that overfishing threatens the creatures near the top of the marine food chain.

4   In one study, Villy Christensen and his colleagues looked at 200 past studies of marine life to learn how fish populations have changed over time. Christensen is a fisheries expert at the University of British Columbia in Vancouver. The oldest studies his team looked at dated to 1880; the most recent were published in 2007. In these 200 studies, researchers counted and described all the different types of life in small oceanic ecosystems.

5   Christensen presented the team's findings in February at the 2011 meeting of the American Association for the Advancement of Science in Washington, D.C. He reported that between 1910 and 1970, the numbers of big predators decreased slowly. In 1970, their populations really started to drop. Around that time, fishing ships began using new tools that led to catching more fish. The numbers have been falling quickly ever since.

6   Now, the number of these big fish in the ocean is very low. Christensen reported that today there is only about one-third as many of the large, fish-eating fish as there was in 1910. That means for every three you might have found in 1910, now you would only find one. Christensen said the future looks increasingly dismal for these giants.

7   "We see no indication that things are improving," Christensen told the audience. "It's a pretty bleak situation."

8   While Christensen looked at the problem from the perspective of the fish, Reg Watson approached it from the perspective of the fishermen. Watson, a biologist also at the University of British Columbia, studied the increase in fishing in recent decades. Like Christensen, Watson reported his findings at the AAAS meeting.

9   In the middle of the 20th century, Watson reported, fishing boats didn't venture far from home—and most fish were caught near the shore. That wasn't true in the 1980s. By then, he said, fishing had moved farther from shore, into the open oceans, and it was helped by the development of new tools and technologies. These advances helped a lot: In the 1990s, fisherman hauled in five times as much fish, by weight, as they had in the middle of the century. But since the 1990s, something has changed. Despite new technologies and more effort, fishing operations have not continued to boost their hauls. If there are fewer fish in the sea, fishing companies may have a hard time keeping up with the demand for fresh fish.

10   The studies by Watson and Christensen don't paint a promising picture for sea predators. These scientists studied historical data to understand the present, and this research is needed to forecast the future of fish and fishing. And the forecast doesn't look good: Large predator fish are becoming harder to find—and there may not be more in the sea for long.

Protecting the Oceans, One Choice at a Time

by Oscar Seever

1   When the US Department of Agriculture (USDA) introduced new dietary guidelines in 2010, one of its key recommendations was to eat seafood twice a week. Seafood is higher in protein and lower in fat than other animal proteins. Also, many fish and shellfish are rich in omega-3 fatty acids. Omega-3s have been shown to have many health benefits, including the support of heart health. If all Americans were to follow this recommendation, however, consumption of seafood in the United States would double.

2   While this would be great for people's health, it could pose a problem for the world's oceans. Current fishing practices are already reducing the populations of many seafood species to the point of collapse. If we want to have access to seafood well into the future, we must take steps to preserve and renew the ocean's bounty and encourage others around the world to do the same. Action from world governments will be vital to sustain seafood populations in the oceans that cover three-quarters of Earth's surface. But there is something you can do as an individual, too. You can exercise the power of your fork and avoid eating seafood with populations that have become endangered.

3   When choosing which seafood to buy and eat, there are two important factors to consider, the species of fish and where it was caught. The bluefin tuna is critically endangered and has been overfished all over the world, largely due to its popularity as a sushi fish. This huge fish, which can grow to be 10 feet long and weigh 1,400 pounds, is popular with fisherman—just one fish can be sold for up to $100,000. But if enough people avoid this fish, the demand would go down. Fishermen wouldn't have as much reason to catch them. Tuna fans can still feed their cravings by choosing more abundant bigeye or yellowfin tuna.

4   The Atlantic halibut is another large fish, which can grow to be 9 feet long and 1,000 pounds. It is particularly vulnerable to overfishing due to its long lifespan. It can live to be 50 years old, and it doesn't reach reproductive maturity until it is between 10 and 14. Halibut caught before they reach maturity never get a chance to reproduce, damaging the entire population. The United States has banned Atlantic halibut fishing in its waters. However, it cannot regulate fishing practices on the "high seas," the large areas of ocean outside of any individual country's control. Luckily, there is a good alternative to Atlantic halibut, its relative the Pacific halibut.

5   For those who like eating lobster, paying attention to where it comes from can protect some lobster populations. Spiny lobsters from the Caribbean and South American are threatened, but spiny lobster populations in Florida, California, and Mexico's Baja California are still in good shape. Your local seafood market should be able to tell you where its seafood comes from. If they cannot, consider a surer option, such as an American lobster from Maine.

6   If this all sounds a bit complicated, don't worry. There is information available on which to base your seafood-eating decisions. The Monterey Bay Aquarium, one of the top aquariums in the country, maintains a complete, easily printable "Buyer's Guide." This list tells you which seafood species from which sources are the best choices, which alternatives to consider, and which species you, the consumer, should avoid. By paying a little attention to the seafood you're eating, you can avoid contributing to the problems faced by endangered fish species. Change won't happen overnight, but every choice you make can help protect an ocean ecosystem near you.

Answer Form

1 Ⓐ Ⓑ Ⓒ Ⓓ
2 Ⓐ Ⓑ Ⓒ Ⓓ   **Number** /3
3 Ⓐ Ⓑ Ⓒ Ⓓ   **Correct**

1 Which of the following **best** sums up how the focus of "Big Fish in Troubled Waters" differs from "Protecting the Oceans, One Choice at a Time"?

A The first article explains why people love to catch large predatory fish like cod and tuna, while the second explains the life-cycle of large fish such as the Atlantic halibut.

B The first article explains why predatory fish are important to the ocean ecosystem, while the second explains where to find information about fish that are rich in omega-3s.

C The first article explains the causes of declining fish populations, while the second explains the connections between the creatures in the ocean food chain.

D The first article explains that overfishing is threatening some fish populations, while the second explains how to save some fish species by making careful decisions about meals.

2 Which of the following pieces of key information is used in both articles?

A Spiny lobsters from the Caribbean and South America are endangered.

B Fish populations are changing or decreasing, leaving some species at risk.

C An increase in smaller fish means a decrease in the food supply for predatory fish.

D The health benefits of eating fish and shellfish is creating a high demand for them.

3   Which statement **best** describes the purposes that shaped the authors' presentations of key information in the two articles?

     A   Both authors are trying to convince the reader to agree with their points of view.

     B   Both authors give facts as evidence to support conclusions.

     C   The author of the first article uses facts and then draws a logical conclusion. The author of the second article uses facts to move the reader to take action.

     D   The author of the first article gives reasons and evidence to support his opinion. The author of the second article uses facts and reasons to predict future trends.

4   Compare and contrast the ways the authors shaped their presentations in the two articles. Describe how their use of key information helped them to achieve their purposes. Use at least **three** details from the texts in your response.

_____

_____

_____

_____

_____

_____

_____

_____

_____

_____

_____

_____

_____

_____

✓ **Self Check**   *Go back and see what you can check off on the Self Check on page 170.*

Read these two essays. Then answer the questions that follow.

The Benefits of Shale Gas

by Henry Chang

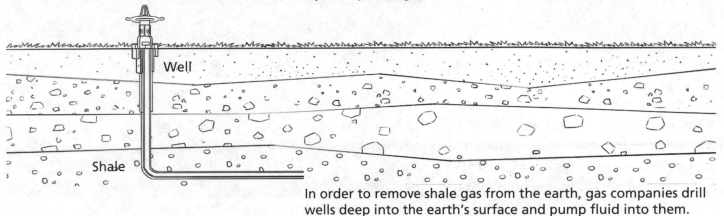

In order to remove shale gas from the earth, gas companies drill wells deep into the earth's surface and pump fluid into them.

1   Shale gas is a type of natural gas found under shale rock, which is common throughout the United States. While people have known for a long time that shale gas existed, until recently there was no way to access it. However, modern technology has changed the situation. We can now tap into a vast supply of shale gas, which we can use to inexpensively heat homes, power automobiles, and produce electricity. Shale gas has become the fastest-growing energy source in the United States and is the cleanest of all fossil fuels. Burning shale gas releases less carbon dioxide into the air than burning coal or oil.

2   Despite its benefits, however, many people oppose the use of shale gas. They think that the process used to access shale gas, hydraulic fracturing, also called "fracking," is harmful to people and the environment because it pollutes drinking water. These opponents are mistaken.

3   To access shale gas, gas companies drill wells several thousand feet into the earth. They pump fluid under high pressure into these wells. This fluid fractures, or breaks up, the shale rock, so the shale gas can be removed from the earth. While this fluid consists mainly of water and sand, it also contains a small amount of chemicals. Those who oppose hydraulic fracturing believe that these chemicals will contaminate drinking water, making it unsafe to drink. However, the risk of this happening is extremely small—and it can be eliminated completely if gas companies avoid drilling near drinking-water sources.

4   The benefits of hydraulic fracturing far outweigh the risks. For one thing, burning shale gas is good for the economy. The high cost of fuel in the United States has led many businesses to move to other countries. The affordability of shale gas will keep this from happening in the future. It may even encourage some of the businesses that have left the United States to return. Using shale gas also benefits homeowners because it reduces their heating and electricity bills.

5   Hydraulic fracturing also creates jobs. As the demand for shale gas increases, gas companies will need more employees. It is estimated that the use of hydraulic fracturing will create more than 500,000 high-paying, safe jobs. Americans need to embrace the use of shale gas. It is the solution to the energy crisis and the key to a productive future for our country.

Stop the Fracking!

by Cynthia Martinez

1   Fracking is destroying the United States. As you may know, fracking is the process of extracting shale gas from the ground. Fracking pollutes rivers, lakes, and streams and contaminates drinking water. Contaminated water contains chemicals that are harmful to people and animals. Fracking also pollutes the air and destroys the land. Fracking even harms people. Reports show that more than 1,000 people have suffered serious illnesses and/or death from drinking water that was contaminated due to fracking.

Gas companies often set up rigs in farmland areas that are used to extract shale gas from the earth.

2   To extract shale gas from the ground, gas companies drill deep into the earth and force fluids into the ground under high pressure. These fluids break up shale rock and release shale gas. While this process might sound harmless, it is definitely not. Up to 8 million gallons of fluid are used each time shale rock is "fracked." About 40,000 gallons of chemicals are mixed into this fluid. Some of these chemicals are carcinogens, or chemicals known to cause cancer in humans. These chemicals seep into the ground surrounding the well and contaminate groundwater. This has happened with nearly every well that gas companies have drilled. Gas companies also leave some of the leftover fluid from fracking in open pits, where it eventually evaporates and causes air pollution. This type of pollution damages the ozone layer and causes acid rain.

3   Truck traffic is another major problem associated with fracking. Up to 1,300 trucks may be needed to bring in enough fluid for a single well. These trucks are much too heavy for rural roads. They cause pollution and destroy roadways. Taxpayers may have to pay millions of dollars to repair roads damaged by these trucks.

4   Farmers who are struggling to pay their bills often welcome gas companies onto their land. They are eager to sign a lease from a gas company. And why shouldn't they? Gas companies may pay farmers a million dollars for the right to drill for shale gas on their land. However, these farmers often do not realize that fracking will destroy their land. Crops may not grow there for many years. Fracking will also pollute farmers' drinking water, making the water in their drinking wells smell like chemicals and gasoline. The open pits created by gas companies may cause livestock to become sick or die.

5   Supporters of fracking say that the process creates high-paying jobs. This is misleading. Fracking might create a few jobs, but these jobs do not pay well, and they are not safe. Many workers at drilling sites now have lung cancer. Are these really the types of jobs we want to create for Americans?

6   The dangers of fracking far outweigh the benefits. The Environmental Protection Agency (EPA) is investigating the effects of fracking. Oppose fracking and do your part to save our country!

Answer Form

1 Ⓐ Ⓑ Ⓒ Ⓓ
2 Ⓐ Ⓑ Ⓒ Ⓓ
3 Ⓐ Ⓑ Ⓒ Ⓓ
4 Ⓐ Ⓑ Ⓒ Ⓓ **Number**
5 Ⓐ Ⓑ Ⓒ Ⓓ **Correct** ⟋5

Answer the questions. Mark your answers to questions 1–5 on the Answer Form to the right.

1 Which statement supports the claim in the first essay that the benefits of hydraulic fracturing outweigh the risks?

A "To access shale gas, gas companies drill wells several thousand feet into the earth."

B "Using shale gas also benefits homeowners because it reduces their heating and electricity bills."

C "Hydraulic fracturing, also called 'fracking,' is harmful to people and the environment because it pollutes drinking water."

D "These chemicals seep into the ground surrounding the well and contaminate groundwater."

2 The author of "Stop the Fracking!" would disagree with which statement from "The Benefits of Shale Gas"?

A "It may even encourage some of the businesses that have left the United States to return."

B "The benefits of hydraulic fracturing far outweigh the risks."

C "As the demand for shale gas increases, gas companies will need more employees."

D "It is estimated that the use of hydraulic fracturing will create more than 500,000 high-paying, safe jobs."

3 Which piece of evidence is discussed only by the author of "The Benefits of Shale Gas"?

A truck traffic

B the process of the use of hydraulic fracturing

C the cleanliness of shale gas

D open pits

4   Read these sentences from "Stop the Fracking!"

> Truck traffic is another major problem associated with fracking. Up to 1,300 trucks may be needed to bring in enough fluid for a single well. These trucks are much too heavy for rural roads. They cause pollution and destroy roadways. Taxpayers may have to pay millions of dollars to repair roads damaged by these trucks.

Do these sentences support the author's main argument?

A   No, because they do not have to do with the process of drilling for shale gas.

B   Yes, because they point out another way that fracking affects taxpayers.

C   No, because they do not have to do with the contamination of drinking water.

D   Yes, because they point out another way that fracking harms the environment.

5   Which of these **best** describes how the two authors support the claim that the chemicals in the fluid used in hydraulic fracturing are harmful to people?

A   The author of "The Benefits of Shale Gas" says chemicals rarely contaminate water, while the author of "Stop the Fracking!" says that the chemicals almost always contaminate water.

B   The author of "The Benefits of Shale Gas" says the fluid contains only a small amount of harmful chemicals, while the author of "Stop the Fracking!" says the fluid consists mostly of harmful chemicals.

C   The author of "The Benefits of Shale Gas" says that gas companies do not drill near drinking-water sources, while the author of "Stop the Fracking!" says that gas companies almost always drill near drinking-water sources.

D   The author of "The Benefits of Shale Gas" says that the water is still safe to drink, while the author of "Stop the Fracking!" says the water is not safe to drink.

6 Write a paragraph evaluating the evidence the author of "The Benefits of Shale Gas" uses to support his claim that burning shale gas is good for the economy. Is the evidence relevant and sufficient? Use details from the essay to support your answer.

_____

_____

_____

_____

7 Below are three claims one could make based on the essay "Stop the Fracking!"

CLAIMS

	Fracking contaminates groundwater.
	Fracking increases truck traffic.
	Fracking creates high-paying jobs.

Part A

Put an "X" by the claim that is supported by the most relevant and sufficient facts in "Stop the Fracking!"

Part B

Write down **two** facts from "Stop the Fracking!" that **best** provide evidence to support the claim selected in Part A.

First fact:_____

_____

Second fact:_____

_____

8 Both the author of "The Benefits of Shale Gas" and the author of "Stop the Fracking!" describe the process of hydraulic fracturing. Write a paragraph explaining how their descriptions of fracking differ. Use details from both essays in your answer.

_____

_____

_____

_____

_____

_____

_____

_____

_____

_____

_____

_____

Performance Task—Extended Response

9 Think about "The Benefits of Shale Gas" and "Stop the Fracking!" Which author do you think presents a stronger argument? What specific claims and evidence make that argument stronger? Write an essay of two to three paragraphs explaining why one of these essays presents a stronger argument than the other. Be sure to use evidence from both essays in your answer.

In your answer, be sure to
- state which author makes the stronger argument
- explain what makes that argument stronger
- use evidence from both essays in your answer

Check your writing for correct spelling, grammar, capitalization, and punctuation.

_____

_____

_____

_____

_____

_____

_____

_____

_____

_____

Media Feature

CCSS

RI.7.7: Compare and contrast a text to an audio, video, or multimedia version of the text, analyzing each medium's portrayal of the subject (e.g., how the delivery of a speech affects the impact of the words).

Comparing Text to Other Media

Think of a recent news story that made you feel sad, excited, angry, or amazed. Maybe it was a natural disaster, or an important sporting event, or something that happened right where you live. How did you first hear the news? Did you read it online? See a TV news report? Hear about it on the radio?

How information is delivered can be as important as the information itself. That's because images and sound often affect how people react to news. The first televised Presidential Debate in 1960 proved just how important images are. Americans who listened to the debate on the radio were positive that Richard Nixon won. But almost everyone who watched it on TV felt just as strongly that John F. Kennedy won! Why? Well, experts thought it was because of the way the men looked. Kennedy was younger and appeared very relaxed. Nixon was older and was sweating throughout much of the debate.

When you read and then view a speech, you can understand how the way in which you receive information can affect your response to it.

The chart below shows some of the benefits of reading a speech, versus watching and hearing it. After you complete the activities on the next page, you will consider limitations as well as benefits of these different ways to experience and understand the content of a speech.

Reading a Speech	Watching and Listening to a Speech
Benefits You can… • take as much time as you like to read through it • reread anything that is unclear • evaluate every detail • study and appreciate word choice • examine the way the information is structured	**Benefits** You can… • see the speaker's expressions and gestures • hear the speaker's emotion • notice which words and ideas the speaker emphasizes • hear the rhythm of the words • see and hear how other people may be reacting to the words

Discuss the differences between reading a news story in a newspaper or magazine versus seeing it on TV or online. Which medium would you rather use to learn about a sporting event? How about a natural disaster or the buzz about a new movie? Why?

197

On page 197 you learned how reading a speech can be a very different experience from watching and listening to one. Now you'll look at a specific example of a famous speech as it appeared in print and on TV. Think about how the medium used to deliver the message affects your response.

Read this excerpt from President John F. Kennedy's inauguration speech. It is considered to be one of the best inaugural speeches in American history. Underline words and phrases that seem especially powerful.

President John F. Kennedy
excerpt from his Inaugural Speech, January 20, 1961

In the long history of the world, only a few generations have been granted the role of defending freedom in its hour of maximum danger. I do not shrink from this responsibility— I welcome it. I do not believe that any of us would exchange places with any other people or any other generation. The energy, the faith, the devotion which we bring to this endeavor will light our country and all who serve it—and the glow from that fire can truly light the world.

And so, my fellow Americans: ask not what your country can do for you—ask what you can do for your country.

My fellow citizens of the world: ask not what America will do for you, but what together we can do for the freedom of man.

Finally, whether you are citizens of America or citizens of the world, ask of us here the same high standards of strength and sacrifice which we ask of you. With a good conscience our only sure reward, with history the final judge of our deeds, let us go forth to lead the land we love…

Now that you've read the excerpt, you'll find out how Kennedy actually looked and sounded when he delivered it. First, you'll hear the speech. The second time, you'll both hear and see it. Take notes on what you noticed as just a listener, and then as both a listener and a viewer. Were the phrases and words you underlined in the text of the speech the same ones that impressed you as you listened and watched?

Discuss the differences between reading Kennedy's speech and then seeing and hearing it. Which experience is more powerful? Why? What are the limitations to each experience? Did reading the text first help you appreciate Kennedy's delivery of the speech?

Unit 6
Integration of Knowledge and Ideas in Literature

Have you ever met a pair of twins who are nothing alike? They might look the same on the outside, but their personalities and likes and dislikes might be totally different. The same is true in literature. Think about a story you've read that takes place in the past, for example during the time of the American Revolution. The story and a true historical account may share many historical details, such as important battles, and real characters, such as Paul Revere or George Washington. But the fictional story also includes events and characters that the author has invented or changed—like the twins, it is different in some very significant ways. As a reader, you can **integrate** the **knowledge** and **ideas** you've learned from reading history with the characters and events in historical fiction. This will give you a deeper understanding of both the historical period and the story.

In this unit you will read literature about a particular time in history and compare it to an actual historical account of the same time. You will learn how authors weave historical information into their fictional texts and how eventually the fictional texts may affect the way readers view the time period. You will even compare a written story to its movie version. These twins may be nothing alike, but their ideas may rub off on each other!

✔ **Self Check**   **Fill out the Self Check on the next page.** ▶

Before starting this unit, check off the skills you know below. As you complete each lesson, see how many more you can check off!

✔ Self Check

I know how to:	Before this unit	After this unit
compare and contrast a fictional text about a time, place, or character and a historical account of the same period.	☐	☐
describe how authors include some historical facts and change others in writing historical fiction.	☐	☐
compare a written story to its filmed version, and analyze the effects of the different techniques a director uses.	☐	☐

Comparing and Contrasting Genres

CCSS

RL.7.9: Compare and contrast a fictional portrayal of a time, place, or character and a historical account of the same period as a means of understanding how authors of fiction use or alter history.

Theme: *A Time of Transition*

Have you ever seen a movie about an important part of history, such as the Civil Rights Movement, that included fictional characters? This kind of movie is a work of **historical fiction**, or a story set in the past that combines made-up characters and events with historical figures and real events from a specific time and place. A **historical account**, on the other hand, is a factual explanation, description, or narrative from or about the past. All the people actually lived, the places existed, and the events in a historical account really occurred.

Study the illustration below. Which details are based on reality and which are fictional?

The image above shows a real person, Martin Luther King Jr., standing next to a fictional character, a young woman who admires him. In a similar way, historical fiction includes real people and events and then alters some historical details to tell a made-up story.

Study the chart to consider how the author of historical fiction draws upon real facts to create a work of fiction.

How Historical Fiction Uses History	How Historical Fiction Alters History
• set in a real time period and place • provides factual information • includes events that actually occurred • uses historical figures, language, and details, such as famous people or typical customs of the times	• plot combines real and made-up events • made-up yet realistic characters interact with real people who once lived • most dialogue is invented • may interpret or change historical details to create a better story

Good readers understand that historical accounts use facts and information to inform readers about history, while historical fiction is meant to entertain readers with an engaging story that combines real and imagined characters and events from the past. As they read, good readers are aware of these differences and are careful to separate fact from fiction.

Read the historical account about the Lewis and Clark expedition.

Genre: **Historical Account**

Journey to the Pacific   *by Rita Hay*

In 1804, Meriwether Lewis and William Clark led the first U.S. expedition to the Pacific Coast of North America. Sent by President Thomas Jefferson to chart a route through unexplored regions of the country, the team of explorers recorded the wide variety of plants, animals, and geography they saw in the wilderness. The expedition journeyed along rivers, over mountains, and through valleys for over a year, encountering hostile tribes, inclement weather, and challenging terrain.

On November 7th, 1805, the "Corps of Discovery" thought they had finally found the Pacific Ocean, but they were mistaken. The wide expanse of open water turned out to be the estuary, or mouth, of the Columbia River. With the help of native guides and determined companions, however, the team finally succeeded; the expedition reached the Pacific Ocean on November 15th, 1805. A long, hard winter and return journey lay before them, but the first half of their mission had been accomplished.

Explore how to answer this question: *"What characteristics of a historical account are present in this passage?"*

This historical account of Lewis and Clark's expedition includes many details about their journey. Underline examples of facts, people, and places that present historical information.

Fill in the first column of the chart below with facts from the account. After reading the fictional story on the next page, add additional details to the second column of the chart.

Historical Facts	Fictional Details

With a partner, discuss how to confirm the accuracy of the statement about the mistake made by the explorers on November 7, 1805.

Read the historical fiction story, and complete the chart by adding fictional details. Then read and answer the question that follows.

Genre: **Historical Fiction**

Close Reading

Which facts from the account on the previous page are also present in the historical fiction story? **Underline** facts that are the same or similar. **Star (*)** any story elements that are clearly fictional, and add them to the chart on page 202.

Sighting the Pacific   *by Jaycee Wright*

As the weary explorers reached the top of the hill, Mr. Lewis let out a cry of delight. "We've made it!" he exclaimed. "The Pacific!"

The men exchanged doubtful glances—just last week, Mr. Clark had rejoiced along with the entire team, confident that the large body of water before them was the ocean. Later, they discovered that the water was just the estuary of the Columbia River. Yet they smelled ocean air! Peter had tried to stay positive as they continued their search, but it was extremely difficult. Would today, November 15th, actually be the day they reached the Pacific Ocean?

"That certainly is a sight for sore eyes!" one of the men exclaimed, and Peter looked up and grinned. After a year and a half of traveling, they had, in fact, come upon the salt waters of the Pacific.

Hint

Compare the answer choices with the facts you underlined in "Journey to the Pacific."

Circle the best answer.

Which fact presented in "Journey to the Pacific" is also included in the fictional story above?

A Peter played a key role as a member of Lewis and Clark's team.

B Some of the explorers felt that the ocean was a "sight for sore eyes."

C Peter tried to keep up his spirits during the expedition.

D The explorers had mistaken an estuary for the Pacific Ocean.

✎ Show Your Thinking

Describe how the author of "Sighting the Pacific" used and altered historical details about the Lewis and Clark expedition to tell a story.

_____

_____

💬 With a partner, discuss the advantages of reading each type of account about an historical event.

Read the following historical account and historical fiction piece. Use the Study Buddies and Close Readings to guide your reading.

Because this is a historical account, I know that it contains true facts and historically accurate details. As I read, I'm going to focus on the historical events and people that are mentioned in the text.

Close Reading

Circle at least three details that help identify this passage as a historical account.

Underline the most important facts that the author presents about the Orphan Train Movement. Look for details that answer *who, what, when, where, why,* and *how.*

Genre: **Historical Account**

Orphan Train Riders   *by Elliot Elmore*

1   By the mid 1800s, the New York City streets were filled with an estimated 30,000 poor and hungry children. Many were homeless or abandoned; they sold newspapers, rags, or matches in order to earn money and lived on the streets in all kinds of weather. Often forming gangs in order to protect themselves, the children led hard lives, but it was the only life they knew.

2   In 1853, Charles Loring Brace, a young minister, took it upon himself to help these children. "When a child stands in front of you in rags with a tear-stained face," he said, "you cannot easily forget him . . . ." Brace founded the Children's Aid Society, an organization devoted to moving children from the streets of New York City to new homes in rural areas across the country.

3   Later referred to as the Orphan Train Movement, the first step in the process was to load needy children onto what became known as "orphan trains." The children were then transported to forty-seven states and Canada. Brace believed that loving families in rural areas would adopt these children. He hoped they would grow up with the education and support needed to become productive members of society.

4   Handbills advertised the arrival of the Orphan Train in town. The orphans were cleaned up and displayed onstage in front of curious crowds. Potential parents poked and inspected the children like livestock; siblings were often split apart. Some children ran away, and some were abused. Others found supportive people whom they considered family for the rest of their lives. Regardless of the outcome, however, most found the experience and transition to a new life to be difficult at best.

5   Yet overall, the program resulted in positive outcomes; two orphans even grew up to be state governors. The mass relocation of needy children across the country was Brace's best effort to connect them with better lives. The Orphan Train Movement was later considered to be the beginning of the foster care system.

Genre: **Historical Fiction**

The Train to Somewhere   *by Lydia Wren*

As I read, I'll think about how this child's experience is similar to and different from the details described in "Orphan Train Riders."

Close Reading

Compare the dates, people, places, and events described in the previous passage to those described in this story. **Underline** any facts that are similar.

Which details come from the author's imagination? Draw a **box** around three story elements that show it is a work of fiction.

1   My heart was in my throat as Robbie and I boarded the train in New York City that April day. A member of the Children's Aid Society led us to our seats and advised us, "Be sure to smile and make a good impression on the people you meet!"

2   At age five, I thought myself lucky—at least I had my older brother at my side. I still could remember Mama humming as she cooked dinner and my father's smiling face, but they had both died. For months we had lived on the streets until the Children's Aid Society sheltered us. Now they were shipping us on an orphan train to a new home and a new life.

3   As the train gathered speed, I caught one last glimpse of the city, the only home I had ever known. The next few days blurred together as our train powered over rivers, lush farmlands, and empty prairies. Where were we going, and what would happen to us? Our destination and future were unclear and unknown.

4   Then one morning we pulled into a small station as our Society escorts did their best to smooth our hair and straighten our clothes. Weary and confused, we were led to a large hall and seated on a stage in front of a crowd of strangers. Many stared, but some walked up to inspect us. Suddenly I was staggered by a terrible thought. What if Robbie and I went to different homes in different towns and were separated permanently?

5   "What do you know about farming?" a man asked Robbie gruffly. Wide-eyed, Robbie stammered a response, and my heart thumped wildly in my chest as I clutched his sweaty hand.

6   "Now Jacob," said a plain woman behind the man. "Don't start off by scaring 'em." She looked at us and smiled. "Are you brother and sister? Would you both like to come live with us?"

7   Some 70 years later, I still remark at how well my luck held. It wasn't just that Robbie and I were raised together or that our lives were all pleasure and no pain. No, it was that the Larsens came to take us home that day, two caring people who became our new family and who made us who we are today.

Hints

Compare paragraph 4 of the historical account with the girl's experience in "The Train to Somewhere." What similarities and differences do you find?

1 Which detail from the historical account best supports the fictional story about a girl's orphan train experience?

   A   Handbills advertised the arrival of the Orphan Train in town.

   B   The children were all adopted into caring families in new homes.

   C   Crowds gathered at the town stations to greet the orphans.

   D   The experience was quite upsetting for the orphan children .

Reread the chart on the first page of this lesson. How does the author of the historical fiction piece alter history?

2 Which statement best describes how the author of "The Train to Somewhere" alters historical details to tell her story?

   A   The author includes historical facts, such as when the Children's Aid Society was formed.

   B   The author describes the experiences and feelings of an imaginary orphan who was sent west on an orphan train.

   C   The author provides specific details about families who agreed with Brace's beliefs about ways to help needy orphan children.

   D   The author explores the adventures of two young children as they start their new lives on a farm in rural America.

Look back at the facts you underlined in the fiction story that indicate which information both texts have in common.

3 Compare and contrast details in the historical account of the Orphan Train Movement to those in the fictional story. Describe how the author of "The Train to Somewhere" has used and altered historical facts. Use at least two details from the texts to support your response.

_____

_____

_____

_____

_____

_____

_____

_____

Read the following speech and historical fiction story. Then answer the questions that follow.

from "The Progress of 50 Years"

by Mrs. Lucy Stone

Lucy Stone was a well-known suffragist in the Women's Rights Movement. Forced to pay for her own education, she was the first woman from Massachusetts to earn a college degree and gained fame for not changing her name after marrying Henry B. Blackwell in 1855. Stone continued to fight for equality for women throughout her career. The following is an excerpt from her last public speech, presented to the Congress of Women at the World's Fair in 1893.

1   Fifty years ago the legal injustice imposed upon women was appalling. Wives, widows and mothers seemed to have been hunted out by the law on purpose to see in how many ways they could be wronged and made helpless. A wife by her marriage lost all right to any personal property she might have. The income of her land went to her husband, so that she was made absolutely penniless. If a woman earned a dollar by scrubbing, her husband had a right to take the dollar. . . . It was his dollar. If a woman wrote a book the copyright of the same belonged to her husband and not to her. The law counted out in many states how many cups and saucers, spoons and knives and chairs a widow might have when her husband died. I have seen many a widow who took the cups she had bought before she was married and bought them again after her husband died, so as to have them legally. The law gave no right to a married woman to any legal existence at all. Her legal existence was suspended during marriage. She could neither sue nor be sued. If she had a child born alive the law gave her husband the use of all her real estate as long as he should live, and called it by the pleasant name of "the estate by courtesy." When the husband died the law gave the widow the use of one-third of the real estate belonging to him, and it was called the "widow's encumbrance." While the law dealt thus with her in regard to her property, it dealt still more hardly with her in regard to her children. No married mother could have any right to her child, and in most of the states of the Union that is the law to-day. But the laws in regard to the personal and property rights of women have been greatly changed and improved, and we are very grateful to the men who have done it.

2   We have not only gained in the fact that the laws are modified. Women have acquired a certain amount of political power. We have now in twenty states school suffrage for women. Forty years ago there was but one. Kentucky allowed widows with children of school age to vote on school questions. We have also municipal suffrage for women in Kansas, and full suffrage in Wyoming, a state larger than all New England.

3   The last half century has gained for women the right to the highest education and entrance to all professions and occupations, or nearly all. As a result we have women's clubs, the Woman's Congress, women's educational and industrial unions, the moral education societies, the Woman's Relief Corps, police matrons . . . colleges for women, and co-educational colleges and the Harvard Annex, medical schools and medical societies open to women, women's hospitals . . . women as a power in the press, authors, women artists, women's beneficent societies and Helping Hand societies, women school supervisors, and factory inspectors and prison inspectors, women on state boards of charity, the International Council of Women, the Woman's National Council, and last, but not least, the Board of Lady Managers. And not one of these things was allowed women fifty years ago, except the opening at Oberlin. By what toil and fatigue and patience and strife

and the beautiful law of growth has all this been wrought? These things have not come of themselves. They could not have occurred except as the great movement for women has brought them out and about. They are part of the eternal order, and they have come to stay. Now all we need is to continue to speak the truth fearlessly, and we shall add to our number those who will turn the scale to the side of equal and full justice in all things.

A Widow's Burden

by Hanna Ingram

1   Though Sarah loved her parents, she began to worry as soon as she received word that her mother and father were coming to the farm for a visit. She hadn't told them the news about Elijah's estate, and she wondered how she would fit everyone at the table during mealtime. In truth, that problem was small compared to her other burdens, but she could do little to remove a single one.

2   Sarah missed her husband Elijah terribly. Last winter, he had caught a chill and died from it. This left Sarah to manage the farm alone. She and her girls could have coped, but a few months ago, her stepson Brad had shown up at her door, court order in hand. He was laying claim to two-thirds of Elijah's farm, his rightful inheritance. Being a woman meant she was only entitled to one third of her husband's property; her stepson was "kind" enough to let her keep the cabin and a small plot of land for a garden. The rest of the farm would be sold. Sarah only hoped she could grow enough to feed her girls and find work in town.

3   Just focusing on her parents' visit brought Sarah more heartache. It was so unfair. As a widow, she was entitled to so little of Elijah's estate, and Brad had claimed most of the furniture, the extra plates, and the silverware, silverware she'd received from her grandmother. She was left with four place settings and four chairs—just enough for herself and the girls for each meal. She had done some mending for Mr. Molloy with the intention of earning enough money to buy back the plates and a chair or two, but she'd had to spend the money on flour, sugar, and more pins.

4   Sarah tidied the house nervously as she waited for her parents to arrive. The last time she had seen them, she recalled, Elijah was still alive. Soon she saw a distant cloud of dust from their wagon as it rolled up the road. The children ran behind it toward the house, and Sarah greeted her parents fondly. Setting aside her own worries, Sarah began chatting about family and friends.

5   At last, the family sat down to eat. Sarah's two oldest girls withdrew quietly, knowing that they were to eat later so as to share their seats and place settings with their grandparents. As Sarah served the dinner she could ill afford, her mother watched her with concern.

6   "Why aren't we all eating together, dear?" her mother asked. "And what is on your mind?"

7   Sarah hesitated, but then she decided to tell the truth. "As a widow, I am only entitled to a few of the things Elijah and I once shared, and Elijah's son Brad has claimed the rest. That's why my home is so bare. We have so little now that Elijah is gone."

8   Her father shook his head sadly. "What about the farm?" he asked.

9   Sarah explained that Brad's court order allowed him to sell most of the land. As a woman, she wasn't legally entitled to keep it.

10   "What a pity!" her father said thoughtfully.

11   "Nonsense," cried Sarah's mother. "This is just the problem I've been describing these many years, Jebediah!" Sarah's father cleared his throat, but her mother continued. "And you know how much I admire Lucy Stone's efforts to provide fair treatment for women!"

12   "Who is Lucy Stone?" Sarah asked, ignoring her father's frown.

13   Her mother explained that Mrs. Stone had been speaking about women's rights for many years and was pushing to modify state laws. She also called for women to be allowed to pursue all professions and occupations. Her mother continued, "Mrs. Stone even refused to take her husband's last name when she married him because she did not want to be considered anyone's property. And this woman is not alone in her fight. Women all over the country are working together so that they will no longer be mistreated as you have been, Sarah. The Women's Rights Movement is gaining support from many!"

14   "For once your mother may have a point," observed her father, taking Sarah's hand to reassure her. "You should have a right to what you and Elijah owned together, Sarah. We will help you get back on your feet, and then we'll fight to get your farm back."

15   Her mother nodded in agreement. Then she added one last thought, "Perhaps when more men and women add their voices to this movement, we will be able to improve the lives of all the women throughout the nation."

16   Later, with stories of women like Lucy Stone in her head and her parents' reassurances, Sarah washed the dinner dishes with a smile on her face. For the first time in months, she could imagine a life for herself where she didn't have to live like a second-class citizen. As for her girls, what new doors of opportunity would this movement open for them?

Answer Form

1 Ⓐ Ⓑ Ⓒ Ⓓ
2 Ⓐ Ⓑ Ⓒ Ⓓ   **Number** /3
3 Ⓐ Ⓑ Ⓒ Ⓓ   **Correct**

1 Which statement **best** describes how the author has drawn an important fact from the speech to create a fictional story?

   A   Lucy Stone speaks about the lack of equality for women, and Sarah experiences the problems it creates.

   B   Lucy Stone delivers a speech, and after they hear it, Sarah and her mother decide to join the women's movement.

   C   The speech is about social change, and the story is about accepting things as they are.

   D   The speech is meant to persuade women, and the story problem encourages a woman to fight for her rights.

2   Which historical detail from the speech is also included in the story?

    A   If a woman wrote a book, her husband owned the copyright.

    B   A widow usually inherited only a small part of her husband's estate.

    C   Married women had no legal rights and could not even sue someone.

    D   Married women did not have any right to raise their own children.

3   Which statement **best** describes how the author of "A Widow's Burden" altered historical facts to tell her story?

    A   In reality, the problem of the inequalities experienced by Sarah could not be put right so easily.

    B   In reality, it would be difficult to prove that women had gained political power in less than fifty years.

    C   In reality, it is unlikely that one woman's speech would be powerful enough to encourage Sarah to agree with her parents.

    D   In reality, the women's movement did not improve the standard of living for women in the 1840s.

4   Compare and contrast details in the speech "The Progress of 50 Years" to those in the fictional story. Describe how the author of "A Widow's Burden" has used and altered historical facts. Use at least **two** details from the texts to support your response.

_____

_____

_____

_____

_____

_____

✓ **Self Check**   *Go back and see what you can check off on the Self Check on page 200.*

Read the historical account and the story. Then answer the questions that follow.

Moving to America

by Marta Vanchenka

1   Starting in the mid-1800s, many people from all over Europe made the perilous journey across the Atlantic Ocean to start new lives in the United States. These immigrants left their native lands for many reasons. They were searching for better jobs, land, safety from war, freedom from unfair treatment, or the ability to practice their own religion. What they all had in common, though, was the belief that moving to the United States would be the best chance to improve their lives.

2   The trip from Europe to the United States was a long and challenging one. It began with a journey to a large port city—such as Bremen, Germany—where precious tickets for steamships to the United States could be purchased. According to a ticket from 1912, it cost $53 for transportation from Germany to the United States. This may not seem like much today, but long ago that was a great deal of money. The trip across the Atlantic Ocean, which usually took about twelve days, was often extremely unpleasant for immigrants. Most were made to travel in steerage—a crowded, uncomfortable area in the lower part of a ship.

3   Many passengers were overcome with joy and relief when they finally spotted the coast of North America. Upon landing, the weary travelers would be examined and interviewed at an immigration station, such as Ellis Island in New York Bay. Between 1892 and 1924, more than 15 million people entered the United States through Ellis Island. This island is close to the Statue of Liberty, the world-famous landmark that promised hope to millions of immigrants. On the base of the statue is "The New Colossus," a famous poem written by Emma Lazarus in 1883. In this poem, America welcomes the world's "huddled masses yearning to breathe free."

4   However, immigrants would find that their journey—and their challenges—had just begun. Some Americans treated the newcomers unfairly. Many immigrant groups feuded with each other as well. Most immigrants had to take difficult and dangerous work in coal mines, factories, and railroads. With patience and hard work, however, they established themselves in society and began raising families. Many of these families preserved the proud traditions of their ancestors and have helped enrich the culture of the United States.

"New York: Welcome to the Land of Freedom," from *Frank Leslie's Illustrated Newspaper*, July 2, 1887.

A Fateful Journey

by Mark Dziak

1   "Father, look at the steamships!" called thirteen-year-old Maryana. "Aren't they amazing?"

2   Maryana, along with her father Mikhail and her sister Sabina, had traveled all the way from Russia to the large coastal port of Bremen, Germany. For weeks they had ridden on ox carts over bumpy roads, sat aboard overcrowded trains, and walked on dirt roads until they could barely take another step. They were exhausted from their journey but still enthusiastic about what lay ahead.

3   Father proudly displayed the family's ship ticket. "This paper is our future, girls," he said solemnly. "This is our ticket to America, the land of opportunity."

4   Maryana and her family eagerly approached the beautiful ship, the *Crown Prince*. Soon, however, they found themselves in a noisy crowd of hundreds of people being led down staircase after staircase to the bare and cold bottom decks. "Welcome to steerage," said a gruff attendant, leading them to some cramped bunk beds.

5   Sabina looked around worriedly and said, "It looks like it's going to be a long trip."

6   With a great rumble, the steam engines fired up, and the ship slowly began to move. The family could hear the people on deck cheering and making their farewells, but in steerage they could not see anything except the cold steel walls. Father tried to cheer them up by talking about the girls' uncle, Pyotr, who had emigrated to the United States many years ago. He had changed his name to Peter and founded a large textile company where he had become very wealthy. Father expected to work there and make a lot of money too.

7   Some people in a nearby bunk heard them talking and joined the conversation. These people also had family members in America, in Pennsylvania. A woman with an infant said that her husband had immigrated first, found a job in the coal mines, and then sent her money to buy a ticket to join him. A sullen-looking young man nearby said that he was alone. Mikhail put an arm around him and smiled, saying, "Look at all these people! None of us are alone!"

8   Suddenly, an older gentleman with a bushy white beard began singing. Maryana did not know the song—it was in another language—but she enjoyed the melody. She began singing as well, and then other people joined in, in languages from Polish to Italian to German to Greek. Soon they were laughing, dancing, and making friends,

9   It was a long and difficult ocean crossing, lasting almost two weeks, but when the call rose that the Statue of Liberty was in sight, the exhausted passengers gave a great cheer. Maryana knew that all of her family's troubles would soon be over. It was the happiest moment of her life.

Answer the questions. Mark your answers to
questions 1–5A on the Answer Form to the right.

1 How does the author of "A Fateful Journey" use historical fact from "Moving to America" in his story?

　Ⓐ He includes details about the long, difficult trip to America.

　B He lists the American cities where immigrants were headed.

　C He describes how steamships looked and operated.

　D He describes the port city in great detail.

2 Which of these features is found **only** in "A Fateful Journey"?

　A dates of important events

　B famous quotations

　C invented dialogue

　D descriptions of ocean travel

3 Which historical detail did the authors of **both** "Moving to America" and "A Fateful Journey" include?

　Ⓐ Tickets cost a great deal of money.

　B Some immigrants were from Greece.

　C Ship passengers slept in bunk beds.

　D Bremen was a large steamship port.

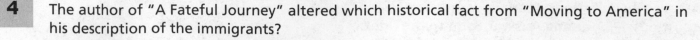
4   The author of "A Fateful Journey" altered which historical fact from "Moving to America" in his description of the immigrants?

     A   Many immigrants traveled to the United States.

     B   Some immigrants worked in the coal mines.

     C   Many immigrants feuded with each other.

     D   The immigrants came from all over Europe.

5   Answer Parts A, B, and C below.

Part A

Which idea do the authors of both "Moving to America" and "A Fateful Journey" include?

     A   the many reasons immigrants wanted to leave Europe

     B   the sufferings of immigrants on their trip to America

     C   the famous poem that welcomes immigrants to America

     D   the process of examining immigrants at Ellis Island

Part B

Find a sentence in "Moving to America" with details that support your answer to Part A. Write that sentence on the lines below.

_____

_____

Part C

Find a sentence in "A Fateful Journey" with details that support your answer to Part A. Write that sentence on the lines below.

_____

_____

6 Describe how the story of Uncle Pyotr in "A Fateful Journey" differs from the historical account of immigrants in "Moving to America." Use details from both passages to support your answer.

_____

_____

_____

_____

_____

7 Read this sentence from "A Fateful Journey."

Maryana knew that all of her family's troubles would soon be over.

Explain how this sentence differs from the historical account of immigrants in "Moving to America." Use details from both passages to support your answer.

_____

_____

_____

_____

_____

8 Compare how both authors described the importance of steamship tickets to immigrants. Use details from both "Moving to America" and "A Fateful Journey" to support your answer.

_____

_____

_____

_____

_____

_____

_____

_____

_____

_____

_____

_____

_____

Performance Task—Extended Response

9 Think about the choices that the author of "A Fateful Journey" made. What historical details did he include? What did he alter? What elements of the story did he invent? Write an essay explaining these choices and their impact on the story. Be sure to include details from both passages in your essay.

In your answer, be sure to
- explain the author's choices of which details to include, alter, or invent
- explain the impact of each choice on the story
- use details from both passages in your answer

Check your writing for correct spelling, grammar, capitalization, and punctuation.

_____

_____

_____

_____

_____

_____

_____

_____

_____

_____

_____

_____

_____

_____

_____

_____

_____

_____

_____

_____

_____

_____

_____

_____

_____

_____

Media Feature

CCSS

RL.7.7: Compare and contrast a written story, drama, or poem to its ... filmed ... version, analyzing the effects of techniques unique to each medium (e.g., lighting, sound, color, or camera focus and angles in a film.)

Comparing Media Techniques

Have you ever gotten "lost in a book," picturing the characters and scenes so clearly you almost felt as if you were there? A writer has very few tools with which to create that world: dialogue and thought, sensory description, and action. Movie directors have a much wider array of techniques that can bring stories to life on screen. Being aware of those techniques can help you appreciate how directors craft a story that affects the viewer on many different levels.

Use this chart to think about how a director creates a fictional world in a movie, and identify what a director can do that an author cannot.

Technique	Characteristics	Effect on Viewer
Camera Shots	• **wide shots:** show a large area or space and establish setting • **medium shots:** show a smaller space or fewer characters • **close-ups:** show only a character's face and expressions	• allows viewer to get a sense of place • viewer becomes involved in the interactions between characters • helps viewer understand how a character is feeling
Editing	• **pacing:** the length of a scene • **cross-cut:** switches back and forth between two actions • **dissolve:** overlapping transition from one scene to the next scene	• long scenes build suspense; quick cuts create excitement • can create suspense or tension • may show time passing or signal a switch in location
Set Design	• **staging:** the set and details used to create the physical word of each scene • **props:** objects present in the scene or used by characters	• staging can affect a viewer's perception of the characters or their actions • props may tell something about a character or add realism
Lighting & Sound	• **lighting, color filters:** bright or low light; overall tone • **sound effects:** sounds added to enhance a scene • **score:** background music used throughout the movie	• create a mood, or the feeling of a different time or place • add to the realism of a scene and may help create a mood • helps the viewer know how to feel

With a friend, watch a few great scenes from one of your favorite movies. This time, notice how camera shots, editing, lighting, and sound affect what you experience. Discuss what you see as you watch.

Think about the first time you saw the villain in a movie you've watched. What did the scene look like? Was the lighting shadowy and dramatic? Was there ominous music playing? What kinds of shots were used?

Now read this scene from a book by Ray Bradbury. Two boys have sneaked from their homes after spotting the arrival of a mysterious carnival train in a nearby field—at midnight. Notice how the author used words and images to create a mood and build suspense. Now think about how a movie director might accomplish those same goals. Complete the director's notes that follow.

Well, the carnival train was crouched there now in the autumn grass on the old rail spur near the woods, and the boys crept and lay down under a bush, waiting…

The train just stood in the middle of the dry autumn field, no one in the locomotive…no one in any of the cars behind, all black under the moon…

"It's so quiet," whispered Will…

But then a tall man stepped down from the train caboose platform… All dark suit, shadow-faced, he waded to the center of the meadow, his shirt as black as the gloved hands he now stretched to the sky.

He gestured once.

And the train came to life.

Director's notes

Goal: To create a scene that _____

_____

_____

Setting	Lighting and Sound	Camera Shots	Directions for Editing
A dry autumn field at midnight, illuminated by a full moon, with woods at one side, including a bush under which the boys can hide. The train sits on a track that cuts through the middle of the field.			

Compare your director's notes with those of a classmate. What choices were similar? Which were different? How would those choices affect the viewer?

Ready® Common Core Language Handbook
Table of Contents

Lesson 1
Phrases and Clauses

CCSS
L.7.1a: Explain the function of phrases and clauses in general. . . .

Introduction **Phrases** and **clauses** are groups of words that give specific information in a sentence.

- A **phrase** may contain the subject or the predicate of a sentence but never both—and sometimes neither. For this reason, a phrase cannot stand alone.

Sentence:	The great American artist Romare Bearden was born on September 2, 1911.
Phrase 1:	The great American artist Romare Bearden *(contains subject)*
Phrase 2:	was born *(contains predicate)*
Phrase 3:	on September 2, 1911 *(contains neither)*

- A **clause** contains both a subject and a predicate. An **independent clause** can stand alone. A **dependent (subordinate) clause** depends on another clause and cannot stand alone.

Sentence:	Although Bearden was born in North Carolina, his family eventually moved to New York.
	subject predicate
Clause 1:	Although Bearden was born in North Carolina *(dependent)*
	subject predicate
Clause 2:	his family eventually moved to New York *(independent)*

Guided Practice Circle *P* for *phrase* or *C* for *clause* to identify the underlined group of words in each sentence. Then write *D* above any dependent clauses.

Hint

A dependent clause often begins with *before*, *after*, or *until*. Phrases can also begin with these words, but phrases cannot have both a subject and a predicate.

1 <u>Before he began his career as an artist</u>, Bearden received a degree in education.   P   C

2 <u>After college</u>, he worked as a social worker in New York City.   P   C

3 <u>He studied the works of many European artists</u>, including Picasso and Matisse.   P   C

4 Bearden also studied <u>African art and Chinese landscape paintings</u>.   P   C

For numbers 1–5, select the group of words that answers each question.

1 Which group of words in this sentence is a clause?

When World War II broke out, Bearden served in the U.S. Army.

A broke out

B in the U.S. Army

C served in the U.S. Army

D When World War II broke out

2 Which group of words in this sentence is a dependent clause?

After that, Bearden spent time in Paris, where he studied art.

A where he studied art

B spent time in Paris

C After that

D Bearden spent time

3 Which group of words in this sentence is an independent clause?

Back in New York once more, Bearden briefly became a songwriter before pursuing art again.

A Bearden briefly became a songwriter

B became a songwriter before pursuing art again

C Back in New York once more

D before pursuing art again

4 Which group of words in this sentence is a phrase?

In the 1960s, while Bearden focused on creating collages that depicted African-American life, he also became active in civil rights.

A he also became active in civil rights

B In the 1960s, while Bearden focused on creating collages

C In the 1960s

D while Bearden focused

5 Which group of words in this sentence is a dependent clause that contains a phrase?

Bearden was supporting young minority artists when he helped establish the Cinque Gallery in 1969.

A Bearden was supporting young minority artists

B when he helped establish the Cinque Gallery in 1969

C was supporting young minority artists when he helped

D establish the Cinque Gallery in 1969

Lesson 2
Adjective Phrases and Clauses

CCSS
L.7.1a: Explain the function of phrases and clauses in general and their function in specific sentences.

Introduction Remember that phrases and clauses are groups of words that give specific information in a sentence. A **clause** has both a subject and a predicate, while a **phrase** may have one or the other but not both.

Some phrases and clauses function like **adjectives**, modifying a noun or a pronoun in a sentence.

- An **adjective phrase** tells "which one," "what kind," or "how many."

My **uncle from Chile** is my mother's little brother.
        (tells which uncle)

- An **adjective clause** also tells "which one," "what kind," or "how many." It usually begins with a relative pronoun, such as *who, whose, whom, which,* or *that*. The relative pronoun often serves as the subject of the clause.

He has a **job that takes him all over the world**.
        (tells what kind of job)

Guided Practice Identify the underlined group of words as an adjective phrase or an adjective clause by writing *phrase* or *clause* on the line. Then draw an arrow from the phrase or clause to the noun it modifies.

Hint

A clause can include several phrases within it. These phrases are often **prepositional phrases**, which are phrases that often describe the location, direction, or timing of something.

1 My uncle told me a funny story about a mistake <u>that he made at a hotel in Paris.</u> _____

2 Uncle Nestor, <u>whose French is not very good</u>, went to the front desk to ask for an extra blanket. _____

3 The clerk <u>at the desk</u> looked puzzled. _____

4 It turns out that Uncle Nestor had confused the word for *blanket* with the word <u>meaning "flag."</u> _____

5 The clerk thought my uncle wanted to wrap himself in a flag, <u>which would not be very warm!</u> _____

For numbers 1–3, choose the group of words from each sentence that is an adjective phrase.

1 Kenya, in eastern Africa, was where Uncle Nestor lived for two years.

A for two years

B in eastern Africa

C where Uncle Nestor lived

D lived for two years

For numbers 4 and 5, choose the group of words from each sentence that is an adjective clause.

2 He also spent a lot of time in Prague, which is a city in the Czech Republic.

A a lot of time

B also spent

C in the Czech Republic

D which is a city in the Czech Republic

4 Uncle Nestor worked for a while on a ship that sailed the Caribbean.

A that sailed the Caribbean

B for a while

C Uncle Nestor worked

D on a ship

5 The captain of the ship was a man named Ramón, whom Nestor knew from Chile.

A of the ship

B knew from Chile

C a man named Ramón

D whom Nestor knew from Chile

3 A man from the island of Crete convinced Uncle Nestor that he should spend some time there.

A that he should spend some time there

B from the island of Crete

C convinced Uncle Nestor

D A man from the island

Lesson 3
Adverb Phrases and Clauses

CCSS
L.7.1a: Explain the function of phrases and clauses in general and their function in specific sentences.

Introduction Phrases and clauses are groups of words that give specific information in a sentence. A **clause** has both a subject and a predicate, while a **phrase** does not.

Some phrases and clauses function like **adverbs**, which means they modify a verb, an adjective, or another adverb in a sentence.

- An **adverb phrase** tells "how," "when," "where," or "why." It is often a prepositional phrase.

Soccer players **wear** protective gear **on the field**.
(tells where; modifies verb *wear*)

Soccer gloves are **thick with padding**.
(tells how; modifies adjective *thick*)

- An **adverb clause** can also tell "how," "when," "where," or "why." It is always a dependent clause.

Gloves **protect** goalies **when they catch the ball**.
(tells when; modifies verb *protect*)

Goalies **need** gloves **because the ball can hurt**.
(tells why; modifies verb *need*)

Guided Practice Circle the word in each sentence that the underlined phrase or clause modifies. Write *how, when, where,* or *why* to explain what the phrase or clause tells.

Hint

Often an adverb phrase or clause immediately follows the word it modifies, but sometimes other words separate the two. The phrase or clause may also come at the beginning of a sentence, *before* the modified word.

1 Goalies are the only players who touch the ball <u>with their hands</u>.

_____

2 <u>As the ball comes toward the goal</u>, the goalie moves quickly.

_____

3 If necessary, the goalie dives <u>onto the ground</u>. _____

4 Sometimes the other team scores <u>because the ball gets past</u>
<u>the goalie</u>. _____

5 The game is over <u>after two halves of play</u>. _____

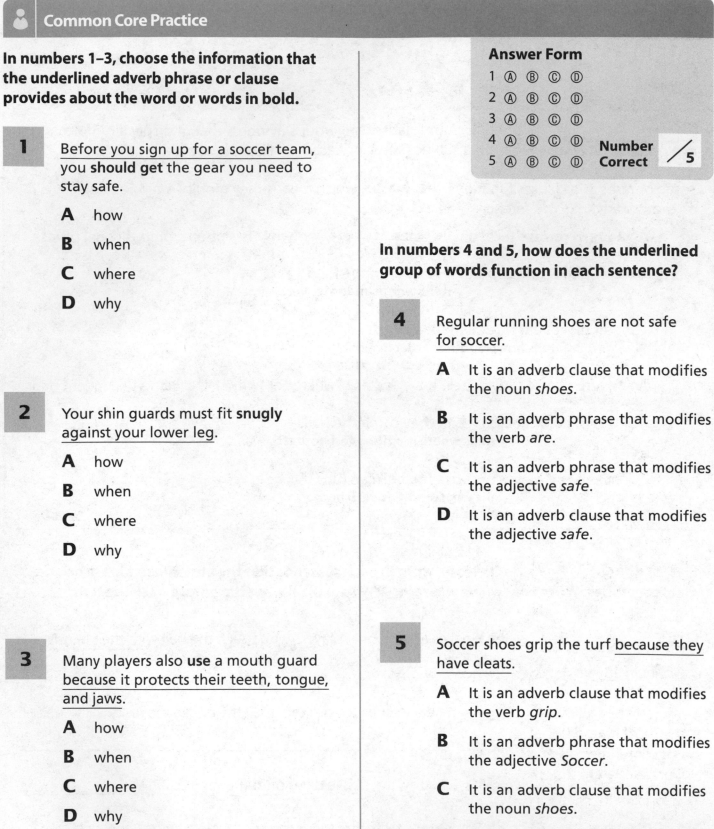
In numbers 1–3, choose the information that the underlined adverb phrase or clause provides about the word or words in bold.

1 Before you sign up for a soccer team, you **should get** the gear you need to stay safe.

   A how

   B when

   C where

   D why

2 Your shin guards must fit **snugly** against your lower leg.

   A how

   B when

   C where

   D why

3 Many players also **use** a mouth guard because it protects their teeth, tongue, and jaws.

   A how

   B when

   C where

   D why

Answer Form

1 Ⓐ Ⓑ Ⓒ Ⓓ
2 Ⓐ Ⓑ Ⓒ Ⓓ
3 Ⓐ Ⓑ Ⓒ Ⓓ
4 Ⓐ Ⓑ Ⓒ Ⓓ   **Number**
5 Ⓐ Ⓑ Ⓒ Ⓓ   **Correct** /5

In numbers 4 and 5, how does the underlined group of words function in each sentence?

4 Regular running shoes are not safe for soccer.

   A It is an adverb clause that modifies the noun *shoes*.

   B It is an adverb phrase that modifies the verb *are*.

   C It is an adverb phrase that modifies the adjective *safe*.

   D It is an adverb clause that modifies the adjective *safe*.

5 Soccer shoes grip the turf because they have cleats.

   A It is an adverb clause that modifies the verb *grip*.

   B It is an adverb phrase that modifies the adjective *Soccer*.

   C It is an adverb clause that modifies the noun *shoes*.

   D It is an adverb phrase that modifies the verb *grip*.

Lesson 4
Simple and Compound Sentences

CCSS
L.7.1b: Choose among simple [and] compound ... sentences to signal differing relationships among ideas.

Introduction Sentences can be described according to the number and type of clauses in them. Remember that a **clause** is a group of words that contains both a subject and a predicate. An **independent clause** is a clause that can stand alone as its own sentence.

- A **simple sentence** contains one independent clause.

subject   predicate
[My great-grandmother Lucy] [was born in Oklahoma in 1911.]

- A **compound sentence** is made up of two or more **independent clauses.** Those clauses are joined by a **coordinating conjunction** such as *and, or, so, but,* or *yet,* with a comma between the first clause and the conjunction.

independent clause 1   independent clause 2
Lucy's sister Rosene was born in 1913, **and** her other sister, Rotha, was born in 1915.

Guided Practice **Write *simple* next to each simple sentence. Write *compound* next to each compound sentence, then circle the conjunction that joins the two clauses.**

Hint

A simple sentence can have a compound subject or compound predicate.

Compound subject:

My brother and I loved Grandma Lucy.

Compound predicate:

She *wrote music and played the piano.*

Both sentences are simple sentences.

1 Lucy's mother and father were both schoolteachers. _____

2 They traveled all over Oklahoma, yet Lucy and her sisters never minded or complained. _____

3 As a young girl, Lucy was always one of the best students in her class. _____

4 Schools were segregated in Oklahoma in the early 1900s, so Lucy and her sisters attended schools for black children.

_____

5 Lucy's family did not have much money but lived happily.

_____

For numbers 1–3, choose the sentence that answers each question.

1 Which of these is a simple sentence?

   A Great-Grandma Lucy married Richmond Bell in 1937, and they moved to Arizona.

   B There was little work in Oklahoma, but in Arizona they got jobs picking cotton.

   C The work was difficult, yet Lucy was glad to have a job.

   D She and Richmond worked hard and saved their money.

2 Which of these is a compound sentence?

   A Lucy and Richmond heard about work in California.

   B They could buy some land and a house in California's Central Valley.

   C Folks were struggling to survive in most places, but in California they had jobs.

   D Lucy and Richmond packed up, hopped on a train, and went west.

3 Which of these is a compound sentence?

   A The couple found a house in the town of Dos Palos.

   B Dos Palos was a small community, but the land was good for farming.

   C Lucy and Richmond bought a cow, raised chickens, and grew vegetables.

   D Their first child was born in Dos Palos in the summer of 1945.

For numbers 4 and 5, choose the answer that correctly combines each pair of simple sentences into a compound sentence.

4 World War II began. Richmond joined the army.

   A World War II began but Richmond joined the army.

   B World War II began, Richmond joined the army.

   C World War II began, and, Richmond joined the army.

   D World War II began, and Richmond joined the army.

5 With the men away, many jobs were open to women. Lucy became a librarian.

   A With the men away, many jobs were open to women, so Lucy became a librarian.

   B With the men away, many jobs were open to women, Lucy became a librarian.

   C With the men away, many jobs were open to women, so, Lucy became a librarian.

   D With the men away, many jobs were open to women so, Lucy became a librarian.

Lesson 5
Complex and Compound-Complex Sentences

CCSS
L.7.1b: Choose among . . . complex [and] compound–complex sentences to signal differing relationships among ideas.

Introduction A **clause** is a group of words with both a subject and a predicate. An **independent clause** can stand alone; a **dependent clause** cannot. A dependent clause usually begins with a **subordinating conjunction** such as *while*, *because*, or *although* or a **relative pronoun** such as *who*, *that*, or *which*.

- A **complex sentence** has an independent clause and at least one dependent clause.

  While many people enjoy music, some scientists think that it also makes them smarter.

  Scientists have done studies that suggest a link between music and reading skills.

- A **compound-complex** sentence has at least two independent clauses joined by a **coordinating conjunction**, as well as one or more dependent clauses.

  Scientists have made some important discoveries about music, and this research has encouraged people who want school music programs to continue.

Guided Practice Identify each sentence type by writing *complex* or *compound-complex*. Underline the dependent clause or clauses in each sentence.

Hint

Remember: A complex sentence has one independent clause. A compound-complex sentence has at least two independent clauses. Both types of sentences have at least one dependent clause.

1. Researchers have found interesting connections between music and brain activity, although the results are not final.

   _____

2. When college students in one study had received musical training before age 12, they were able to remember more words from a list than students who had not received training. _____

3. In another study, students had higher reading scores after seven months if they had received daily music lessons, and their scores remained high after a year. _____

4. Most schools do not want to cut music programs, but some schools have no choice because they do not have enough money.

   _____

For numbers 1–4, choose the sentence that answers each question.

1 Which of these is a complex sentence?

A Schools have had to cut not only music but also art.

B Many students love music, and most of them like art.

C Teachers value music and art, and many have fought to keep these programs.

D While some children take private music lessons, many students can't afford them.

2 Which of these is a compound-complex sentence?

A Some schools have found ways to offer music instruction to their students.

B These schools receive money from outside organizations that donate money.

C A foundation is an organization that raises money for causes, and some foundations focus on music programs.

D Music may raise students' test scores, so these foundations see music programs as an investment in the future.

3 Which of these is a complex sentence containing more than one dependent clause?

A A foundation in Tennessee bought musical instruments for students in Memphis who could not pay for their own instruments.

B Only ten percent of families in the Memphis City Schools could afford to rent an instrument, so the foundation provided the money.

C During the next eight years, the school district was voted one of the "Best Communities for Music Education in America" four times!

D Because the foundation believed in the importance of music, all students in Memphis now have access to instruments, which has changed children's lives.

4 Which is the **best** way to combine the sentences into a compound-complex sentence?

Music relaxes some people. Other people get energy from music. Music increases their heart rate.

A Music relaxes some people and gives other people energy and increases their heart rate.

B Music relaxes some people, but other people get energy from music because it increases their heart rate.

C Music relaxes people, and it increases their heart rate while it gives energy to them.

D Because music relaxes some people and it gives energy to others, music increases their heart rate.

Lesson 6
Using Different Kinds of Sentences

CCSS
L.7.1b: Choose among simple, compound, complex, and compound-complex sentences to signal differing relationships among ideas.

Introduction Building your sentences in different ways can help you eliminate wordiness and make clear connections between ideas. There are four basic types of sentences:

Type	Definition	Example
Simple	has one **independent** clause	Jousting was a medieval sport.
Compound	has two or more **independent** clauses	Medieval knights had to be experts in battle, and jousting was one way to prepare for battle.
Complex	has one **independent** clause and one or more **dependent** clauses	Although jousting was a form of entertainment, it also let knights practice important skills.
Compound-complex	has two or more **independent** clauses and one or more **dependent** clauses	Jousting wasn't as dangerous as combat, but a knight could still be hurt when he fell off his horse.

Varying the sentence types when you write can also make your writing more interesting to read.

Guided Practice Underline the independent clause or clauses in each sentence. Then write *simple*, *compound*, *complex*, or *compound-complex* to identify the sentence type.

Hint

The independent and dependent clauses in a complex or compound-complex sentence may be in any order. For instance, the dependent clause may come first.

Example:
While a knight had to be brave, he also had to be respectful, and he had to be loyal to his king.

1 A knight's training began early in life, and it ended in the knight's teenage years. _____

2 Jousts kept knights in great condition for real battles.

_____

3 When spectators attended jousts, they often rooted for a favorite knight. _____

4 Although jousts often ended in bloodshed, the matches were a popular part of life, and townspeople regularly gathered to watch these events. _____

5 Jousting competitions were usually part of a larger tournament that included other events as well. _____

For numbers 1–4, choose the best way to combine the sentences to eliminate repetition and make the relationships between ideas clear.

1 Jousts could be dangerous. Often knights broke bones. This would happen even though knights wore armor.

A Although jousts could be dangerous, knights wore armor and still broke bones.

B Because knights wore armor, they broke bones, and jousts were still dangerous.

C Jousts could be dangerous, and although knights wore armor, they still often broke bones.

D Because jousts could be dangerous, knights broke bones, but knights wore armor.

2 Special lances for jousting had to be made to avoid serious injury. This was because battle lances were such dangerous weapons.

A Battle lances were such dangerous weapons that special lances for jousting had to be made to avoid serious injury.

B Special lances for jousting had to be made to avoid serious injury although battle lances were such dangerous weapons.

C Because the special lances for jousting had to be made to avoid serious injury, battle lances were dangerous weapons.

D Battle lances were such dangerous weapons because special lances for jousting had to be made to avoid serious injury.

3 Knights had many obligations and duties. They had to be strong and kind.

A Knights had to be strong and kind, but they had many duties and obligations.

B Knights had many duties and obligations, and they also had to be strong and kind.

C Knights had many duties and obligations because they had to be strong and kind.

D Although they had to be strong and kind, knights had many duties and obligations.

4 A knight had a hard life. He fought to honor his king both on and off the battlefield.

A A knight had a hard life, so he fought to honor his king both on and off the battlefield.

B Although he fought to honor his king both on and off the battlefield, a knight had a hard life.

C A knight had a hard life after he fought to honor his king both on and off the battlefield.

D Because he fought to honor his king both on and off the battlefield, a knight had a hard life.

Lesson 7
Misplaced Modifiers

CCSS
L.7.1c: Place phrases and clauses within a sentence, recognizing and correcting misplaced . . . modifiers.

Introduction

A **misplaced modifier** is a phrase or clause that is intended to modify a certain word in a sentence but is in the wrong place. As a result, it connects the wrong words or ideas to each other and confuses the reader. For example:

> We sat and talked about camping **in the kitchen**.

- The phrase *in the kitchen* is meant to modify *sat*, but instead it suggests that the camping happened in the kitchen. Now, look at another example.

> I served breakfast to my family, **which I made myself**.

- The clause *which I made myself* is misplaced. It suggests that the speaker made her family, not breakfast.

- To fix a misplaced modifier, move it as close as possible to what it should modify:

> We sat **in the kitchen** and talked about camping.

> I served my family breakfast, **which I made myself**.

Guided Practice

Rewrite each sentence to correct the misplaced modifier.

Hint

If a dependent clause begins with the relative pronoun *who* or *which* and gives information that is not crucial to the meaning of the sentence, use commas to set off the clause from the rest of the sentence.

Example:
The muffins, *which smelled delicious*, were still warm.

1 I baked blueberry muffins and scrambled some eggs in the oven.

_____

2 My cousin Rob told us while he ate where he and Josh had camped.

_____

3 Rob had taken my nine-year-old brother camping, who is in college.

_____

4 Rob had photos of the lovely lake on his phone near their campsite.

_____

5 We put a drawing of the lake on the fridge that Josh had made.

_____

For numbers 1–4, choose the answer that best corrects the misplaced modifier in each sentence.

1 Rob told us about hearing a strange noise in the night after breakfast.

A After breakfast, Rob told us about hearing a strange noise in the night.

B Rob told us about hearing a strange noise after breakfast in the night.

C After breakfast, Rob told us in the night about hearing a strange noise.

D In the night, Rob heard a strange noise that after breakfast he told us about.

2 Dad let Josh borrow his fishing rod to take on the trip, which was old but still worked.

A Josh borrowed for the trip, which was old but still worked, Dad's fishing rod.

B For the trip, Dad let Josh borrow his fishing rod, which was old but still worked.

C To take on the trip, Josh borrowed a fishing rod from Dad, which was old but still worked.

D The fishing rod that Josh borrowed to take on the trip from Dad was old but still worked.

3 Rob told us how Josh had caught a fish as he was washing the dishes.

A Rob as he was washing the dishes told us how Josh had caught a fish.

B Josh told us that, as Rob was washing the dishes, he had caught a fish.

C Josh had caught a fish, and Rob was washing the dishes and told us about it.

D As Rob was washing the dishes, he told us how Josh had caught a fish.

4 Next summer my cousin invited me to go camping by the lake with his family.

A My cousin invited me to go camping by the lake with his family next summer.

B By the lake next summer, my cousin invited me to go camping with his family.

C My cousin by the lake invited me next summer to go camping with his family.

D My cousin with his family next summer invited me to go camping by the lake.

Lesson 8
Dangling Modifiers

CCSS
L.7.1c: Place phrases and clauses within a sentence, recognizing and correcting . . . dangling modifiers.

Introduction A **dangling modifier** is a phrase or clause intended to modify a certain word, but that word is not actually stated in the sentence, or it is stated but the dangling modifier seems to modify a different word. Below are two sentences with dangling modifiers:

> **Driving past the mountains,** they were snow-covered and majestic.
> **After traveling all day,** the motel was a welcome sight.

In the sentences above, who was driving past the mountains? Who was traveling all day?

- One way to fix a dangling modifier is to add the word that was meant to be modified, often by making it the subject of the sentence.

> **Driving past the mountains, <u>we</u>** saw that they were snow-covered and majestic.

- Another way to fix a dangling modifier is to make it a dependent clause with its own subject. You might also have to rearrange the sentence.

> The motel was a welcome sight **after <u>we</u> had been traveling all day.**

Guided Practice **Rewrite each sentence to correct the dangling modifier.**

Hint
To correct a dangling modifier, you might need to reword other parts of the sentence completely.

1 Sleeping soundly through the night, my bed was comfortable.

_____

2 After eating a good breakfast, the cave tour sounded more fun.

_____

3 Before leaving for the cave tour, the brochure gave us directions.

_____

4 Climbing into the car, my camera dropped and broke.

_____

5 Waiting in line for the tour, clouds started forming.

_____

For numbers 1–4, choose the revision that best corrects the dangling modifier in each sentence.

1 Explaining how the cave was made, we learned some amazing facts from the guide.

A While learning how the cave was made, the guide told us some amazing facts.

B Learning some amazing facts, the guide explained how the cave was made.

C Explaining some amazing facts, we learned from the guide how the cave was made.

D As the guide explained how the cave was made, we learned some amazing facts.

3 Buying souvenirs at the gift shop, the clerk showed Ty some hats.

A The clerk showed Ty some hats, buying souvenirs at the gift shop.

B While Ty was buying souvenirs at the gift shop, the clerk showed him some hats.

C Buying souvenirs, the clerk at the gift shop showed Ty some hats.

D While the clerk showed Ty some hats, he was buying souvenirs at the gift shop.

2 Walking out of the cave, a cloudburst soaked Emilia.

A A cloudburst soaked Emilia as she was walking out of the cave.

B Walking out of the cave was a cloudburst that soaked Emilia.

C Emilia was soaked as she walked out of the cave by a cloudburst.

D A cloudburst out of the cave soaked Emilia as she was walking.

4 Driving home, the rain stopped for a few minutes.

A Driving home for a few minutes, the rain stopped.

B The rain stopped driving home for a few minutes.

C For a few minutes driving home, the rain stopped.

D As we were driving home, the rain stopped for a few minutes.

Lesson 9
Commas with Coordinate Adjectives

CCSS
L.7.2a: Use a comma to separate coordinate adjectives (e.g., *It was a fascinating, enjoyable movie* but not *He wore an old[,] green shirt*).

👥 Introduction

When you use more than one adjective to describe a noun, sometimes the adjectives need commas between them—but sometimes they do not.

- If the adjectives make sense no matter what order you put them in, they are called **coordinate adjectives.** Coordinate adjectives should be separated by a comma.

  > The Civil War was captured on film by **brave, dedicated** photographers.
  >
  > *(Reordering the adjectives as **dedicated, brave** would also make sense.)*

- If the adjectives would *not* make sense if reordered, do not put a comma between them.

  > The Civil War was the **first major** conflict to be widely photographed.
  >
  > *(Reordering the adjectives as **major first** would not make sense.)*

- In a series of three or more adjectives, some might be coordinate adjectives and others might not. Put in commas only where they are needed.

  > The photos offered **many fascinating, realistic** images of wartime.

👥 Guided Practice

Correct each sentence by adding and deleting commas as needed.

Hint

If you can add the word *and* between the adjectives, they are coordinate adjectives and must be separated by commas.

1 The Civil War proved to be a remarkable important moment in the history of photography.

2 Photographers had to carry their heavy bulky, camera equipment with them as they traveled.

3 The pictures showed young tired, wounded soldiers surviving in difficult, wartime conditions.

4 The photographers inspired numerous, future, news journalists.

5 The many terrible dangers of war were depicted, but so were strong courageous acts of leadership.

For numbers 1–5, choose the answer that best shows how the underlined part of each sentence should be rewritten. If the sentence is already correct, choose D.

1 Photographers took pictures of <u>bearded, Union generals</u> posing for the camera.

  A bearded Union generals

  B bearded, Union, generals

  C bearded Union, generals

  D correct as is

2 <u>Courageous loyal foot soldiers</u> were also photographed on the battlefield.

  A Courageous loyal, foot soldiers

  B Courageous, loyal foot soldiers

  C Courageous, loyal, foot soldiers

  D correct as is

3 Images were taken by <u>special roving camp photographers</u> who traveled with troops.

  A special, roving camp photographers

  B special roving, camp photographers

  C special, roving, camp photographers

  D correct as is

4 When soldiers died, photographs provided cherished mementos for <u>proud, loving, family members</u>.

  A proud loving family members

  B proud loving, family members

  C proud, loving family members

  D correct as is

5 Photographer Alexander Gardner provided the <u>first, prolonged coverage</u> of the war.

  A first, prolonged, coverage

  B first prolonged coverage

  C first prolonged, coverage

  D correct as is

Lesson 10
Eliminating Wordiness and Redundancy

CCSS
L.7.3a: Choose language that expresses ideas precisely and concisely, recognizing and eliminating wordiness and redundancy.

Introduction

Good writers know that every word counts. When revising your writing:

- **Use fewer words.** Edit your writing to remove unnecessary words and phrases.

Delete Phrases That Don't Add Meaning	*Wordy:*	**This paper will focus on** the Great Migration **and the reason why** it had a huge impact on urban life in the United States.
	Concise:	The Great Migration had a huge impact on urban life in the United States.
Use One Word in Place of a Phrase	*Wordy:*	**During the time that** World War I broke out, factories in Northern cities **had a need for** more workers.
	Concise:	**When** World War I broke out, factories in Northern cities **needed** more workers.

- **Delete repeated information.** Delete or combine words and phrases that repeat ideas.

Avoid Repeating Words or Ideas	*Repetitious:*	By the end of 1919, a million African Americans **had left, leaving** the South for **cities** and **urban areas** like Chicago, New York, and Detroit.
	Better:	By the end of 1919, a million African Americans had left the South for cities like Chicago, New York, and Detroit.

Guided Practice

Revise each sentence to eliminate wordiness and repeated ideas.

Hint

Ask yourself: Which words can I delete without changing the main idea? Which phrases can I replace with just one word?

1 The Great Migration was the largest, biggest mass movement of people in U.S. history.

_____

_____

2 In the early 1900s at the turn of the century, most African Americans lived in the South.

_____

_____

3 They worked as sharecroppers, farming the land as part of the sharecropper system.

_____

_____

For numbers 1–4, choose the answer that best revises the sentence without changing its meaning.

1 African-American people and families wanted to live free from poverty and violence.

A African-American people and families wanted to live free from violence.

B African-American families were free from poverty.

C African-American people and families wanted to live free.

D African-American families wanted freedom from poverty and violence.

2 Newspaper ads telling about jobs that were located in the North and West were able to convince people to move to those areas of the country.

A Newspaper ads for jobs in the North and West convinced people to move to those regions.

B Newspaper ads for jobs were able to convince people to move to those areas of the country.

C Newspapers that were located in the North and West convinced people to move to those regions.

D Newspaper jobs were able to convince people to move to those areas of the North and West.

3 Sometimes one family member moved first; later the whole family was reunited together.

A Sometimes one family moved; later they were reunited together.

B Sometimes one family member moved and was reunited.

C Sometimes one family member moved first; later the whole family was reunited.

D Sometimes one family member and the whole family reunited later.

4 By 1970, the year the Great Migration is considered to have ended, the South was home to fewer than half of all African Americans in the United States.

A When the Great Migration ended in 1970, fewer than half of all African Americans lived in the South.

B By 1970, the year the Great Migration ended, few African Americans lived in the South.

C The Great Migration is when the South was home to fewer than half of all African Americans in the United States.

D By 1970, the year the Great Migration is considered to have ended, the South was home to half of all African Americans in the United States.

Lesson 11
Using Context Clues

CCSS

L.7.4a: Use context (e.g., the overall meaning of a sentence or paragraph; a word's position or function in a sentence) as a clue to the meaning of a word or phrase.

Introduction When you come across an unfamiliar word, look for **context clues**— nearby words that hint at the meaning of the word. Study these four types of context clues.

Context Clue	Signal Words	Example
Restatement	*or, in other words, that is to say*	Women's rights advocates, **or supporters**, met in Seneca Falls, New York, in 1848.
Example	*like, such as, for example, for instance*	Leaders often faced fierce opposition **such as name-calling, disrespect, and even threats of harm.**
Cause and Effect	*as a result of, because, and thanks to*	**Because of these leaders' efforts to gain equal rights,** women secured the right to vote in 1920.
Comparison and Contrast	*also, like, as well, but, yet, however, although*	Proponents of women's rights, **like those who support other causes,** are committed to their beliefs.

Other clues to a word's meaning are the word's position in the sentence and its part of speech.

- Below, the position of *cause* after *can* shows it is a verb, "to make something happen."

  > Stirring speeches **can cause** people to change their minds about an issue.

- Below, the position of *cause* after *the* shows it is a noun, meaning "a goal or issue."

  > Elizabeth Cady Stanton dedicated herself to **the cause** of women's rights.

Guided Practice **Underline a context clue that helps you understand each underlined word. Draw a line from the clue to the word. With a partner, identify each type of clue you used.**

Hint

When you come across an unfamiliar word in a sentence, don't just look in the same sentence for clues. Also look in sentences that come before and after the word.

Until 1920, suffrage, or the right to vote, was denied to women.

Some prominent figures supported the cause. For example, the

famous reformer Frederick Douglass spoke out for women's rights.

Many small meetings took place, but a convention held in Seneca Falls

in 1848 helped the movement grow. Thanks to their persistence,

women won the right to vote more than seventy years later.

For numbers 1–4, use context clues to figure out the meaning of each underlined word.

> Women's suffrage organizations faced determined <u>resistance</u> from groups who argued that a woman's place was in the home, not in the political arena. Plenty of women strongly agreed that they deserved more rights. Yet many of them still <u>deplored</u> the idea of women having a voice in the government.

1 What does the word <u>resistance</u> mean in the paragraph?

A opposition

B agreement

C questions

D approval

3 What does the word <u>deplored</u> mean in the paragraph?

A failed to understand

B disapproved of

C agreed with

D investigated

2 Which words provide a clue to the meaning of <u>resistance</u>?

A "in the political arena"

B "in the home"

C "groups who argued"

D "in the government"

4 Which words provide a **contrast** clue to the meaning of <u>deplored</u>?

A "Plenty of women"

B "strongly agreed"

C "deserved more rights"

D "having a voice"

Lesson 12
Greek and Latin Word Parts

CCSS
L.7.4b: Use common, grade-appropriate Greek or Latin affixes and roots as clues to the meaning of a word (e.g., *belligerent, bellicose, rebel*).

Introduction   Many English words have Greek and Latin roots and affixes.

- A **root** is a word part that contains the core meaning of the word. In the word *science*, for example, the root *sci* means "knowledge."

Root	Meaning	Root	Meaning
belli	"war"	*flect, flex*	"bend"
tract	"draw, pull"	*sci*	"knowledge"
hydr	"water"	*form*	"shape, form"

- An **affix** is a word part added to a root. Affixes include **prefixes**, which come before the root, and **suffixes**, which come after the root.

Prefix	Meaning	Suffix	Meaning
de-, dis-	"do the opposite"	*-ous, -ious*	"characterized by"
re-	"again, anew"	*-ent*	"inclined to"
con-	"with"	*-able, -ible*	"capable of, tending"

Guided Practice   Read the passage. Circle the roots in the underlined words. On a separate piece of paper, write the meanings of the word parts and define the word.

Hint

A root's meaning will sometimes not fit well with the definition of the word. You'll need to make an inference (an educated guess) to see the connection between the root and the meaning.

My dog Sam has a belligerent personality. The moment he becomes conscious of a cat, he gives chase. No matter what I do to distract him, nothing works. The problem is intractable.

One day, Sam approached a stray cat, which raised its spiky fur, bared its teeth, and took off after *him*. Sam returned later, dehydrated, hot, and humble. But did Sam reform his behavior? No! My dog is just too inflexible to change his habits.

For numbers 1–4, read each sentence. Then answer the question.

1

When I bring Sam his leash for a walk, his response is effusive.

The prefix *ef-* means "out," and the root *fus* means "pour." What is the meaning of effusive as it is used in the sentence?

A showing quiet pleasure

B showing great enthusiasm

C showing boredom and weariness

D showing confusion

2

Being a quadruped, Sam is often frustrated by my slow pace.

The prefix *quadr-* means "four," and the root *ped* means "foot." What is the meaning of quadruped as it is used in the sentence?

A a four-foot-long animal

B a four-footed animal

C a four-speed bicycle

D a four-wheeled scooter

3

When we turn toward home, Sam reacts badly to the brevity of our outing.

The root *brev* means "brief," and the suffix *-ity* means "degree." What is the meaning of brevity as it is used in the sentence?

A slowness

B suddenness

C shortness

D frequency

4

He sits down on the sidewalk and is tenacious about staying there.

The root *ten* means "hold," and the suffix *-ious* means "characterized by." What is the meaning of tenacious as it is used in the sentence?

A happy and content

B full of rage

C unable to move

D unwilling to give in

Lesson 13
Using a Dictionary or Glossary

CCSS
L.7.4c: Consult general and specialized reference materials (e.g., dictionaries, glossaries . . .), both print and digital, to find the pronunciation of a word or determine or clarify its precise meaning or its part of speech.

Introduction
Many words have more than one definition. Some words also function as more than one part of speech. A dictionary can tell you a word's definition and part of speech.

- A **dictionary** lists words in alphabetical order. Each entry gives the word's pronunciation, the part of speech it can function as, and the word's meaning or meanings.

Attempt has more than one meaning, so each definition is numbered.

attempt (ə'tem[p]t) *n.* 1. an act of trying to achieve something 2. an effort to surpass a record *v.* 3. to make an effort to achieve or complete 4. to try to climb to the top: *The group decided to attempt Mount Mitchell.*

This sample sentence clarifies one of the meanings of *attempt*.

Pronunciations are in parentheses. A stress mark (') shows which syllable to stress. Pronunciations often depend on the part of speech.

figure (fĭg'yər) *n.* 1. a symbol, such as a number 2. a famous person 3. the shape or form of someone or something *v.* 4. to calculate, do math 5. to believe or conclude: *I never figured it would rain.*

Abbreviations show the part of speech: *n.* stands for *noun* and *v.* stands for *verb*.

- A **glossary** is an alphabetical list of terms used in a book. Each entry explains the meaning of a word as it is used in that book.

Guided Practice
Use the entries above and your own dictionary to answer the questions about the underlined words in the passage.

Hint

When looking up a word with multiple definitions, be sure to read them all. Don't just stop with the first or second definition.

Warning: The Asian longhorned beetle has invaded the United States! A wood-boring beetle, it could underline{decimate} our forests. This super-pest is underline{indigenous} to China and other Asian countries. Since the beetle's detection in the United States, government agencies have underline{attempted} to underline{eradicate} it. Who could have underline{figured} that a small bug could make so much trouble?

1 Which definition helps you understand the meaning of *attempt*?

_____

2 What part of speech is the word *attempt* as used in the passage?

_____

3 Which definition helps you understand the meaning of *figured*?

_____

4 Use your dictionary to find the meanings and parts of speech of *decimate*, *indigenous*, and *eradicate* as they are used in the passage. Write your answers on a separate piece of paper.

Use the dictionary entries to answer numbers 1–4.

introduce (ĭn'trə dōos'), (ĭn'trə dyōos') v. **1.** to present one person to another: *Let me introduce you to Larry.* **2.** to cause someone to experience something for the first time: *Ingrid introduced me to Dutch food.* **3.** to bring something to a place for the first time **4.** to preface: *Phil introduced the film with a brief talk.*

1 Which definition matches how introduced is used in this sentence?

The Asian longhorned beetle was likely introduced to the United States as a stowaway in wood packing materials from Asia.

A Definition 1

B Definition 2

C Definition 3

D Definition 4

depression (dĭ prĕsh'ən) n. **1.** a pit or a hollow **2.** great sadness **3.** a reduction in activity **4.** a period in which an economy declines

2 Which definition matches how depression is used in this sentence?

A female beetle chews depressions in the bark of a hardwood tree and lays her eggs in them.

A Definition 1

B Definition 2

C Definition 3

D Definition 4

conduct (kən dŭkt') v. **1.** to manage or direct **2.** to lead or guide someone: *Stefan will conduct you to your rooms.* **3.** to behave   **conduct** (kŏn' dŭkt') n. **4.** the way a person behaves **5.** the management of something

3 Choose the correct pronunciation of conduct as it is used in this sentence.

The government has enlisted help, and volunteers now conduct searches for Asian longhorned beetles.

A kŭn' dŭkt'

B kən dŭkt'

C kŭn' dŭkt'

D kŏn' dŭkt

4 Choose the correct part of speech of conduct as it is used in this sentence.

Environmental organizations now conduct frequent beetle-egg hunts.

A noun

B verb

C adjective

D adverb

Lesson 14
Using a Thesaurus

CCSS
L.7.4c: Consult general and specialized reference materials (e.g., . . . thesauruses) both print and digital, to [find a word and] determine or clarify its precise meaning . . . .

Introduction

You can use a **thesaurus** to find synonyms and antonyms for words.

When a word has more than one meaning, each definition is numbered.

Sometimes there is a sample sentence.

Some words have more than one pronunciation and part of speech.

concern (kən sûrn') *v.* **1.** to be of significance or importance to: *Staying healthy concerns all of us.* **interest, involve, pertain, influence** **2.** to worry someone: *Your rash concerns me.* **distress, disturb, trouble, worry, disquiet** *n.* **3.** a matter or issue: *My financial affairs are my private concern.* **affair, consideration, matter, issue** **4.** a worry: *A lingering cough is a concern.* **worry, care, anxiety** **5.** a business: *The bakery is a concern that has operated for twenty years.* **business, enterprise, company, firm**

fragment (frăg' mənt) *n.* **1.** a bit of something: *This fragment of pottery is from your vase.* **bit, chip, shred, sliver, segment** *Antonyms: whole, total*
fragment (frăg mĕnt') *v.* **2.** to break into small pieces: *The loud noise fragmented the glass.* **break, shatter, smash** *Antonyms: unite, combine, mend*

Guided Practice

Use the passage and the thesaurus entries to answer numbers 1–5.

Hint

If you ever want to replace a word with a synonym, consider the age and background of your audience. How familiar will your audience be with the word you choose?

 Air pollution <u>concerns</u> people because of its negative impact on health and the environment. Air pollution contains particulates, which are tiny <u>fragments</u> of solids or liquids that are suspended in air.

1 Which words are synonyms of *concerns* as it is used in the passage?

_____

2 Which definition matches *concerns* as it is used in the passage?

_____

3 Which words are synonyms of *fragments* as it is used in the passage?

_____

4 Which words are antonyms of *fragments* as it is used in the passage?

_____

5 Which synonym would be the best choice to replace *fragments* if you were writing for very young children? _____

For numbers 1 and 2, read the sentence. Then use the thesaurus entry to answer the questions.

---

contribute (kən trĭb′yōot) *v.* **1.** to give something, such as time or money, to a cause: *Ryan contributed five dollars to the fundraiser.* **donate, give, grant, bestow** *Antonyms: take, receive* **2.** to help make something happen, to be a cause of something: *Your good wishes contributed to my happiness.* **add, aid, help, assist, support, influence** *Antonyms: curb, impede, detract*

Answer Form

1 Ⓐ Ⓑ Ⓒ Ⓓ
2 Ⓐ Ⓑ Ⓒ Ⓓ
3 Ⓐ Ⓑ Ⓒ Ⓓ
4 Ⓐ Ⓑ Ⓒ Ⓓ

Number Correct ___/4

For numbers 3 and 4, read the sentence. Then use the thesaurus entry to answer the questions.

---

appropriate (ə prō′prē ĭt) *adj.* **1.** suitable: *Sandals are appropriate shoes on a hot day.* **correct, suitable** *Antonyms: inappropriate, unsuitable* **appropriate** (ə prō′prē āt′) *v.* **2.** to use something for a purpose: *Will the city appropriate funds for a new pool?* **allocate, assign** *Antonym: withhold* **3.** to take something for one's own use, often without asking the owner's permission: *Gwen appropriated her sister's bike for the day.* **take, commandeer, seize**

---

1 The burning of fossil fuels such as fuel oil, gasoline, and natural gas contributes significantly to air pollution.

Which is an antonym for <u>contributes</u> as it is used above?

A grants

B detracts

C adds

D assists

2 Volunteer organizations contribute time and energy to promoting methods of reducing pollution.

Which is a synonym for <u>contribute</u> as it is used above?

A donate

B aid

C impede

D influence

3 The use of appropriate control devices can reduce the level of emissions.

Which is a synonym for <u>appropriate</u> as it is used above?

A withheld

B suitable

C commandeered

D seized

4 Should governments appropriate funds to combat pollution?

Which is an antonym for <u>appropriate</u> as it is used above?

A take

B correct

C withhold

D allocate

Lesson 15
Figures of Speech

CCSS
L.7.5a: Interpret figures of speech (e.g., literary, biblical, and mythological allusions) in context.

Introduction

Writing often includes **figures of speech**, expressions that suggest ideas and feelings beyond the actual meanings of the words. One figure of speech is an allusion.

- In an **allusion**, a writer refers to a well-known person or situation, such as from a literary work, the Bible, or mythology.

- Writers use allusions to deepen a reader's understanding of the person or situation they are writing about. An allusion brings vivid, meaningful associations to mind.

Study the allusions in the chart.

Example	Meaning
Gus was a good student, but algebra was his **Achilles' heel.**	Achilles is a mythological hero who died when an arrow struck his heel, his only weak spot. This **mythological allusion** means that algebra is Gus's weak point.
Gus didn't understand algebra, and it had been an **albatross** around his neck for weeks.	The albatross is a seabird killed by the sea captain in the poem "The Rime of the Ancient Mariner." Its death brings worries and problems. This **literary allusion** means that algebra is a problem for Gus.
Tomorrow Gus would meet his **Goliath** when he took the math test.	In the Bible, Goliath is a giant warrior who battles a boy. The **biblical allusion** means that the math test seems like a menacing monster.

Guided Practice

Underline each allusion. Identify it as literary, biblical, or mythological. Then discuss its meaning with a partner. Write your ideas on a sheet of paper.

Hint

You might recognize some of these allusions. But if you are unsure, circle the words you think are an allusion in each sentence. Type the words into a search engine to find out what the allusion refers to and what it means.

1. Every time Gus tried to do an algebra problem, he felt like he'd tumbled down the rabbit's hole.

2. Mom said to Gus, "Is anything wrong? You look like you're carrying the weight of the world on your shoulders."

3. Gus debated whether he should tell Mom his worries or just eat, drink, and be merry while he could.

4. His sister Bianca said, "Chill, Gus! You're just making much ado about nothing!"

5. Gus felt like Big Brother had been watching him and wondered, "How does Bianca know my worries?"

For numbers 1–4, use the information in the chart to choose the meaning of each underlined allusion.

Answer Form

1 Ⓐ Ⓑ Ⓒ Ⓓ
2 Ⓐ Ⓑ Ⓒ Ⓓ
3 Ⓐ Ⓑ Ⓒ Ⓓ
4 Ⓐ Ⓑ Ⓒ Ⓓ

Number Correct ⟋4

Dr. Jekyll and Mr. Hyde	from a novel, a person with a split personality—one kind, the other mean
Job	in the Bible, a man who patiently endured terrible suffering
Hercules	a hero of Greek mythology who put great effort into doing impossible tasks
Gordian knot	in Greek legend, a knot that, when cut by Alexander the Great, enabled him to conquer Asia

1 Bianca had a personality like <u>Jekyll and Hyde</u>, but today she was feeling kind.

  A Bianca was sometimes nice and sometimes nasty.

  B Bianca was like a two-headed monster.

  C Bianca was sometimes helpful but often not.

  D Bianca was changeable.

2 <u>With the patience of Job</u>, Bianca explained how to solve equations in many different ways.

  A Bianca often gave in to temptation.

  B Bianca was good at playing tricks on people.

  C Bianca was not quick to become discouraged.

  D Bianca had the strength of a Greek god.

3 Gus made a <u>Herculean effort</u> to understand algebra.

  A Gus made a chart to solve his problem.

  B Gus made a huge attempt to solve his problem.

  C Gus had great faith and prayed instead of studying.

  D Gus barely tried because he expected life to be easy.

4 At last Gus severed the <u>Gordian knot</u>, and algebra was no longer a problem!

  A Gus could not take the test because of an injury.

  B Gus no longer cared if he failed algebra.

  C Gus quit algebra to avoid failing.

  D Gus was finally able to do algebra.

CCSS
L.7.5b: Use the relationship between particular words (e.g., synonym/antonym, analogy) to better understand each of the words.

👥 **Introduction**   In this lesson, you will study **analogies**, or the types of relationships between pairs of words. The example below is an analogy.

near is to **distant** as **hidden** is to **exposed**

Near and *distant* are antonyms, and *hidden* and *exposed* are antonyms. So, *near* and *distant* have the same type of relationship as *hidden* and *exposed*. Their relationships are **analogous** to each other.

Sometimes analogies are written with colons.

- A **colon (:)** separates the words in each pair. The colon stands for the phrase *is to*.
- A **double colon (::)** separates the pairs of words. The double colon stands for the word *as*.

near **:** distant **::** hidden **:** exposed
    is to   *as*   *is to*

Antonym analogies are just one type of analogy. There are many other types, as this chart shows.

Type of Analogy	Example
Synonym	friendly : nice :: rapid : fast
Cause/Effect	fire : scorch :: drought : wither
Part/Whole	foot : leg :: leaf : branch
Item/Category	horse : animal :: car : vehicle
Tool/User	camera : photographer :: stove : chef

👥 **Guided Practice**   **Choose the word that completes the analogy. Write the word on the line. Then identify the type of analogy, and write it next to the analogy.**

Hint

First, figure out the relationship between the first pair of words. Then, choose the word that will make the second pair of words have the same type of relationship as the first pair of words.

1 cent : dollar :: inch : _____ _____
    foot   meter   worm

2 saw : carpenter :: telescope : _____ _____
    constellation   lens   astronomer

3 tragedy : sorrow :: triumph : _____ _____
    victory   hero   pride

4 eagle : bird :: shark : _____ _____
    tuna   ocean   fish

For numbers 1–5, choose the word that correctly completes each analogy.

1 sink : kitchen :: classroom : _____

 A students

 B textbook

 C school

 D learn

2 laptop : computer :: ring : _____

 A jewelry

 B doorbell

 C circus

 D bracelet

3 joke : laughter :: virus : _____

 A computer

 B cure

 C crying

 D illness

4 cozy : uncomfortable :: odd : _____

 A strange

 B ordinary

 C painful

 D cold

5 hammer : builder :: microphone : _____

 A louder

 B volume

 C audio

 D singer

Lesson 17
Denotation and Connotation

CCSS
L.7.5c: Distinguish among the connotations (associations) of words with similar denotations (definitions) (e.g., *refined, respectful, polite, diplomatic, condescending*).

Introduction

Words can have two kinds of meaning. A word's **denotation** is its basic meaning, or dictionary definition. A word's **connotations** are the feelings associated with it.

- A word or phrase can have **positive**, **negative**, or **neutral** connotations.

Positive Connotation	Neutral Connotation	Negative Connotation
Ian **requested** a glass of water.	Ian **asked for** a glass of water.	Ian **demanded** a glass of water.

- A word's or phrase's connotation partly depends on its context.

Positive	Negative
The **ice-cold** water was refreshing on the hot day.	The **ice-cold** water made Ian shiver.

When writing, choose words that will produce in your readers the feelings you want them to have.

Guided Practice

Read the sentences. Write *P* if the underlined word has a positive connotation. Write *N* if the word has a negative connotation.

Hint

Ask yourself: How does this word make me feel? If the word makes you feel good, it has a positive connotation. If it makes you feel bad, it has a negative connotation.

1 Ian and Atsuko were <u>contenders</u> in the storywriting contest. _____

Ian and Atsuko were <u>rivals</u> in the storywriting contest. _____

2 Atsuko was known for her <u>mysterious</u> plots. _____

Atsuko was known for her <u>bewildering</u> plots. _____

3 Ian's characters were <u>ridiculous</u>. _____

Ian's characters were <u>amusing</u>. _____

4 Ian <u>displayed</u> his large vocabulary. _____

Ian <u>flaunted</u> his large vocabulary. _____

5 Atsuko's main character behaved <u>rashly</u>. _____

Atsuko's main character behaved <u>boldly</u>. _____

6 Everyone <u>snickered</u> at Atsuko's surprise ending. _____

Everyone <u>chuckled</u> at Atsuko's surprise ending. _____

For numbers 1–3, choose the word that has the same denotation as the underlined word and also has the most negative connotation.

1 After school, a <u>bunch</u> of students gathered by the riverfront.

   A mob

   B crowd

   C group

   D collection

For numbers 4 and 5, choose the word that has the same denotation as the underlined word and also has the most positive connotation.

2 Atsuko, strolling home, was <u>surprised</u> to see her classmates huddled together.

   A amazed

   B astonished

   C shocked

   D astounded

4 Ian was in their midst, so they were certainly <u>planning</u> something.

   A concocting

   B devising

   C scheming

   D plotting

5 Suddenly they turned toward her and <u>announced</u>, "You won first prize."

   A stated

   B said

   C uttered

   D exclaimed

3 Atsuko kept a <u>watchful</u> eye on her classmates as she approached them.

   A close

   B attentive

   C suspicious

   D keen

Photo Credits

Page 16, Heiko Kiera/Shutterstock

Page 35: Photograph of Othniel Charles Marsh. From David Starr Jordan, *Leading American Men of Science*. H. Holt and Company (1910). Public domain.

Page 35: Photograph of Edward Drinker Cope. From *The Century Illustrated Monthly Magazine,* Vol. 55, p. 11. Public domain.

Page 36, Jorg Hackemann/Shutterstock

Page 87, David Dohnal/Shutterstock

Page 121, jl6612227/Shutterstock

Page 190, Tom Grundy/Shutterstock

Page 211: "New York—Welcome to the Land of Freedom," from *Frank Leslie's Illustrated Newspaper,* July 2, 1887, pp. 324–25. Courtesy Library of Congress, LC-USZ62-113735. Public domain.

Illustration Credits

Page 201, Cenveo, Inc.

All other illustrations by Six Red Marbles